LUNCH WITH

ALSO BY JAN WONG

Red China Blues: My Long March from Mao to Now

Jan Wong's China: Reports from a Not-So-Foreign Correspondent

lunch with

JAN
WONG

Anchor Canada

National Library of Canada Cataloguing in Publication Data

Wong, Jan
Lunch with

ISBN 0-385-25982-4

1. Celebrities – Canada – Interviews. 2. Celebrities – Interviews. I. Title.

FC25.W636 2001   920.071   C2001-930560-5
F1005.W66 2001

Cover photograph by Denise Grant Photography
Text design by Kim Monteforte/Heidy Lawrance Associates
Printed and bound in Canada

Published in Canada by
Anchor Canada, a division of
Random House of Canada Limited

Visit Random House of Canada Limited's website: www.randomhouse.ca

TRANS 10 9 8 7 6 5 4 3 2 1

To my mother, Eva Wong,

and my father, Bill Wong,

Montreal restaurateur

par excellence

IF

(WITH APOLOGIES TO RUDYARD KIPLING)

If I were dressed in Armani
And coiffed with élan,
If my bons mots were
Quoted and doted upon,
If my gestures and carriage
Bespoke a great style,
If I showed no emotion
Beyond my sweet smile,
If my actions were selfless
My mind chaste and pure,
If my causes were worthy
And très, très du jour,
If I knew that I never
Did anything wrong,
Then, only then,
Would I Lunch with Jan Wong

Jeanie Davis, Toronto
Letter to *The Globe and Mail*,
November 17, 1997

contents

FELLOW SCRIBBLERS

POLITICAL ANIMALS

Movie Makers

Winners and Losers

Family Matters

LUNCH WITH

the importance of lunch

"HOW WOULD YOU LIKE TO TAKE MARGARET ATWOOD TO LUNCH?"

It was just before Labour Day weekend, 1996. My editor called me at home, presumably because I was the only one not on my way to the cottage. After turning down an interview with *The Globe and Mail,* Margaret Atwood had changed her mind. The Queen of CanLit would now deign to meet me for lunch.

All that weekend, I read *Alias Grace,* Atwood's new novel. On Tuesday morning, I was so nervous that I went early to Arlequin, her favourite neighbourhood restaurant. I wanted to ensure everything was just right: the best booth in the no-smoking section (because Atwood didn't smoke) and a large bottle of mineral water (in case she arrived thirsty). For myself, I ordered pita bread to nibble on while I scribbled notes.

Afterward, I wrote the standard famous-author interview with its invisible journalist. My editor, Cathrin Bradbury, asked for a rewrite—in the first person. "We want the readers to feel as if they're right there sitting with you," she said.

Atwood had given me one hour, an eternity on television but barely adequate for print. So I added attitude and atmospherics. I described how Atwood wanted to switch to another, "quieter" table even though at 11:30 a.m.—*her* designated time—we were Arlequin's only customers. I wrote about her refusal to order lunch—"I can't talk while I'm eating"—even though a lunch interview was *her* idea. I recorded how she blanched when asked about her Pelee Island cottage, as though rabid fans would rent boats and circle the place.

Readers loved it. And the Atwood interview became the prototype for "Lunch With," a weekly column in *The Globe and Mail*.

The experience taught me an important lesson: how celebs behave can be more interesting than what they say. *For Better or For Worse* cartoonist Lynn Johnston was hypercritical of our Old Spaghetti Factory waitress, to the point of filling out a scathing comment card. It made me wonder how she behaved when there wasn't a reporter present jotting down every muscle twitch. Many lunches later, I realized Johnston and Atwood were afflicted by "celebrityitis," a rare condition characterized by an avowed desire for privacy while actively participating in a national publicity tour.

In a letter to the editor, Barbara Dawn Salo wrote, "Jan Wong is the Diane Arbus of journalism. Absolutely everyone is a freak to her. She strips her subject buck naked and shoves her camera very, very hard into their flesh. The resulting picture is twisted, a distortion of reality." In another letter to the editor, Roselyne Campbell disagreed: "Some people may think her writing is spiteful, but I thoroughly enjoy her sense of humour. She writes with a frankness and honesty I find most refreshing."

I figured "Lunch With" would last six months.

Before absolutely everyone wised up, I was determined not to pull my punches. If the emperor wore no clothes, that's what I would report. Readers quickly grasped that this was the naked lunch. You'd think I'd never eat Lunch in this town again. But nearly four years later, the publicists still call. Celebrities apparently believe that public-relations maxim: there's no such thing as bad publicity.

Some colleagues consider Lunch a dream job: gorging

among the gorgeous and the great. Others consider it a humiliating comedown from my previous posting as *The Globe*'s Beijing bureau chief. Two years into the column, one reader, Dr. Max Himel, wrote me a long letter calling it "terrible," "dreadful," and "too cute for words." He added that he regretted he could not accept an invitation to lunch. "I have never been able to develop a taste," he wrote, "for hemlock tea."

Personally, I see Lunch as a logical career move. My six years overseas as a foreign correspondent taught me to poke holes in the well-constructed façade. And before China, I dealt with armies of publicists in my eight years as a business reporter (shipping, banking, financial services). Totalitarian dictatorships everywhere have humongous P.R. machines. At the Bank of Boston, for instance, it was called Corporate Communications. In China, it's called, and I'm not kidding, the Ministry of Propaganda. My years in China toughened me for the celebrity beat. After witnessing the 1989 Tiananmen Square Massacre, I'm only mildly unnerved by a celebrity hissy fit.

Now and then, for relief from the self-obsessed, I'll take a noncelebrity to Lunch. They have included a beggar, a mentally handicapped woman, and my own Aunt Ming. Occasionally, noncelebrities propose, ahem, themselves. Many are struggling artists or tenured academics. Then there was the caller who said, "I'm a Boring White Male. You haven't done that category. Why don't you take me to Lunch?" I passed.

Over time, it has dawned on a few celebs that there is no such thing as a free Lunch. Refuseniks include Hilary Weston, Martha Stewart, Howard Stern, Jesse Helms, and Ross Rebagliati, the Olympic snowboarder who nearly lost his medal for smoking marijuana secondhand. But the majority accept an invitation to Lunch because they have something to sell. They're pushing their book, movie, or political party. They're flogging their bank merger, television show, or pay-per-view service, such as the one where you commune with your dead child for only $200 U.S. These celebs know they need free ads because the public is far too skeptical about paid ones. Hence the far-flung publicity tour, in which journalism becomes handmaiden to marketing.

In the twenty-first century, celebrity has blossomed into a multibillion-dollar business. Publicists demand to see stories in advance. They negotiate play. ("Put my puff piece on page one, or the deal's off.") They delineate No-Ask Zones: Andrea Bocelli's blindness, Rosie O'Donnell's sexual orientation. Some flacks try to bundle hot clients with lukewarm ones. "You can have Tom Green," one agent told me, "but you gotta do Mike Bullard, too." (Bullard's actually pretty hot himself, which is why I'd already Lunched him. But some publicists don't worry about details.)

"Lunch With" aims to be a weekly Consumer Reports on Famous People. So I do not do deals. And I do not go off the record. Why should I know something I can't share with the reader? Publicists sometimes want to tag along, but I politely discourage chaperones. If they insist, I warn them they may end up in the column as the appetizer. That usually does the trick.

No one, incidentally, has ever walked out on Lunch, although dress manufacturer Peter Nygård did call an abrupt halt to our meeting, while we were enjoying a lovely platter of sandwiches. Mostly, a meal has a civilizing influence on people. Breaking bread together engenders intimacy. And etiquette keeps them in their seats. (Or perhaps they just want dessert.)

Let me be the first to admit that I am celebrity-impaired. I've never seen *Baywatch*. I didn't even know who Tom Green was until he achieved fame on Mike Bullard's *Open Mike* show. I once agreed to interview author Michael Ignatieff only because I confused him with author Michael Ondaatje. (Midway through my research I figured I had the wrong Michael when *The English Patient* never popped up.) Alas, neither Ondaatje nor Bullard made the final cut for this book.

Celebrities hate it when everyone already knows all about them, yet they also hate it when you don't. (That's another symptom of celebrityitis.) That Labour Day weekend of 1996, I managed only bare-bones research before the Lunch with Atwood. I knew she had dedicated *Alias Grace* to someone named Jess; I just didn't realize Jess was her daughter. That got me into trouble, as you shall see. I also knew that Atwood had been raised in the bush up north, but didn't know why. When asked what her father had done for a living, she snapped: "Look it up in the file." That's six words. "Entomologist" is one.

That Lunch with Atwood taught me a valuable lesson. "Lunch With" now starts with intensive research. I read the celebrity's books. I watch their movies and television shows and listen to their CDs. I read the stacks of articles (and sometimes books) that others have written about them. The trick is to sit down to lunch knowing everything that's publicly known. Only then can you move the interview into a new realm. You can also spot the little white lies. And recognize the same tired old answers to the same tired old questions.

I've never killed a Lunch after the interview. On rare occasions, I have backed out after doing the research because the person seemed boring. I once cancelled out of kindness, too. Frank McCourt had soared to the top of the bestseller lists with *Angela's Ashes,* and his brother, Malachy, was riding on Frank's coattails. Malachy's *A Monk Swimming* sold 330,000 copies in two years, not bad considering the tepid reviews, but a mere fraction of the 10 million copies of *Angela's Ashes* that Frank sold. And Malachy's memoir turned out to be a dreary list of every poor sap he had screwed, emotionally and otherwise. I didn't see the point in trashing the brother of a famous person at Lunch. (So I'll do that now in one paragraph.)

The myth is that I get one great meal a week. In truth, I try for a place that either fits or fights the subject. Thus, a

beggar named Nancy Hallam was Lunched at Centro, one of
Toronto's swankiest restaurants. A brawling beauty queen was
Lunched at a steak house called Barberian's. As for the chair-
man of McDonald's, he was given a choice: Wendy's or Burger
King. After agonizing for two days, George Cohon invited me
for microwaved hot dogs at one of his favourite charities.

After the Atwood non-Lunch where I noshed on bread and
water, I learned that, for the sake of journalistic excellence, I
have no choice but to endure the hardship of appetizers and
desserts. That encourages my guests to do the same—thereby
prolonging the interview. If my guests order a glass of wine, I
also order a glass. When they have drained theirs, I push mine
across the table, saying, "I haven't touched it. Wouldn't want
it to go to waste."

Alas, I never have time to scarf down as much as I'd like. I've
learned to talk with my mouth full. But the better the quotes,
the less I get to eat. That's because I take voluminous notes,
using a tape recorder only for backup. I have also perfected the
technique of holding pen and fork in the same hand at the same
time. So far, I've managed to avoid writing on my face.

But Lunch isn't just about quotes. It's also about food. A
French philosopher once said you are what you eat. So I pay
attention to what the celeb eats and doesn't eat. Guess what
Fred Goldman, who sued O.J. Simpson for the murder of his
waiter son, orders with his scrambled eggs? It isn't orange
juice. And for the record, I have never once mentioned when
guests had spinach stuck in their teeth. But I'm not promising
I never will.

A "Lunch With" interview is like a final exam, and not just
for my guest. Including aperitifs, I often have no more than an
hour and 15 minutes. So I strategize. Should I start with a safe
topic, like the celebrity's new book, or should I zero in on bra
size? (I ask this only of those who have had careers in cleavage.)

I routinely ask height and weight. And I always ask age *and* birthdate. That often catches them out if they're trying to shave off a couple of decades.

I think, What do I *really* want to know? So I'll ask Miss Canada how she posed naked for *Playboy* at, um, that time of the month. I'll ask Jukka-Pekka Saraste, conductor of the Toronto Symphony Orchestra, how he persuades his kids to practise the piano. And I try to imagine what the imaginary reader and I would chat about if we stayed behind for a second cup of coffee after the celebrity left. We'd probably agree, for instance, that maestro manners are different from yours and mine. At a Japanese restaurant, Jukka-Pekka Saraste took the collective dish of marinated spinach, meant for his publicist, himself, and me, slid it across the table, and ate the whole thing by himself.

Naturally, there's postprandial fallout. Margaret Atwood and Margaret Trudeau both called to chew me out. During Lunch, author Jeffrey Archer threatened to sue. After Lunch (but before publication), Peter Nygård also threatened to sue. No one, though, has actually sued. But it's yet another good reason to turn on a tape recorder. Now and then, the celebrity opts for revenge—as you will see.

Journalistically speaking, though, I enjoy Lunch. Here are some of my favourites. Bon appétit!

THE PROTOTYPE

margaret atwood

September 7, 1996

Margaret Atwood, CanLit icon and author or editor of forty-three books, has just admitted she can't spell.

"Spell *busy*," I say, to assess just how orthographically challenged she is.

"B-u-s-y," she says meekly.

"Spell *macaroni*."

She doesn't even attempt it. "I mix up my a's and e's," she explains.

Before I can toss another word at her, Atwood, fifty-six, recovers her equilibrium. In her trademark elongated nasal twang, she drawls: "When I announced in high school I was going to be a writer, my mother said, 'You'd better learn to spell.' I said, 'Others will do that for me,' and they have."

We are sitting in Arlequin, her hangout in the Annex, an upscale Toronto neighbourhood of brownstones and boutiques. Her publicist had faxed me to meet Atwood here for lunch. I am allotted one hour with her before she leaves for Lake Erie's Pelee Island—a rest on the eve of a looming book tour.

I arrive ten minutes early, dropping Atwood's name to get a good table. The apparently well-read waiter is impressed. He seats me in a spacious red leatherette banquette in no smoking,

assuring me that Atwood doesn't smoke. For me, this is a
no-lunch lunch. I can't waste a precious moment cutting or
chewing. But to avoid drooling while Atwood eats, I order
bread and hummus.

She arrives and frowns at the table. "Too noisy," she says,
even though the restaurant is deserted at 11:30 a.m.—her
choice of time for lunch. She eyes the banquette at the very
back. "Why don't we move back there?" I look at the bread and
hummus and the glasses of water and say, "That's smoking." She
finally sits down. For her, this will also be a no-lunch lunch. "I
can't eat and talk at the same time," she explains, ordering a café
au lait. "Just a little coffee. Mostly milk," she says to the hover-
ing waiter. "Do you have 1 per cent or 2 per cent?"

With her translucent skin, longish nose, pale blue eyes,
and Botticelli mass of brown curls, Atwood looks like a petite
version of Cher in *The Witches of Eastwick*. She is five feet three
and a half inches ("I used to be five-four but I'm shrinking")
and wears a black sweater, a straw hat, black sandals, and
black-striped loose pants. For a photographer's benefit, she has
applied mascara and a lick of lipstick.

Her latest book and ninth novel, about an obscure
nineteenth-century Canadian murderess, is a departure from
her usual novels about contemporary relationships. To prepare,
she immersed herself in the literature of the time. "Have
you read Victorian lurid thrillers?" I shake my head, feeling
dumb. "Well, I have," she says. Some readers find her books
dauntingly dense, but she is one of the few Canadian novelists
whose books sell very well. Based on advance orders for *Alias
Grace*, "it's a success, don't worry," Atwood says. Asked for
specifics, she becomes as prudish as one of her characters. "We
don't discuss numbers in our family."

Atwood virtually created CanLit. "There is no one king of
CanLit. But there is a queen, and that's Atwood," says John

Pearce, editor-in-chief of Seal, which publishes Atwood in mass-market paperback in Canada. I wonder if she's recognized when she goes out. She nods. "This is Canada, so they just usually…" She pantomimes: first a long stare, then a whisper in the ear of an imaginary companion.

I ask the routine questions about her family. Atwood says her daughter is studying English and philosophy at McGill University. I ask what her name is. Atwood balks. I nod, feeling faintly embarrassed that I didn't think about stalkers and kidnappers. Belatedly, I realize that Atwood has very publicly dedicated *Alias Grace* to Jess, who is, of course, her daughter.

A pleasant inquiry about her imminent departure for Pelee Island sparks another Atwood rebuke. "I would never have told you that," she says. (She didn't, but I already knew.) Would her fans really circle in a boat, hoping for a sighting? I mean, there is civilized fame, such as hers, and uncivilized fame, such as Pamela Anderson Lee's. "How would you feel if you were having dinner and people drove up to your house?" says Atwood, sipping her café au lait. The waiter hovers, wondering why neither of us is ordering lunch.

Later, I learn that Atwood hangs this sign on her office wall: "Wanting to know an author because you like his work is like wanting to know a duck because you like paté." Keeping secrets is part of her style. She doesn't tell anyone what she is working on—not her agent, not her publishers, not even her devoted assistant and spelling helpmate, Sarah Cooper. It's out of self-defence. Creating a make-believe conversation with an editor, Atwood parodies herself. "Well, actually, I'm writing a novel set in the future with characters running around in Dutch Cleanser can outfits," she says, alluding to her 1985 novel, *The Handmaid's Tale*. While that book was still in the embryonic stage, she once made the mistake of describing it to novelist Graeme Gibson, her partner and father of Jess.

"Don't you think you're going a bit too far?" he replied.

When writing, Atwood used to distract herself by leaping on her back-yard trampoline. "I don't hop, skip, and jump any more—too old." Now she relaxes by baking pies in the gloomy kitchen of her Edwardian home—blueberry, rhubarb, pumpkin, and peach. Atwood writes her first draft longhand on yellow legal pads, then types it into her computer, using four fingers—and a thumb for the space bar. In 1995, she published a book of poems, a collection of speeches, and a children's book and edited, with Robert Weaver, an anthology of short stories.

Despite her years of success, Atwood still suffers prepublication jitters. She feels old stings, such as an unkind review way back in 1985. With *Alias Grace*, will the critics—and her public—agree with the bookstores? "On the one hand, my job is over. On the other hand, I have insomnia and nightmares. It's like waiting for exam results." When she can't sleep, she sips hot milk and honey and rereads her favourite old books. Such as? "You know, murder mysteries."

In a sense, *Alias Grace* is Atwood's first murder mystery. It is a Victorian melodrama based on the real-life story of Grace Marks, a sixteen-year-old maid convicted of a double murder in Canada in 1843. Does Atwood believe Marks committed murder? "I'm not saying," she says stonily. "I'm not going to spoil it for the reader. People at the time came away with either [impression]."

"Is everything all right?" the waiter asks.

Atwood and her researchers found out how parsnips were stored (in the ground), what female prisoners wore to sleep in the 1850s (coarse yellowed smocks), and the correct way to make a Tree of Paradise quilt (dark triangles for the leaves, light triangles for the fruits). They delved into newspaper accounts, court transcripts, and the judge's trial notes, though not always with gratifying results. "It turns out that he was the judge with the most illegible handwriting that ever existed," Atwood says.

She left intact significant facts, but invented freely where there were holes. On and off, "counting the part when I threw most of it out and started again," the novel took about two years to write. "It's very much like a detective story, but the ending is still up in the air," Atwood says. "That's the difference between history and a murder mystery."

Her assistant arrives to whisk her away. With a sigh of relief, I order lunch.

After the story ran, Margaret Atwood's assistant, Sarah Cooper, phoned to tell me how angry her boss was. When Cooper failed to tongue-lash me with sufficient vigour, Atwood grabbed the phone. Without bothering to say "Hello, this is Margaret Atwood," she lit into me for naming her daughter and for using the words "stalkers and kidnappers."

I apologized for any distress I had caused her.

Atwood then demanded The Globe and Mail *zap the article from its electronic database. We would be hearing from her lawyer, she warned. "I suppose you think that I am a book burner," she drawled. As a matter of fact, she did remind me of Communist Chinese book burners who rewrite history to suit their agendas and send recalcitrant writers to the gulag. But I kept that thought to myself.*

The Globe's database is a record of everything we print, including errors. (Corrections are noted at the top of the electronic version.) I told Atwood that deleting material from it was beyond my powers. She'd have to deal with my editor.

Her lawyer did send us a letter. Atwood herself lobbied The Globe *at every level. The editors listened to her complaint, but rejected her request. Our research showed that she had often discussed*

Jess in the media and had allowed her to be photographed for Maclean's magazine and other publications. Atwood's friends later suggested that she had overreacted because her only child had just left home for university.

BEAUTIES

danielle house

November 21, 1996

The "Lunch With" column was launched in late 1996 with Miss Canada International, who was embroiled in assault charges after decking a young woman in a bar.

Miss Canada International is late. She arrives in spike heels, chaperon in tow, blaming a sluggish Toronto subway. Danielle House, who grew up in Daniel's Harbour, Newfoundland (pop. 400), has been on a subway only once before in her life. She is a little shell-shocked. "Two guys started screaming profanities, and were kicking each other," said House.

So did she wade in and throw a punch?

House, twenty, straightens her fringed white moire sash, emblazoned with "Miss Canada International 96–97," shakes her lovely cascade of brown hair, and allows herself a small, painful smile. Last month, she gave new meaning to the phrase "femme fatale" when she allegedly punched her ex-boyfriend's date in a campus bar at Memorial University in St. John's. Police said the woman suffered facial cuts and a chipped tooth. House pleaded not guilty to assault.

Canadian pageant officials unwaveringly backed House.

After all, this isn't a nation of wimps. This is a country where an ambassador's wife once slapped her social secretary, where the prime minister once throttled a chanting protester, and where our peacekeepers occasionally end up killing people. Alas, officials of an international pageant in Jamaica didn't understand and banned her from participating. "It's a lot of foolishness the way things were handled," said House, with a gentle Newfoundland lilt. Instead, she'll appear in Saturday's Grey Cup football parade in Hamilton, take in a Maple Leafs hockey game in Toronto that evening, and skate on Sunday for an Easter Seal fundraiser. Toronto's King Edward Hotel has offered her its Royal Suite.

We are lunching at Barberian's, a steak house in downtown Toronto, because her chaperon told me House hates pasta and salad. "She's the only girl I've ever looked after that just eats meat and potatoes," marvels Sylvia Stark, who also heads the Miss Canada International pageant.

The reigning Miss Universe, from Venezuela, was nearly stripped of her title last August for gaining twenty-seven pounds. House, a dead ringer for a Barbie doll, isn't worried. "I hate salad," she says. "I've never eaten salad. At two points in my life, I tasted salad and …" She shudders at the memory, and orders a steak, medium-rare. When it arrives, the waiter hovers with a trayload of toppings for her baked potato.

"Sour cream?" he asks.

"Yes, please."

"Bacon bits?"

"A few."

"Feta cheese?"

"Yes, please."

It's a mystery how she can wear a size three skirt. House, who won her crown in Toronto last August, competing against nine others, says she never exercises. And she swears she isn't bulimic. A first-year nursing student at Memorial University, her favourite dorm breakfast is ham, two fried eggs, hash brown potatoes, orange juice, and tea. She is partial to McCain's Deep Deluxe Cakes. And when she watches David Letterman, "I'll usually warm up a can of SpaghettiOs."

House, who is five feet eight, said she was 131 pounds when she weighed herself a few months ago. But since "all that started," she says, she's lost a little weight. "People said I went into a bar and started a cat fight, that tables were thrown, fists were thrown. I just wish everybody knew what I knew," she says, adding she can't tell much more until her court date. She does say she dated the man for fifteen months, that he struck her, and that she tried unsuccessfully to break off with him. He left her in July, a month before she was crowned, and is now harassing her, she says.

"He wants to control my life. When I started to move on with my life, I wasn't allowed to. He wants to take my crown from me," she adds, near tears. She says she is still afraid of him.

She finishes her steak and scoops out every bit of baked potato, sour cream, bacon, and feta cheese. The cole slaw lies untouched. "I hate vegetables," she says, ignoring everything green, including the pickles. But she loves meat, especially fresh-killed game. "Bear, caribou, and moose are all delicious, but personally, I prefer caribou."

The daughter of a lobster fisherman and part-time hunting guide, House hopes to get her moose-hunting licence. She has no qualms about shooting and gutting animals and hacking off their antlers. Nor does she doubt she can heft the carcass. "You quarter them, you know." Her roommate recently shot her first caribou, and described the thrill of carrying the quartered animal through the marsh. "It's not for everyone," House concedes. "But it's a very routine thing in Newfoundland."

I tell her I was a freshette princess in college and I challenge her to a friendly arm-wrestling contest. After the waiter clears away the plates we start with our left hands, straining with tiny, ladylike grunts. "The table's shaking," her chaperon whispers, and calls it a draw.

Then we try the right, her punching arm. Miss Canada International, who has no discernible biceps, wins hands down. I don't feel any better when she tells me I am older than her father. At least she says her arms hurt.

After the alleged barroom brawl, ordinary Canadians wrote letters of support for their sock-it-to-'em beauty queen. Last Sunday, an admirer sent a dozen roses. Still, House fears bystanders at the Grey Cup parade might throw garbage at her. But as she finishes off her cheesecake with strawberry sauce and gets up to leave, a businessman at a nearby table gives her a thumbs-up sign. "I heard you talking about what you like to have for breakfast," he says. "Good luck."

Miss Canada International gives him a thousand-watt smile.

danielle house (continued)

DETHRONED BEAUTY QUEEN CONFRONTS THE NAKED TRUTH

November 13, 1997

House must have liked my column. A year later, her publicist came calling again, and House became, so far, the only person I've ever Lunched twice. I caught up with her after she was defrocked, first by pageant officials, then, in another sense, by Playboy.

As a *W5* camera crew records her every move, Danielle House scans the menu for red meat. Last year, the carnivorous Newfoundland beauty queen gave new meaning to the term "femme fatale." In a barroom brawl, she bopped the new girl-friend of her old boyfriend. The other woman suffered a broken nose, two black eyes, a chipped tooth, a swollen lip, and a bruised left temple. A St. John's Provincial Court judge gave House a suspended sentence and a year's probation. Then the Miss Canada International pageant stripped her of her crown. Now House has stripped for *Playboy*. She graces the December cover, clad only in red and green boxing gloves, a tiara, and a smile. She's also hired a Hollywood agent, stashed away a pile of U.S. dollars, and snared all the media attention she wants.

"I wasn't thinking of it in terms of a career move," says House of the punch-out. "But it's true. In terms of publicity it's worked out." Last time we lunched—when she launched this column exactly one year ago—she stayed in a budget hotel, rode the subway, and had been outside the Maritimes only once. Now, dethroned and defrocked, she's ensconced in the Four Seasons Hotel, rides a Lincoln Town Car, and is about to relocate to Los Angeles. But some things haven't changed. Back then, she had no boyfriend. Despite the *Playboy* pictorial, there's still no man in her life. "Everyone's like, 'Guess you had a dozen guys ask you out.'" She shakes her head sadly. She still loves her meat—both eating and hunting. There's no fresh-killed moose at the Four Seasons Studio Café, so she orders a ten-ounce char-grilled steak and mashed potatoes. "I still haven't gotten into eating vegetables."

House, who is part Inuit, remains a knockout: heart-shaped face, hazel eyes, chestnut hair, and a body like Barbie's. After her May 9 conviction, pageant officials repossessed the title, crown, satin sash, and her favourite prize, a Roots leather jacket.

Two days later, *Playboy* called. House had already hired a

publicist, one whose client list included Heidi Fleiss, the Hollywood madam, and Paula Barbieri, O.J. Simpson's ex-girlfriend. The publicist negotiated a sum for House so big that Hugh Hefner had to approve the deal.

"Very good six figures," she says, sipping a Pepsi. "Quite a bit more than [super-model] Cindy Crawford. I understand she got $100,000." The Miss Canada International pageant is seeking a chunk. Nor is the punchee, Annalee Gosse, turning the other cheek. She has sent a lawyer's letter. "I'm very willing to settle if she'll let me make a substantial donation to a charity of her choice," says House, who is wearing a décolleté black suit, sheer black stockings, and a diamond crucifix.

In addition to her lawyers, agent, and publicist, she's hired a financial adviser and an accountant. But her only splurge is a laptop to e-mail friends and scan in contracts. Before signing with *Playboy*, House flew home to Daniel's Harbour to see her father, a lobster fisherman. (Her mother, forty, had died suddenly in March.) "Dad said, 'It's your choice. You know I'll be here and I'll always be here.' Then he laughed and said, 'But I'm not going to see it.' "

Next, House informed her probation officer. After an assessment, the officer decided House didn't need anger-management counselling—recommended by the judge—after all. It's true. When asked if *Playboy* scheduled the shoot around her menstrual cycle, House doesn't throw a punch. She smiles and confesses she had her period the entire week of the shoot. Fearing the white-sheet scenes, not to mention the ivory satin corset, might cramp her style, she confided in the make-up lady.

"Tampons," House was advised. "You clip off the string." As for pubic hair, "They ask you to make it tidy. I shaved myself." And extra make-up? "Just on the boobs."

Playboy installed her in a Beverly Hills hotel. Twice, she dined poolside at Hefner's mansion—with forty of his closest friends and their kids. He wore his trademark pyjamas, of course, but hardly noticed her. "He hung out with men, mostly." On location at a Santa Monica beach house, *Playboy* provided champagne to help her relax. The magazine ordered take-out Chinese the first day. From there, it deteriorated to pizza. The high point was hamburgers. Seven people worked on the shoot, swelling to eleven the day they used live doves as props. "It was so nice," says House in her Newfoundland lilt. "They perched the doves on my shoulders, all around me."

The real poop, please. "I'd get up and I'd be covered with crap," she concedes. "I tell you, I had a very good shower that night." Alas, not a single dove picture made it, but there is a white-sheet scene.

What's it like to be famous for being beautiful, violent, and naked? Isn't House afraid of becoming a mere punchline? "It's a really good opportunity. But it's just a stepping stone," she says of the *Playboy* pictorial. So far, only one friend, a Newfoundland pageant organizer, has denounced her. House, who dropped out of nursing school because of her legal problems, is looking forward to acting lessons and modelling. "Mom would have wanted to come to L.A. with me," she says, her eyes misting over. "She'd be buying copies of *Playboy* and handing them to all her friends."

House eventually settled her suit with Annalee Gosse. Terms weren't disclosed.

The details of the Playboy *photo shoot were too much for some* Globe *readers as they explained in two letters to the editor published November 19, 1997. T.L. Cooper complained that my "Lunch With Danielle House far overstepped the bounds of decorum and good judgment I expect of* The Globe and Mail," *and William J. Russell*

*wrote, "It is unfortunate that crudities are becoming common fare in
Canada's National Newspaper. Jan Wong's recent candid lunch conversation with alleged beauty queen Danielle House regarding her
menstruation problems while posing nude for* Playboy *was hardly
breakfast reading ... More discretion regarding items worth reporting is certainly in order."*

don cherry

LEARNING TO STAY ON TOP OF THE GAME
WITHOUT HIS ROSE

May 14, 1998

Even in the gloom of his own Don Cherry Sports Grill, Don
Cherry stands out. But can those two pink studs in his collar
be ... pierced earrings? "You're the first to know," says Cherry,
resplendent in red and black hound's-tooth blazer, red tie, and
shirt with a collar so high and starched and tight he looks like
he's in traction.

His right-wing rants on CBC's *Hockey Night in Canada*
have made him the macho megamouth defender of our national
sport. But you'd never guess from his wardrobe. "People were
writing in that it was very obvious I was a latent homosexual,"
says Cherry, sixty-four. "I had to ask someone what 'latent'
meant." At the moment, thirty-one of his shirts are having
their monogrammed cuffs and three-and-a-half-inch collars
replaced. Cherry, who's afraid they'll shrink at the cleaner's, has
his daughter-in-law handwash them; he personally stretches
the collars while they're still damp. The shirts occupy one

whole closet in his Mississauga home. His double-breasted suits fill the other three.

"I took all the closets," he says. "When Rose was alive, she got three-quarters of one." Rose was Cherry's wife, who was diagnosed with liver cancer in January 1997. Last May, she checked into the hospital. Three weeks later, she was dead at sixty-two. Rose wouldn't let Cherry tell anyone she was sick. "She didn't want to bother Ron," he says, referring to Ron MacLean, his sidekick on *HNIC*'s "Coach's Corner" segment. So Cherry kept working. Finally, the CBC issued a press release saying he would miss the Stanley Cup playoff final because of a family illness.

The next morning, a Sunday, Cherry drove to the hospital. "She waited till I got there from church." He twists the diamond-studded hockey ring on his wedding-band finger. "I was holding her hand when she died." He gulps his Coke. "You gonna eat?" he says gruffly. As he orders tortellini, I confess I'm no fan of hockey violence. My two young boys only play soccer and take karate. Cherry, who sells thousands of Rock 'em Sock 'em hockey-highlight videos every year, sputters.

"Karate! And you're worried?"

Rose was the only woman Cherry ever dated. He was twenty, a Grade 9 dropout from Kingston, Ontario, playing with the American Hockey League team in Hershey, Pennsylvania. She was eighteen, a secretary at the chocolate factory. On their first date, he invited her to a game, where she watched him get into a bloody fight. "She thought we were nuts, like you do."

Rose followed him to places like Trois-Rivières, Sudbury, and Spokane. In 1981, after five years coaching the Boston Bruins with Bobby Orr and the Colorado Rockies, Cherry joined *Hockey Night in Canada*. "I could tell when I did a good 'Coach's Corner.' Rose wouldn't speak to me for a day." Their biggest fight was over hockey. After making a coaching error that resulted in an overtime goal that eliminated the Bruins from the 1979 playoffs, Cherry couldn't bear to watch any more. When Rose insisted on watching, he stormed home to Kingston for two weeks. "It's the only marriage where the husband went home to his mother because the wife wanted to watch hockey."

Remembering Rose, he laughs and, sometimes, verges on tears. He's supporting Rose's Place, a hospice in her memory to help families of terminally ill children. Once a month, he drives three hours to Kingston, stays by her grave for several hours, then drives back to Toronto. "We were always together, all the time. When I was in a meeting, I could hardly wait to go home," says Cherry, the son of an electrician and pro baseball player.

He hates eating alone, and would phone Rose to wait for him. On the road, he'd call her every morning just to talk. He never fished, sailed, or golfed. He preferred homebody hobbies—feeding goldfish and collecting Royal Doulton china—and was happiest sitting at the table munching her muffins. "Rose and I used to settle the world from eight to nine-thirty every morning."

Cherry still gets Rose's muffins. His Filipina-Canadian daughter-in-law, Lisa, discovered the recipe. But now he eats them standing by the kitchen sink. After Rose died, Cherry reverted to a hockey-player diet. "Single guys," he says, "find out that twenty-four bottles of beer will fit in the vegetable bin." Lisa began stuffing his freezer with precooked meals after she found him eating beans out of a can and rinsing the spoon under the tap.

Lisa and Tim, who runs this restaurant, live across the street. When Cherry forgets to close his garage door, they stand in their guest room and use a spare remote to beep it shut. She also irons his shirts. His daughter, Cindy, handles his money. When Rose died, Cherry didn't even know where he banked.

She doled out the money sparingly. "So here's the big-time Don Cherry getting $60 at a time." She demanded his hotel receipts the moment he came home. "I'd say, 'Could I at least get in the door?'" With no one to give him the deep-freeze treatment when he comes home, he's less cautious about dropping Cherry bombs on live television. He assumes some viewers tune in to catch the moment he self-destructs. His CBC contract goes, he says, "from week to week."

At the recent Nagano Olympics, he dumped on freestyle skier Jean-Luc Brassard for complaining about carrying the Canadian flag. And he attacks Swedes for "parachuting in here taking jobs from Canadian boys." But he is no racist. "If you're a Canadian, you're a Canadian. We all came from somewhere."

On Tuesday, he'll hit the road for a month of playoffs. When Rose was alive, he thought of quitting to spend more time with her. "But what's the sense of stopping work now?" he says, pausing to sign a customer's autograph. "What am I going to do?"

A year later, Don Cherry quietly remarried. His new wife is a blonde named Luba, nearly twenty years his junior. Cherry was delighted that many people assumed she was his daughter. His "Coach's Corner" remains the highlight of Hockey Night in Canada.

margaret trudeau

IN A HOT FLASH, MENOPAUSE FREES
THE FLOWER CHILD

February 13, 1997

At forty-eight, Margaret Sinclair Trudeau Kemper is finally, happily infertile. "You're free," she says, having just completed two terrible years of menopause. Her fame has always been linked to fecundity. There was the fairy-tale marriage to a bachelor prime minister when she was twenty-two and he was fifty-one. Then, in quick succession, three baby boys, two (exactly two years apart) on Christmas Day, the third on Gandhi's birthday. Later, with her second husband, a fourth son arrived and then a fifth child, her only daughter.

Pierre Trudeau first spied Margaret thirty years ago in Tahiti. He had been "an ugly duckling," she says, "a creepy intellectual ... until Trudeaumania." He wanted children, and there she was on the beach. "I was eighteen, sitting with my parents, probably in my little bikini. Perfect." She half-rises from her chair at Juniper, a trendy Ottawa restaurant, to show off her now Rubenesque figure, slapping her rump for emphasis. She doesn't work out, but takes stairs two at a time. At this lunch, she nibbles a salad to keep her curves from maxing out.

Menopause was rough, almost breaking up her second marriage. At forty-six, she stopped menstruating, had mood swings, and dyed her hair blonde. The hot flashes were "like shifting gear without the clutch in," she says. "My doctor examined me and said, 'Everything's shrinking very nicely.' Well, I didn't want everything to shrink." Last summer, she suffered a "huge sadness." She couldn't stand being around anyone. Fried (pronounced freed) Kemper, her husband of thirteen years, took their two children and moved out to their cottage. Her doctor prescribed estrogen, and she reconciled with Kemper—and redyed her hair brown. Her blue eyes are still enormous, her smile still dazzles. She is wearing a gauzy scarf, snug grey sweater, and tight jeans.

Kemper, an Ottawa real-estate agent one year her junior, was rich when they married in 1984, two weeks after her divorce from Trudeau. Then his real-estate business went into voluntary receivership. They still have a ski chalet and two cars—a Ford Explorer and an old Mercedes—but Margaret feels poor. "We had a bit of a sad week because my Visa bill came in, and Fried got to it before I could hide it," she says, her voice suddenly a baby-doll simper. "He's so shocked at how expensive Christmas is. Aren't we all? But with Martha Stewart hanging over us, a little plastic wreath on the door does not work."

After the divorce, the three boys moved in with Trudeau, who oversaw their homework and banned television. On weekends, Margaret indulged them with pizza and rented videos. Justin, twenty-five, teaches snowboarding in B.C.; Sacha, twenty-three, a philosophy graduate, spent the summer in military boot camp; and Michel, twenty-one, a Dalhousie student, portages through Algonquin Park each summer.

"I don't want my kids to become victims of the drug culture," says Margaret, whose father was a Liberal cabinet minister. "But I'm hip enough to understand that drinking a beer and having a joint with your friends is different from snorting cocaine or shooting heroin." But not hip enough, it seems, to avoid the wrong end of a generation gap. "We have one earring and two tattoos in the family," she says, grimacing. One tattoo is a tricolour raven over an entire back shoulder—needled on a beach in Thailand. "We were very angry. We insisted he go through an AIDS test," she says. "And this was a boy who used to scream when he got a splinter." (The test was negative.)

She sighs. "They laugh at me. They say, here I was, a hippie revolutionary." Back in the seventies, Margaret was Canada's Fergie and Princess Di combined. Instead of managing her small army of servants at 24 Sussex, the flower child wanted to serve them. "What an ungrateful little bitch," says Margaret in a stage whisper. She didn't suck toes, but she began hanging out with Mikhail Baryshnikov, Jack Nicholson, and the Rolling Stones. She became anorexic, acted in two terrible movies, and smoked marijuana.

At 24 Sussex? "That would have been illegal." Pause. "I have no memory of it." I bite my tongue to avoid blurting that if you remember the sixties, you probably weren't there. But what about now? She shakes her head. "But if they would just legalize marijuana and capsulize it, I'd take it every day instead of a drink because I like the buzz and the warmth."

When she had Justin two years after the October Crisis, Trudeau told her that if terrorists took them, there would be no deals. "He told me to roll over in the gutter, hold the baby to me, and scream with all my might because I would be harder to pick up. You can imagine how I felt." In 1977, on her sixth wedding anniversary, Margaret told *People* magazine about her husband's fondness for garter belts and the effect her nipples had on state visitors. Shortly after, they announced they were separating. There were no support payments. "He was mean to me in that way. But you know what? Good for him."

These days, she only dances while she dusts, with the stereo turned way up. "Now, give me servants!" she says, gazing heavenward. Her big thrill is a part-time job stuffing envelopes and organizing events at WaterCan, a nonprofit agency devoted to bringing clean water to the Third World. "It's Barbie goes to the office," says Margaret, who formerly hosted a television talk show in Ottawa. "I'm excited about my stapler."

She notes she is the same age Trudeau was when he met her. "I want him to think well of me," she says wistfully, adding that she wishes he had been the father of her daughter, apparently without considering her current husband's feelings. (In 1991, at age seventy-one, Trudeau had a daughter with lawyer Deborah Coyne, who was then thirty-six.)

Margaret's brooch frames a tiny photo of Alicia, now eight. "If she's anything like me, she'll have a strong sexual urge because she's a born mother. I'll tell her that until she's forty-eight, she'll have to battle her impulses and desires."

During our long lunch in Ottawa, I kept wondering when Margaret Trudeau would retract her blithe statement about wishing Pierre Trudeau had been the father of her only daughter. She never did. I can imagine the screaming in her household the morning the interview ran. That afternoon, she phoned to say she had never said such a thing. I grabbed my notebook and read her back the quote. "I wish I had never met you," she said, and hung up.

Soon after, amid a flurry of rumours that she was obsessed with Princess Diana's young sons, Margaret Trudeau was hospitalized for depression. Then, in late 1998, Canadians were stunned and saddened when an avalanche swept the Trudeaus' youngest son into icy Kokanee Lake in eastern B.C. Michel Trudeau's body was never recovered. The stress of coping with her son's death broke up her marriage to Fried Kemper. She resumed calling herself Margaret Trudeau, which is what the public has always called her. And she announced plans to cohost a television talk show for aging baby boomers.

In September 2000 Pierre Trudeau passed away. Margaret was at his side during the last days, and sat front and centre, with her two sons, at the state funeral.

peter nygård

FASHION DESIGNER'S TAN REFLECTS
THE DARK SIDE OF LIFE

April 24, 1997

On a visit to Winnipeg, someone tipped me off about some sexual-harassment settlements involving Peter Nygård, who had created a personality cult about himself as a socialite and the biggest manufacturer of women's clothing in Canada. Intrigued, I invited him to Lunch. Over sandwiches in his office, we had a lovely time talking about his lavish entertainment habits. But the atmosphere changed when I asked about the sexual-harassment suits and his child-support payments, or lack thereof. He terminated the interview.

The next day, Nygård's lawyer began phoning, faxing, and mailing legal threats. The Winnipeg Free Press, The Globe's sister newspaper, had already printed several stories about Nygård and sexual harassment. It, too, was feeling heat from his lawyers. All this made The Globe's editors nervous. They set higher and higher hurdles for publication, which made me want to pursue the truth even more rigorously. Among other requirements, I had to go back and tape crucial interviews with former employees, obtain legal files from an ex-girlfriend who once picketed him for child support, and exact promises from various sources that they would testify on The Globe's behalf if we ever went to court. David Roberts, in our Winnipeg bureau, searched court documents pertaining to Nygård's child-support payments. My own observations of elevator lifts in his old black boots weren't good enough; I needed a former Nygård assistant on tape confirming that he indeed wore lifts. (I got that.)

I spent weeks nailing the story. Each time I submitted a draft,

the editors kicked it back and raised the bar. I cut more and more
material. The part about sexual harassment, the original catalyst for
the story, shrank to seven sentences and is restricted to his side of
events. But I'm stubborn. I wrote and rewrote. One fine April day, my
column was finally approved. I read it through. Then I realized they
had rewritten the ending so that it clunked, loudly, with lawyerly
prose. I objected. I was told to shut up and be grateful. At least we
could mention the sexual-harassment complaints. So, after six months
of rewrites, the Peter Nygård column finally made it into print.

Peter Nygård is a touchy-feely kind of guy. He grabs me by the
shoulders. "Stand here," says Canada's biggest clothing manufacturer and designer, pulling me onto a fish tank set flush
with the floor. "Glass is very strong."

As I climb the stairs behind him, on a grand tour of his
Toronto office, past the tanning salon, open-pit fireplace,
indoor waterfall, and caged pink parrot named Buyer ("Give
me an order! Not enough!"), I notice what seem to be two-inch
lifts in his black boots. For the next two hours, the lifts will be
about the only thing I don't dare ask about.

Over a sandwich lunch in his vast showroom and office, I
do ask Nygård, fifty-six, about his playboy lifestyle, his out-of-
wedlock children, and his court-mandated child-support payments. I also ask Nygård, who was recently chosen as one of
Canada's most eligible bachelors by Air Canada's *EnRoute* magazine, about his thinning hair and too-perfect teeth.

Nygård, whose family immigrated to Canada from
Helsinki when he was twelve, grew up in Deloraine, Manitoba,
in a converted coal bin without indoor plumbing. These days,
his silk and polyester separates are sold across Canada. Huge
posters of his grinning, tuxedoed self have adorned Eaton's and
the Bay. His privately owned Nygård International Ltd. has

2,400 employees, 135 stores, a Los Angeles distribution centre, factories in Winnipeg and Saskatoon, and imports 60 per cent of its inventory from Asia and Mexico. He pats a chunk of the Berlin Wall he bought as a coffee table. "It's a constant reminder for me how lucky we were to live on the right side of that wall," says Nygård, who lives mostly in the Bahamas, a "non-resident for tax purposes" in Revenue Canada parlance.

Nygård started out in Winnipeg in Eaton's home furnishings. In late 1966, he joined the sales staff of Tan-Jay, a local clothing manufacturer, soon acquiring 20 per cent with $48,000 of mostly borrowed money. Three months later, when the owner died of cancer, Nygård, then twenty-seven, became president. Eager to join the fashion ranks, he grew out his Eaton's-era brushcut, worked on a perpetual tan, and began collecting Excaliburs, flashy replicas of antique roadsters. He built hedonistic office-homes. The Winnipeg one is a cross between the Flintstones and the OK Corral, with a sink of lava rock and a bed made of logs. His Bahamas home, featured in Robin Leach's *Lifestyles of the Rich and Famous*, has a stone-grotto jacuzzi and a seventy-foot-high treehouse office. George Bush went twice to gawk, bringing Barbara the second time.

At a Fourth of July party in 1986 at his office-home in Marina del Ray, California, Nygård painted an elephant white and dressed Great Danes in tuxedos. His Toronto office-home opening in 1987 attracted Premier David Peterson, Mayor Art Eggleton, Miss Helsinki, and actress Susan Anton. In 1992, when he and 44,000 other Canadians were awarded "commemorative medals" in the dying days of the Mulroney government, Nygård threw a black-tie gala to celebrate. (Videos of the 1992 party— and his daughter's Sweet Sixteenth—are part of his press kit.)

But Nygård's thirtieth anniversary passed recently without the usual champagne-soaked, feather-costumed party. "Business has been tough for ten years, and it's going to be tough for another ten years," he says in a slight Finnish accent. Anniversaries also remind him of his age. A lifetime of tanning has left his skin like a baseball mitt. His trademark blond mane doesn't quite cover his bald spot. He denies that he has implants. "I put a thickener into my hair, a mousse, and blow it dry," he says. And when I ask Nygård if he dyes his hair, he quips: "I add a little grey to the sides to give me a distinguished look."

Nygård says he is six foot two. I can't bring myself to ask if that's with or without lifts. I apologize for dwelling on his looks, but he does seem obsessed. A bronze bust of himself adorns the Toronto lobby. Everywhere, there are more huge, blown-up photos of him in a tuxedo, his favourite get-up. When I admire his perfect teeth, he bares them to give me a good look. "They're bonded," he says. "I even buy them as presents for my favourite people."

He says he has no idea how many favourite people he's had. "My life is such that if I need a date it's not hard at all." His only marriage, to a model, lasted three years and was childless. "Maybe marriage takes a lot of hard work. I'm much happier this way."

Maybe not. "Deep down inside, I'm longing for a relationship like my dad has with my mother," he admits. "They've been married for fifty-six years." Asked how many children he has, Nygård claims one son and two daughters with a woman who now lives in Seattle. But there have been a few others, including a son with Kaarina Pakka, a flight attendant. In 1993, Pakka picketed his Toronto headquarters for increased child-support payments. Nygård's company sued her for slander. Later, his assistant faxed me to say the missing money was Pakka's fault for sending cost-of-living documents to Toronto instead of the Bahamas. (When Nygård learned I had interviewed Pakka, he invited her and their son, now nine, to spend last Christmas with him, their first contact in years.)

In Winnipeg in 1977, a judge ordered Nygård to pay $150

a month to the Children's Aid Society to support another out-of-wedlock son, who was then two. In 1989, Nygård's lawyers urged the court not to "go overboard" with a wealthy man and suggested that the child, by then fourteen, continue to live modestly. But a judge ordered Nygård to up the monthly payment to $730. In 1992, when the son turned eighteen, Nygård's office argued that he wasn't a full-time student and therefore was not entitled to support. But the same judge, noting that the mother had sold almost everything she owned to raise her child, ordered Nygård to increase monthly support to $1,000.

"They [the women] tricked me into an unwanted type of entrapment," says Nygård icily. "I pay more than my fair share."

Now he wants me out. As I fetch my coat, I ask about some sexual-harassment complaints filed last spring with the Manitoba Human Rights Commission. Nygård, who says his company paid the three complainants to avoid further legal expense, denied any wrongdoing. His company paid the women about $18,500 in damages and lost wages and agreed to establish a sexual-harassment policy. The commission did not proceed with the case. It was settled last May. Nygård calls the complaints "blackmail" for bigger severance payments. "In hindsight, we should have fought it, but that's hindsight."

The Globe held its breath for weeks. *We never heard from Peter Nygård, or his lawyer, again. Nygård stopped doing a lot of interviews, but he continued to entertain lavishly. For the 2000 Oscars, he invited six hundred celebrities for a black-tie dinner at the Beverly Hills Hotel. Actor Tony Curtis was spotted among the guests. When asked if this was his first time at one of Nygård's Oscar parties, Curtis said, "Peter who? I never heard of the guy."*

keith martin

MD/MP, NEVER HOME, SEEKS SF

November 24, 1999

The conservative Reform Party, now called the Canadian Alliance,
has always been saddled with a right-wing, intolerant image. So I
was intrigued when an aide to Dr. Keith Martin, a Reform member
of Parliament, called seeking a little ink. Dr. Martin, the aide con-
fided, had just won second place in a beauty contest. I was also
intrigued because Dr. Martin represented Esquimalt, B.C. That was
where my grandfather, who arrived as a coolie in the 1880s to build
the Canadian Pacific Railway, had found work as a houseboy. And
it was there, in the summer of 1999, that several rusting boatloads
disgorged their cargo of nearly six hundred illegal Chinese migrants.
I was curious as to what Dr. Martin, himself an immigrant,
thought of them.

Dr. Keith Martin is tall, dark, and handsome. No wonder
staffers on Parliament Hill voted him 1999's second-sexiest MP.
Context is everything; first place went to that other Martin MP,
Paul. (Really.) Unlike the jowly finance minister, this Martin
resembles an exotic Pierce Brosnan. He's thirty-nine, eligible,
and has a thirty-two-inch waist. At six foot one, he weighs 175
pounds—without his dark suit and silk tie—the result of
working out five times a week at the gym.

This Martin is also lonely. "Very lonely," he says over dim
sum at Toronto's Bright Pearl Seafood Restaurant in the heart
of old Chinatown. He's so lonely, in fact, that his office pestered
"Lunch With" to take him out for a meal, something no other

right-minded politician has ever done. Either Dr. Martin is truly desperate for female company, or he harbours leadership ambitions for the Reform Party, currently led by the much-maligned Preston Manning, a previous "Lunch With" guest. (Manning agreed to Lunch, but only after I had pestered *him*. Alas, he didn't make the final cut for this book.)

Dr. Martin denies his leadership ambitions. He won't comment on his lack of female company. Indeed, he blushes when asked to confirm his last romantic date, way back in 1994, a year after he was first elected to Parliament. It was with a nurse in his Victoria, B.C., riding of Esquimalt–Juan de Fuca, wasn't it? "How did you know that?" asks an alarmed Dr. Martin, the Reform Party's health critic. He refuses to comment further on his social life, or the lack thereof. He also denies rumours that he's gay. "I'm not. Not by a long shot. Never was. Am not now. Never will be. I adore women."

Women don't adore him back, he contends, because of his dual profession. "Two of the worst things that happened to my social life was being a doctor and an MP. If I say I'm an MP, forget it. They don't think I make enough money." When women discover he's a doctor, he says, they "don't treat you as a regular guy. So I say I work in a hospital. I don't elaborate. They usually lose interest." The turnoff may actually be his hours. He normally works until 10 p.m., then gets sushi or take-out Chinese, something he grew to love as an impoverished med student. "You have to be comfortable with your solitude," says Dr. Martin, one of about ten bachelors on Parliament Hill.

At lunch, he's adept with chopsticks. But, mindful of his waist, he avoids spring rolls, not to mention braised chicken feet. He eats slowly, a surprise considering he once competed at family meals with four voracious younger brothers.

In addition to his duties as an MP, Dr. Martin hosts a weekly radio call-in show with constituents and a weekly cable television talk show. A recent guest: Rubin (Hurricane) Carter, who spent nineteen years in U.S. jails for murders he did not commit. Vacations are even less leisurely. Sometimes he practises medicine on native reserves. Last summer, he spent the parliamentary recess in Prince George, B.C. He worked mornings in a detox centre, afternoons for other doctors' practices, and nights and weekends in a hospital emergency room. If only he had more time, he'd help save a few endangered species in Africa.

His riding became the flashpoint last summer after illegal Chinese migrants floated here aboard rusty freighters and were detained at Esquimalt. "Of all the issues in the past six years, this one has received the most calls," says Dr. Martin. "It is not racism to send people back for queue-jumping and tell them to apply through regular channels."

He himself was a child-immigrant from London, England. His green eyes come from his Irish mother, his black hair and genetic tan from his father, who is half Portuguese, half East Indian. His parents worried that racism in England might curtail opportunities for their sons. In 1968, his family immigrated here, by boat because his mother was afraid of flying. "I just remember five [out] of seven days of throwing up." Dr. Martin now calls himself "a whatever" ethnic. Growing up in Scarborough, just east of Toronto, he suffered a decade of epithets. "Paki-bashing was in," he recalls. "I'd be jogging as a child, and adults would scream racist things—Paki, nigger, any combination."

Later, as a young doctor in South Africa during apartheid, he was thrown off trains in Pretoria for being dark. And he was congratulated for being white when he was smuggled into black townships like Soweto. He grew up wanting to save the world. He thought he'd do that, in microcosm, by becoming a doctor. And he'd do it in macrocosm by running for office and pushing through an anti-land-mine bill. He's called for a $10-a-carton tax on cigarettes. Currently, he's pushing for a two-tier health system that, he contends, would allow the rich to subsidize the poor.

Since his 1993 election, he's renounced his MP pension, flown on supersaver tickets, and, while on an antipoaching patrol on the African savannah, tried to save a two-tonne injured white rhino. "I put in thirty-two litres of fluid through her ear and spent hours trying to save her. The next day, she had fallen into a river ravine and we couldn't get her out. We had to shoot her." He pauses. "Sorry to bore you. I didn't mean to get off on a tangent."

Relax, honey. This isn't a date. Besides, he's so pretty he could talk about the International Monetary Fund—which he does, briefly—and no red-blooded female would lose interest. What he doesn't want to talk about is his love life. "It actually impedes my ability to do work," he says.

Told that "Lunch With" is a priceless opportunity for a free personals ad, he reluctantly cooperates, providing we mention land mines, endangered species, and health care. (We just did.) So Dr. Martin offers his idea of a dream companion: "Nice, compassionate, highly intelligent, very physically active, a girl who loves sports, has great curiosity, someone who likes to do things, explore." He wants children eventually, so he also sets age parameters: mid-twenties to mid-thirties. But no preference for, um, looks? "Looks will go," he says endearingly. "I want somebody who's attractive to me, a woman who touches your soul and captures your imagination."

If this description fits you, write: Dr. Keith Martin, MP, 678 Confederation Building, House of Commons, Ottawa, K1A 0A8. No postage required.

Fred Lum's sexy photo of Keith Martin was worth a thousand e-mails. Dr. Martin's office was deluged in the days following the story. At last report, he was still unattached. In 2000, as I had suspected, he entered the leadership race for the Party Formerly Known as Reform. Dr. Martin was considered a long shot to head the Canadian Alliance, behind Preston Manning, the former Reform Party leader, and Stockwell Day, the Alberta treasurer.

PIONEERS

dr. henry morgentaler

LIFE IN A BULLETPROOF VEST

November 3, 1998

I took Dr. Henry Morgentaler to lunch just before Remembrance Day 1998. Tensions were high because an unknown assailant, who had murdered one abortion doctor and ambushed several others, usually struck around November 11.

Dr. Henry Morgentaler is shown to the best table in the restaurant. But for Canada's most famous abortionist, it's the worst table. It's surrounded, back and side, by glass walls, with choice sniper positions all along the rooftops on Bloor Street in Toronto. But Morgentaler doesn't switch tables. Nor does he regret not wearing his bulletproof vest to lunch. "I find it very cumbersome," he says, ordering a glass of white wine at the Royal Ontario Museum's restaurant, Jamie Kennedy at the Museum.

He's seventy-five now, and still at the vortex of the abortion struggle. A week earlier, a sniper killed Dr. Barnett Slepian in Buffalo, the third U.S. obstetrician to be murdered since 1993. In Canada, snipers have wounded three gynecologists since 1995, all around Remembrance Day. "My security people tell me I'm the prime target," says Morgentaler, who knew Slepian. "There's a killer out there. And Buffalo is two hours from Toronto." So he's fixing the curtains in his Toronto home. He's also taking tranquillizers to help him sleep. But for someone who has had so many death threats he's lost count, he doesn't seem all that anxious.

The Nazi death camps either break you or they make you fearless. As the eldest son of two socialist Polish Jews, Morgentaler survived five wartime years in the Lodz ghetto. At twenty-two, he spent the last nine months of the war at Auschwitz and Dachau. His number isn't tattooed on his arm because, by then, the Nazis were too rushed. "But I remember my number: 95077," he says, spooning some black bean soup.

His brother survived the camps. His parents and his sister did not. Morgentaler, who speaks seven languages, including Yiddish, has a white beard and receding grey hair. He's dressed in a tweedy suit, an unfashionably wide yellow tie, and Mephisto walking shoes. He's slight—just five foot five and 140 pounds. "But I have a high moral stature," he says, his eyes twinkling behind his silver-rimmed bifocals. Morgentaler, who lost all his teeth in the camps, orders something soft: roasted salmon with red-pepper sauce.

He arrived by ship in Montreal in February 1950, with his pregnant wife, no overcoat, and just $20. McGill University rejected him, apparently because he was a Jew. Instead, after passing a special entrance exam, he studied medicine at the Université de Montréal. Morgentaler became a general practitioner, not a gynecologist. In 1967, in his capacity as president of the Humanist Association of Canada, he went before a House of Commons committee. Abortion—the botched back-street kind—was then the leading cause of death among women of childbearing age. He made headlines advocating legal abortion on demand. After his daring speech, desperate women besieged his Montreal office. He turned them away. He had only been expressing a philosophical position, he explained. He had no intention of risking his licence, or a prison term. "I was caught in my own rhetoric," he says, taking a bite of salmon. "I felt like a coward and a hypocrite."

He hadn't realized how much the concentration camps had sensitized him to suffering and injustice, or changed his attitude to legalities. In 1968, two months after his speech, Morgentaler began performing his first illegal abortions. "I was put in the camps by a government law," he says. "The fact that abortion was illegal didn't bother me. Some laws are wrong or stupid."

Over the years, he has performed 65,000 abortions himself, with another 100,000 done by other doctors at his eight clinics. Always, he worried about losing a patient. "It would have devastated me personally, but it also would have been terrible for the cause. It would have been front-page news. But we've had a perfect record."

In 1988, Morgentaler won a landmark Supreme Court ruling that effectively legalized abortion. But in the preceding two decades, he had endured four trials, numerous arrests, eight raids on his clinics, a fire-bombing, and ten months in jail. His legal battles cost $2 million, mostly paid by his supporters but $300,000 of which he covered himself.

Perhaps he wouldn't have been easy to live with under any circumstances, but the strain of his public battle took a toll on his private life. His first two wives won't speak to him. His only daughter shuns him. A few years ago, he separated from Arlene Leibovitch, thirty years his junior and the mother of his fourth child. Then, last February, a month before his seventy-fifth birthday, he proposed marriage and she accepted.

Morgentaler, who keeps in shape playing table tennis with their ten-year-old son, Benny, still operates four afternoons a week. Using vacuum suction, a technique he brought to Canada, he performs twelve to fifteen abortions each day. Each operation requires five minutes. "When I look back, I have a sense of accomplishment," he says, savouring a crème brûlée. "I helped so many women out of a bad situation. I changed the law, trained so many doctors, opened clinics. I also changed public opinion." Fewer unwanted babies are born, he notes, so fewer kids are abused and fewer grow up to commit violent crimes. But the anti-abortion groups, some of which called him "a Nazi baby-killer," haven't given up.

"I'm aware someone might pump a few bullets into me," he says, sipping a decaf. "But that won't deter me because I believe what I do is important. We have a safer, better society as a result. I felt it was my duty. And I've never regretted it."

A few days after our Lunch, Morgentaler went underground. But he survived both sniper threats and Lunch. Seven months later, the U.S. indicted James Charles Kopp on murder charges in the October 1998 shooting of Dr. Barnett Slepian. The FBI posted a $500,000 (U.S.) reward for Kopp and put him on its Ten Most Wanted list. In January 2000, Canadian authorities issued a Canada-wide warrant for Kopp for the attempted murder of Dr. Hugh Short, who in 1995 was wounded in the elbow by a high-powered rifle at his home in Ancaster, Ontario. Canadian police said that Kopp was also a key to investigations into the shootings of doctors in Winnipeg and Vancouver. Authorities posted a $543,000 (Canadian) reward for his arrest and conviction.

Canada's abortion rate showed a steady increase in the 1990s, according to Statistics Canada. In 1997, Canadian women had one abortion for every three live births, compared with one for every five live births a decade earlier. That was the year the Supreme Court of Canada struck down a law prohibiting abortions except in circumstances "endangering the life or health" of the mother.

helen gurley brown

ORIGINAL *Cosmo* GIRL STILL LIVING IT UP

January 29, 1998

Helen Gurley Brown is a walking contradiction: a twenty-two-year-old's shape on a seventy-five-year-old body. The odd result is a nubile body that creaks along so it doesn't fall down and break a hip. At lunch, Brown wears three-inch heels, a skin-tight Lycra top, and a matching size-two miniskirt. As she settles into a velvet loveseat at Toronto's Four Seasons Hotel, you can't help noticing her stomach is flat as a board. Her bosom isn't. But she's always talked about being a flat-chested "mouse-burger" all her life. What gives? A boob job?

"I pad," Brown says coldly. "Honey, isn't there anything else we can talk about?"

Who would have thought she'd mind? Brown is, after all, the Queen of Cleavage. For thirty-two years, she put "fabulous bosoms"—her words—on *Cosmopolitan* covers, boosting circulation to a fabulous three million copies an issue. Or rather, Brown *was* the Queen of Cleavage. In 1996, with circulation dropping, Hearst Magazines dethroned her in a palace coup. It didn't want a septuagenarian editing a product targeted at twenty-two-year-olds.

Hair should be a less touchy topic. But isn't Brown a brunette? Why is her fluffy pageboy reddish blonde? "It's a hairpiece," she says through gritted teeth. Brown slapped it on after doing forty laps in the hotel pool this morning. She also did forty laps the night before, penance for scarfing down cookies and three scoops of ice cream for dinner.

At lunch today, she hogs the breadbasket, taking all the focaccia and cornbread, although she doesn't actually eat any. When her salad comes, she eats it with her fingers. "I hate metal against my teeth," she says. Only an iron regimen keeps her five-foot-four frame at 101 pounds. On waking each morning, she does an hour of sit-ups and push-ups, followed by another half-hour of the same at her office. She's been known to commandeer airport meeting rooms to exercise.

"I know my face would look better if I weighed 105," says Brown, who does look a tad haggard after all those push-ups. "But it's so much fun at my age to have a flat stomach." She takes estrogen. She's also had painful dermabrasion for acne scars and an even more painful facelift, not to mention a nose job and silicone injections in her cheeks and forehead.

Looking in the mirror, perhaps Brown thought she would edit *Cosmo* forever. But with her age fast approaching her weight, the *Cosmo* girl is now the *Cosmo* granny. A former secretary turned advertising copywriter, she launched herself with *Sex and the Single Girl*, a combat manual she wrote during the swinging sixties. Her husband suggested turning the concept into a magazine. Long before Zippergate and Monica Lewinsky, *Cosmo* magazine condoned the office romance with the married boss. Revolutionary for its time, it offered monthly home-wrecking, as opposed to home-making, hints.

Not that Brown has done any such thing herself, at least not since she got married. She lost her virginity at age twenty, then played the field for sixteen years. And while she says she never once became pregnant, she remains ferociously pro-choice. At thirty-seven, a spinsterish age for the times, she married David Brown, the movie producer (*Kiss the Girls*). In nearly forty years of marriage, Brown says, she's been faithful to her husband, and he to her.

She grew up poor. Her father was killed in an elevator accident when she was ten. So it fell to Brown to support her invalid older sister, who died recently a few months short of her eightieth birthday. Brown's schoolteacher mother always encouraged her to use her brain and not have babies too soon, if ever. She became class valedictorian. Unfortunately, there was no money for college. To save money, she once tried to get a discount for a root canal, offering to skip the Novocaine. (The dentist refused.)

Brown hasn't lost the thrifty habits of her youth. She always scoops up leftover petits fours after dinner at good French restaurants. She always takes home the miniature liquor bottles from business-class flights. She always keeps free hotel soaps. She even takes the bus to work, paying senior-citizen fare. "It's only 75 cents. Taxi fare to my office is $5.50. Why spend the extra $5?"

It turns out that Brown once rejected a job application from the woman who would one day replace her. Years earlier, Bonnie Fuller had submitted a portfolio of fashion pages. "The art director at the time thought they could be better," says Brown carefully. "I made the final decision. It turns out Bonnie's fashion pages in *Cosmo* are *fabulous*."

When Hearst replaced her with Fuller, it kept intact Brown's salary, rumoured at $1.2 million (U.S.). It also gave her a Mercedes and a new title: editor-in-chief of its thirty-five international editions. Brown lays a manicured, silicone-injected hand on my arm. "I critique every one of the little darlings every month with little yellow stick 'ems," she says. "Some of the editors listen, and some of them don't."

Cosmo now has more sex and more celebrity covers. Circulation has increased about 10 per cent to 2.7 million in the last half of 1997, compared to the last half of 1996. But Brown doesn't approve of revamping the vamp. "There's a *Cosmo* format. If you don't like it," she growls, "then don't work for *Cosmo*."

Not surprisingly, the planned lengthy transition didn't work. When Fuller called her up for a rare lunch in 1997, Brown said as much. "It was totally none of my business, but they're using those bloody out-of-focus pictures more and more. I think it's dumb. I wouldn't have said a word, except it impacts my life. All the other international editors are picking it up."

Since Hearst took away her power, Brown has been to see her shrink at least twice. "They gave me what I call a soft landing. It was time for me not to be editor any more. But, yes, it hurt." With not much else to live for, she lives for dessert. Pushing aside her mostly uneaten chicken potpie (which she did eat with a fork), she orders chestnut-chocolate cake with rum-raisin ice cream. "I certainly don't think I'm a great beauty, or glamorous," she says, delicately spitting out a raisin. "But I'm not bad for my age."

A mere eighteen months after she replaced Helen Gurley Brown at the helm of Cosmopolitan, *Bonnie Fuller left for* Glamour *magazine. There, Fuller displaced yet another aging editor, seventy-year-old Ruth Whitney, who two years earlier had told the* Wall Street Journal *that she had no intention of retiring.*

gillian guess

GUILTY OF LOVE, AND DEFIANT TO THE END

June 19, 1998

Gillian Guess made headlines as the first juror in North America to be accused of having sex with a murder defendant while serving on his jury. As her bizarre case unfolded in Vancouver, I was sure she'd reject an overture for Lunch. But you always try. A noon interview conflicted with her courtroom schedule, she said. To my astonishment, she agreed to meet for dinner.

Guess who's coming to dinner? Not just Gillian Guess, Canada's first babe-juror, but her daughter, too. As Guess slides into a booth at Kamei Royale, a Vancouver sushi restaurant, you can't help noticing her tight black bell-bottoms and bubble-gum-pink lipstick. Her fifteen-year-old daughter, in contrast, is defiantly plain in a baggy navy sweatshirt. You'd dress like that, too, if your mom was accused of having sex with a defendant in a double-murder trial while serving on the jury. At forty-three, Guess gives new meaning to the term "courting trouble." She's also accused of obstructing justice by swaying fellow jurors to acquit her lover, Peter Gill, and five other defendants.

Police subsequently tapped her phone and eavesdropped on her bedroom. During her trial, Guess retaliated with courtroom outbursts, mid-trial interviews, and her own Web site, complete with sultry photo, real address and home phone number.

"Mom! You gave the home number?" says Alana Loewen, shocked.

Canada's most famous juror nods.

"Mom!" Alana wails.

According to the terms of her bail, Guess wasn't allowed to see Gill during her trial. At least he isn't on *her* jury. His 1995 murder trial, at $1.2 million, was one of the most expensive in B.C. history. Guess, who is on legal aid, believes the tab for her trial will reach $8 million. That includes three months of police wiretapping. "Every bodily function we had was listened to," says Guess, sampling some tempura after a long day in court. "It shocked me into celibacy. The sad thing is there's never been more opportunity in my life. I'm getting swamped with marriage proposals, flowers at my door."

Alana sighs and drains her Coke. Guess can't be stupid— she's enrolled at Simon Fraser University working on a master's degree in (what else?) law and psychology. But she's clearly missing some basic component, such as common sense. She insists the judge never told her to avoid having sex with a defendant. "I fell in love, and I'm facing ten years in jail."

It certainly was lust at first sight. "He had on a three-piece Gucci suit, short combed-back hair, glasses, totally manicured nails, the biggest, most beautiful brown eyes I'd ever seen. He looked like a choirboy." Actually, Gill was a convicted drug dealer. But never mind. During the courtroom courtship, he made eyes at her. She suggestively sucked candies. And she wore red boots to signal she was thinking of him. Guess concedes that jurors sleeping with defendants is "a moral, ethical problem." Asked point blank if she slept with Gill during his trial, she falls silent. But her daughter nods vigorously.

"In five years," Guess says, "there's been three men in my life, including Peter Gill. They're making me out to be a slut." She reels off the racy elements: "Interracial sex [Gill is East Indian]; difference in age—I'm ten years older; the forbidden fruit; the danger; the murders."

Her thirteen-year-old son, Adam, sometimes accompanies her to court. His high-school friends have been supportive about the his-and-her trials, Guess says. "I know it's been a real trauma for the kids," she adds.

"It's not a trauma for me," retorts Alana, her braces glinting.

"How can it not be?" Guess sighs.

"Because I deal with things differently from you," Alana says. "I look at it now with a sense of humour because if I didn't, I'd be a mess."

Guess was born in England and grew up in Ottawa. Her 1973 marriage to a drummer lasted a year. Her second marriage, in 1982, to a medical researcher in B.C. produced Alana and Adam and a life in Saudi Arabia and Oman. When that marriage also failed, she obtained $800 a month in child support, picked out a new surname, and moved back to Vancouver. Now she is mulling over offers of movie and book deals. Every day, she downloads from the Internet news items that are often critical of her. "They don't have the evidence, so it's the crime of the short skirt," Guess says. "They've called me a 'bottle blonde.'"

Her hair, we agree to say, is "apricot blonde." She's wearing false eyelashes, large triangular earrings, gold bangles, high-heeled platform sandals, and a sexy black vest. Alana fingers the gold-studded collar of her mother's filmy white blouse. "It looks like she's ready to go line dancing," she says, with the extreme contempt only a fifteen-year-old can muster. "And the vest is short and tight."

"I kept the vest done up because I saw this in the sun-light," says Guess, pointing to the shadow of her décolleté bra. "No way I wanted pictures of this." Guess blames the affair on stress from her former part-time job as an RCMP victim coun-sellor. "The courtroom became my fantasy. I could leave all the dead bodies, rapes, behind, so I could just make eyes with this good-looking guy."

She doesn't want anyone to get the wrong idea, though. "I would sit by the phone for weeks, but I don't call a man. I don't pursue men." But the more she got to know the real Gill, the less she liked him. "He gained a lot of weight, grew his hair long again, was riding his motorcycle." He was—surprise—violent, and once bit her hard on the calf. Also—surprise—he'd been seeing several other women. (He's married but separated.) Does Guess think she was used? "In my heart, I don't think so," she says. "I think I looked better, my body was better than it had ever been. I know at one point he did fall in love with me."

"You don't know," Alana says.

"Yes, I do," Guess says. "You'll understand when you grow up."

"Oh, Mom."

Gillian Guess lost. She was convicted of obstructing justice and sentenced to eighteen months in jail. She served four days and was released pending her appeal. "It feels good. Guess is back," she told reporters outside the courthouse after her release.

Her bail conditions required her to report weekly to a probation officer. She was also prohibited from having contact with her ex-lover and acquitted murder defendant, Peter Gill. When the Crown appealed Gill's acquittal, Guess fought against being subpoenaed in the case. In 1999, the B.C. Court of Appeal ruled that she couldn't be forced to testify. Then Guess decided, surprise, surprise, to testify after all.

She has since said under oath that she and Gill kissed on their first date—during a daytime break from court—under an oak tree in Stanley Park. While she was a juror on his case, Gill would follow her, meet her at bars, and leave messages on her answering machine instructing her to wear red in court to show she was thinking of him.

The affair, she said, lasted eleven months, until her arrest for obstruction of justice. During her appeal of her own conviction, Guess ditched lawyer after lawyer. "I felt like I was being babysat," she explained. For a while, she considered representing herself. The word was she had run through virtually every possible lawyer in Vancouver. The local Legal Aid Society would not comment. At Harvard Law School, sympathetic students posted a Web page offering hypothetical legal grounds for a Guess appeal under U.S. law. Harvard professor Charles Nesson invited a discarded member of her legal team to speak to his law class. "It sounded like the wackiest case I'd ever heard of," said Professor Nesson.

james houston

THE FAR NORTH TRUE AND FREE

November 20, 1997

I first met James Houston, one of Canada's top experts on the Arctic, at a literary festival in Sechelt, B.C. He delighted his audience with his eloquence and humour. I had to admit that until then I'd never heard of him. It seemed that many other Canadians hadn't, either. So when Houston came to Toronto to promote a book, I jumped at the chance to take him to Lunch.

James Houston, neglected hero of Canadian culture, plucks out the bulging eye of a grilled sea herring. "I pretty well eat everything in the world except lemon pie." A white man who lived among the Inuit for fourteen years, Houston was the first to ship their soapstone sculptures to the outside world. He taught them printmaking. And he forced the Hudson's Bay

Co. to pay them in dollars; until then, it tracked fur trades with brass tokens.

At seventy-six, Houston has a jutting jaw and wavy, silver hair. Dressed in tweeds and a silk tie, he is a prolific author and a master designer at Steuben Glass, where his sculptures of Arctic wildlife average $5,000 (U.S.). It's hard to imagine him building an igloo in forty-five minutes. The Inuit taught him that, and how to eat eyeballs, too. "It's like a grape," he said, delicately spitting out a membrane at Nami, a Japanese restaurant in Toronto, which offers the closest equivalent to raw blubber. The Inuit also taught him to eat raw fish and seal, a process he discusses in his bestselling autobiography, *Confessions of an Igloo Dweller*. He especially loves the marrow in the cracked thigh bone of a freshly killed caribou. Also raw?

"Oh, yes! Oh, goodness!" said Houston, who was born in Toronto and was raised on meat, potatoes, and, yes, lemon pie. Though his Presbyterian father, a textile salesman, wasn't exactly rich during the Depression, the family summered at Lake Simcoe. (It was there that Minnie, their Ojibwa maid, muffed the recipe for lemon pie, traumatizing him forever after.)

Houston always loved sketching. At twelve, he studied with the Group of Seven's Arthur Lismer, then the best children's art teacher in Canada. The Second World War cut short his studies at the Ontario College of Art. After five years with the Toronto Scottish Regiment, he studied drawing in Paris at l'Academie de la Grande Chaumière. In 1948, Houston was sketching in Moose Factory, near James Bay, when a bush pilot offered him a free flight to the Quebec Arctic. Dazzled by the pristine tundra, the young artist refused to leave. He had only a toothbrush, a can of peaches, and two words of Inuktitut: *igloo* and *kayak*.

That first day, Houston, then twenty-eight, chose between raw seal—on a bed of gravel—and rotting Arctic char. Seal scared him more. The second day, he shared the tinned peaches; some Inuit held a slice in their mouths for more than an hour. The third day, he sampled seal.

"If someone's starving to death, there's no end to what they'd do. I'd take a bite out of you," said Houston, who was in Toronto to promote his twenty-fifth book, *The Ice Master*, a novel about a nineteenth-century whaling expedition. Escargots, he noted, entered gastronomy when food was scarce after the French Revolution. His new friends nicknamed him Saomik (The Left-handed One). They taught him to speak Inuktitut and handle a dog team. But he flunked the course on sea ice. The odd Inuit falls through once in his life; Houston fell in five near-fatal times. "You run back home, pumping your arms or they'll freeze like armour. Then the women strip you and you jump in your sleeping bag." He jokes that a friend once speculated the plunges weren't entirely accidental.

Houston initially communicated by sketching. In return, the Inuit pressed carvings into his hands. Stunned by their beauty, he took them to the Canadian Handicrafts Guild in Montreal and to curators around the world. As the man most responsible for creating this multimillion-dollar art industry, Houston finds the switch from the politically incorrect word *Eskimo* grating. "Do they know what Inuit is in Japan? In Germany?" he said, referring to the two main buyers of soapstone carvings.

Houston married Alma Bardon, a *Montreal Star* reporter sent to interview him. On their honeymoon, she climbed a forty-foot frozen waterfall and became the second white woman to cross Baffin Island by dogsled. They settled in Cape Dorset and had two sons, to whom they spoke only Inuktitut. It was years before the boys discovered, tearfully, that they weren't Inuit. Houston became the first federally appointed civil administrator of West Baffin Island, a domain of fifty-eight families in an area half the size of Germany. One year, after ten nomadic families in another jurisdiction starved to death, Ottawa built schools and nursing stations. Igloos gave way to permanent dwellings, which required white man's petroleum and ended the nomadic life. "It was all the decent things that decent Canadians wanted to do. But it changed life beyond all recognition."

By 1962, his marriage was crumbling. Alma and the boys left Cape Dorset and moved to Montreal, then England. He moved alone to Manhattan. At forty-one, he took a designing job at Steuben Glass, rising early every morning to write. One book, *White Dawn*, led to a Hollywood movie and made him rich. He and Alma divorced in 1967—she runs an Inuit art shop in Lunenburg, Nova Scotia—and that year he married Alice Watson, an American editor. They divide their time between an eighteenth-century home in Stonington, Connecticut, and a fishing cottage in the Queen Charlotte Islands.

Houston notes that the Inuit actually don't eat blubber, raw or otherwise. (They burn it for fuel.) But he's grown to love raw seal. "It's beautiful red, a lovely texture, not fishy at all," he said, tucking into a plate of sashimi. "And young seal liver is the most exquisite thing you could eat."

dr. ruth

SHORT AND SEXY AND SQUARE

July 7, 1999

Dr. Ruth spots the Crowne Plaza chef peeking from the kitchen. She beckons him over to take her order: sunnyside eggs, fried potatoes, coffee. "And three tablecloths, please." At four foot seven and shrinking, Dr. Ruth doesn't want to disappear behind the table.

As if. In her custom-made silk dress—cobalt blue with red and orange flowers—she's showier than the fruit salad. The beaming chef promises her two cushions instead. They hoist her to eye level, but cause her size-4B blue suede Ferragamos to dangle far above the floor.

All this could have been avoided if Dr. Ruth had accepted an invitation to picnic at Toronto's first and only nude beach. After all, she's the one who advises folks to have sex "at a secluded place on a beach." "Ah, but did you see the word I used? Secluded," says the doyenne of the sexually explicit. "I don't want to be a voyeur," she continues. "Either [that or] I get undressed also, and I'm seventy-one years old."

Press her, though, and the truth emerges. The world's leading sexpert is actually a prude in silk clothing. "I would not have taken off my clothes. I have always been old-fashioned and a square." For a square, she has had (another recommendation) sex in the back of a car.

"And yes, it was good. That's because I'm short."

Dr. Ruth is tiny enough to shop for slacks in the children's department. For dresses—always with pockets—her tailor comes twice yearly from Italy. But for years, she bunched excess pantyhose in the toes of her shoes. "Fortunately, finally, because of the Chinese and Japanese market, Bally and Ferragamo have pantyhose in extra-small."

Her appetite isn't extra-small. She dabs the last chunk of fried potato into the last drop of runny yolk. With a contented sigh, she sits back and sips her coffee. Ruth Westheimer was fifty-two when she got *Sexually Speaking*, her first radio call-in show. She has since written seventeen books, with three more in the works. She also has a syndicated column, a private psychotherapy practice in New York, and her own Web site (www.drruth.com). Dr. Ruth attributes her success to her age, her chutzpah, and a fervent belief, after surviving Nazi Germany, in sticking up for what you believe in. Her success is all the more remarkable, considering she did everything she now tells people not to do.

She expected the first man she had sex with to marry her. He did not. Figuring she was "small and ugly," she married the first man who asked. The marriage lasted five years. She married again because she was pregnant. The man left soon after the birth of their daughter, Miriam. As a single mom, she worked as a dollar-an-hour cleaner while going to school at nights on a scholarship for Holocaust victims. (She holds a Ph.D. from Columbia Teacher's College.)

The third time, she got it right. Skiing in the Catskills, she met Fred Westheimer, who was short enough to avoid nudging her off the T-bar. The marriage produced a son, Joel, and lasted thirty-six years—despite separate bedrooms because Fred snored. He died of heart failure two years ago. She stopped colouring her hair after his first stroke and she wore her wedding ring until recently, when she won a tiny diamond ring for getting the lowest score at a bowling fundraiser for inner-city kids. But she still dyes her eyebrows and she can still dance all night. And she still skis, this past spring at Whistler, B.C. "I do not go on black-diamond [trails] any more," she says, referring to the most dangerous runs. "And I always ski with an instructor."

Dr. Ruth was the only child in a prosperous household in Frankfurt. "My mother worked as a maid in my grandmother's house. She got pregnant. We were Orthodox Jews. My father did the honourable thing and married her." Dr. Ruth found this out accidentally when, out of curiosity, she looked up records in her mother's village. "I got the date of their marriage and I did the calculation," she says, her grey-green eyes twinkling. "And I thought: Maybe that's why I went into the field of contraception."

She was five when the Nazis came to power. In 1938, at age ten, she boarded a train alone for Switzerland. She took only one of her thirteen dolls, but "gave it to another little girl on the train who was crying." She spent six years in an orphanage there, training to be a maid. She never saw her family again, and believes that they all died at Auschwitz. At seventeen, she made her way to Palestine and became a sniper for the Zionist underground. She says she never killed anyone, but was once badly wounded herself.

Dr. Ruth, who now collects prewar dolls, can still hurl a grenade. She's not bad with a water pistol either, as she discovered at a fair with her grandson, Ari. "We came home with fourteen stuffed animals and a goldfish." But enough about guns. She's in Toronto to push her latest book, *Dr. Ruth's Pregnancy Guide for Couples*, cowritten with a gynecologist. "What about the book? Will you mention it at least?"

Okay, so did she have good sex when she was pregnant? "I knew you would ask that," she crows. "Of course not. My daughter is forty-one. I wish somebody had written that book then."

Sexually speaking, though, she's had a wonderful life. Losing her virginity, in a barn in Israel, was "wonderful" and virtually bloodless. "There were a few tiny spots. I wish everyone would do it this way. Oh, it was a beautiful night."

As for her sex life now, Dr. Ruth is "going out," but wouldn't call it "dating." "I'm looking around. I don't necessarily have to get married, but I'd like to find a good companion. Somehow, someplace, somebody will find me interesting. Put that in your paper."

MUSIC MAKERS

bryan adams

A Vegan Who Says Cheese

October 20, 1999

Bryan Adams wants to eat at Prego. At least, that's what his publicist said. But when the rock star arrives forty minutes late, he suggests moving to a nearby deli. Alas, I've already raided the breadbasket, not to mention that the staff at Prego are all atwitter, so it wouldn't be polite to leave. Adams sits down.

His publicist has also nixed a photographer, the celeb logic of which escapes *The Globe*'s photo department. After all, Adams is in Toronto to launch *Made in Canada*, his book of photographic portraits of eighty-nine Canadian women. He'll be autographing copies of it at the opening of an exhibit of these photographs at the Royal Ontario Museum. Given that proceeds from *Made in Canada* go to the Canadian Breast Cancer Foundation, *The Globe* makes him an offer he can't refuse. There's a loaded camera on the table. If Adams will take a picture of himself, we'll pay him our $225 freelance rate, which he can donate to the Breast Cancer Foundation. He says yes.

But first, he scans Prego's menu. He sets it down. Stars don't eat from menus. Adams, after all, is a three-time Oscar nominee, with 55 million records sold, plus duets with Celine Dion, Sporty Spice, Bonnie Raitt, and Luciano Pavarotti. Although has been a vegan for the past decade, surprise, none of the salads—mesclun, romaine, endive—appeal to him. "We have arugula," says the waiter, mentioning a leafy green that's not on the menu.

"Arugula," Adams nods. "With lime and oil."

"Lemon and oil dressing?" the waiter says.

"Lime," Adams says.

Next he wants a pizza. There are two on the menu, but neither will do. Adams wants a plain pizza, with a bit of cheese. The waiter nods and rushes off. But wait. Vegans aren't supposed to eat eggs, milk, and cheese. "I love cheese, but I can't eat it," says Adams. "I pull it all off. It's just for flavour."

We first met last March when he shot me for *Made in Canada*. Had I studied the faxed invitation a bit more closely, I would have realized the photographer was *the* Bryan Adams, not just another guy named Bryan Adams. "I remember we talked about lunch," he says.

He did. During the photo shoot, he casually asked if I'd lunch him for this column. I laughed politely. A no-name photographer? After I reread the fax, I spent the next six months chasing down his publicist. "Are you serious? You really didn't know who I was?" says Adams. "I'm not the least bit offended."

He turns forty in two weeks. But he's a walking video of his hit song "18 til I Die," in shiny black Gucci jeans, a tight grey sweater, and, despite his voluble veganism, leather biker boots. His acne-ravaged skin contributes to his eternally boyish look. His complexion only settled down in his thirties, when he became a vegan. Perhaps that's why he won't allow photographs of himself. At a TV studio in Toronto recently, he specified no close-ups. And he kept checking the monitor to make sure. Like a student, Adams carries a backpack. Inside it, he tucks a trendy new cellphone with a tiny earpiece. Fear of brain cancer, he explains. But when he takes a call at lunch, it looks like he's lost his mind. He sits there hunched over, chatting by himself to his backpack.

Adams, who was born in Kingston, Ontario, always wanted to be a drummer. His father, who loathed rock music, disapproved. At ten, Adams got a Spanish acoustic guitar for Christmas, but no lessons. So he listened to records and figured out the chords by himself. To this day, he can't read music. He plays entirely by ear, and can mimic a melody after hearing it only once. And although he has a $3-million recording studio in Vancouver, he "writes" by switching on a tape recorder.

At five feet eight inches and 150 pounds, Adams is surprisingly scrawny. When his salad arrives with the correct lime dressing, he tucks his napkin into the collar of his sweater and digs in. His pizza arrives. He eats it. He does not pull off the cheese.

He was always, he says, serious about music. At fifteen, he dropped out of high school in Vancouver, determined to carve a career in music. "There was something inside of me—I knew I would stay in music, whether work in a record store, a roadie [the guys who slog gear], or work in a band," he says. "My first band was Shock, and we were shockingly bad."

He grew his famously dirty blond hair "past my nipples." At this lunch, it is relatively short and looks greasy. Either he's applied gel or he may just be badly in need of a shampoo. He won't say which. "I have a bath once a week," he deadpans, "even if I don't need it."

He didn't speak to his father for years. When his parents split and his mother moved in with her boyfriend, Adams was seventeen. He got his own apartment—and took his sixteen-year-old brother with him. Today, he is close to his whole family, especially his mother, whom he calls "the classic British eccentric." He pauses and looks slightly menacing, "And I mean that in the sweetest, most endearing way."

In 1976, when he was sixteen, he went to hear a band called Sweeney Todd. After the show, he sought out the producer and said he could sing way better than the lead vocal-ist. He got the job.

"You have to have insane self-confidence that you're going to get through this," he says, explaining how he copes with being a high-school dropout. "You end up getting an education another way. I ended up reading a lot of books I should have read, way after school."

Adams, who has dual citizenship, now lives in London. He once flubbed the updated lyrics to "O Canada" at an NHL all-star game in Vancouver, but considers himself a staunch Canadian. His blue-grey eyes are sharp. Unaided by glasses, contacts, or laser surgery, he can read my list of questions side-ways and across the table. He isn't happy about the section on his love life. Sample: Is he still with his long-term girlfriend, Danish model Cecilie Thomsen, a Bond girl in *Tomorrow Never Dies*? Answer: No comment. Sample: He cuddles with super-model Linda Evangelista on the cover of a CD he did for breast cancer research in the U.S. Did they have an affair? If not, why not? Answer: "That's for me to know and you to find out," he says with a grin. "I love women."

He certainly loved photographing them, even though, between his schedule and theirs, it was a logistical nightmare.

"I didn't have any trouble with anybody," he says diplomatically.

Indeed, a mole confirms the majority of big names were utterly cooperative. Still, some women demanded a limo pickup. Others requested touchups and airbrushing before approving their photos. Ontario lieutenant-governor Hilary Weston, who has six fur coats in her front closet, didn't want to be portrayed as a socialite. *Flare* magazine, which sponsored *Made in Canada*, conducted long negotiations over her pose. In the end, she vetoed the photo *Flare* liked and chose a more regal one. Actress Sarah Polley was out of sorts because the last time *Flare* ran a photo of her, the accompanying article noted that she had stood the writer up three times. ("Not cancelled," said the mole. "She just didn't show up.")

Inevitably, many prominent women are missing. About ten women didn't make the final cut. In addition, scheduling didn't work out with Sheila Copps, Kate Nelligan, and Buffy Sainte-Marie. As for Adrienne Clarkson, Canada's new governor-general, "her name never came up," says Adams. The final battle was over the book cover. *Flare* magazine wanted to put Pamela Anderson Lee, naked but for a Canadian flag, on the cover. Adams wanted Donna, a Vancouver friend he had known since he was seventeen. He won.

Donna, whom he won't identify by her last name, had breast cancer. She is beautiful, with liquid dark eyes, a gentle smile, and a head rendered bald by chemotherapy. "She died shortly afterward," he says. "She never saw her photo."

After lunch, we walk across the street to the Royal Ontario Museum. He can't wait to see my reaction to my portrait. After all, I got to wear, briefly, a $700 Armani outfit and have my hair done by a New York stylist and my face painted by a make-up artist who even has her own agent. But in the photo, I'm out of focus, my eyes are shut, and the clothes make me look like a Viet Cong peasant. Never mind. Sarah Polley, who refused all hair and make-up treatment, ended up with only half a face.

Inside the exhibit, Adams takes his own photo for *The Globe*. It turned out blurry, but it's unmistakably Bryan. He'll get the $225—and the photo credit.

The day the column ran, Suzanne Boyd, editor of Flare, *couriered a letter to Richard Addis,* The Globe's *editor. "Unfortunately, one has come to expect negativity from Ms. Wong. But it's doubly disappointing, considering Ms. Wong agreed to be photographed for this book, and one can only wonder if her motive truly was to support the fight against breast cancer."*

That raises an intriguing question. When celebrity hearts bleed, to what degree are the motives altruistic and to what degree are they trying to burnish their images? There's no question that Bryan Adams lost a dear friend to breast cancer. But his efforts also won him a mountain of flattering media coverage. Nowadays, a celebrity is expected to have an issue as much as he or she is expected to have a personal trainer. At twenty-five, Leonardo DiCaprio, for instance, became chairman of Earth Day 2000. DiCaprio, who drove a gas-guzzling Lincoln Navigator, had no previous record of environmental activism. To be sure, in our celebrity-driven culture, causes recruit famous spokespersons who can easily get booked on Leno or Letterman. At lunch one day, I couldn't help overhearing the two women at the next table. One was a publicist, the other a charity staffer. Throughout lunch, they talked pure business: how to procure clients such as Celine Dion for fundraisers for cystic fibrosis.

When Flare *lost the fight to Bryan Adams over the book cover, it still put the flag-wrapped Pamela Anderson Lee on its magazine cover that month. The magazine couldn't have made a worse choice. Women with breast implants suffer a higher death rate from breast cancer, doctors say. The implants don't cause cancer, so far as anyone knows, but they make detection that much tougher.*

Six months after my Lunch with Bryan Adams, the director of the Vancouver Art Gallery resigned after refusing to hang Adams's collection. "The gallery's curators were unwilling to support Bryan Adams as a noteworthy, artistic Canadian photographer," said the minutes of a meeting. The gallery's board split over the issue. One member reflected that "the Hollywood crowd" could be "important and useful to us." Another noted that Adams has a "credible art collection and could be useful to us." Still another opposed the exhibit, asking, "What price are we willing to sell our walls for?"

jukka-pekka saraste

THE MAESTRO WHO MAKES HIS KIDS CRY

November 28, 1996

The burning question for parents is: How does the conductor of the Toronto Symphony Orchestra get his kids to practise piano? "We fix a certain time every day," says Jukka-Pekka Saraste. "With us being there, of course. Fifteen minutes a day, around 5 p.m."

So does Saraste, forty, sit there nodding benign approval at his sons, Severi, nine, and Frans, seven, nurturing their fragile egos, reinforcing emerging self-esteem? No, he does not. He makes them cry. "I think you have to show passion when you deal with kids," he says. "Sometimes I'm really aggressive with them. Then they get mad and cry a bit."

Saraste (pronounced SAH-ras-tay) has just finished a tennis game with a doctor friend. He arrives for lunch at Yamase, a Toronto Japanese restaurant, with a TSO publicist in tow, and gulps a glass of cranberry juice. Since he moved here from Finland in 1994, he has been marketed as a sex symbol by the normally staid orchestra, currently celebrating its seventy-fifth season. Mass mailings feature brooding black-and-white shots of Saraste in tight jeans and Eurotrash beard. At a recent concert, ushers handed out programs that featured nine, count 'em, nine photos of Saraste, including a full-colour cover of him in sunglasses, stonewashed jeans, and scraggly hair posing against a deep blue sky. Beethoven merited one.

Sex, apparently, sells. At that same concert, a middle-aged woman uttered a tiny shriek when the TSO's poster boy strode on stage. Although a stronger economy hasn't hurt, many credit Saraste with nudging the TSO into the black. For the record, Saraste wasn't wearing jeans at lunch, and his front teeth protrude unevenly. He is surprisingly short—five feet seven inches—and bears no resemblance to the glamour photos. He looks more like a pouting adolescent trying to grow a beard who accidentally fell face first into a lawn mower.

I wonder if he actually spends a lot of money trying to look like that, and ask where he cuts his hair. "In Finland," he replies. He isn't kidding. Luckily, he has retained his job as conductor of the Finnish Radio Symphony Orchestra, or his hair might be down to his waist. On those twice-yearly trips back to Helsinki, he visits the same female barber who has cut his hair for the past fifteen years. And in between? "As you can see," he says, shaking his head and laughing.

Does Saraste think he's sexy? "I'm a very serious musician," he says. "I want people to come for the right reasons." Back home, he points out, he is not a sex symbol. "In Finland, nobody markets anything." His ticket sales there are expected to cover a mere 3 per cent of costs, compared to 50 per cent at the TSO. That may explain why desperate TSO marketers have built a personality cult around Saraste. They put his breezy signature in lights on the symphony's electronic billboard outside Roy Thomson Hall. (Jukka-Pekka is Finnish for John-Peter.) They even stencilled it, in mauve paint, on the sidewalk. Why mauve? "To tell you the truth, the paint was donated," says the publicist, looking slightly embarrassed.

Saraste, who is said to earn several hundred thousand dollars a year, doesn't have to worry about cheque forgers. He never writes any. An accountant friend handles the bills, including the $30,000 he pays annually in Toronto private-school tuition for Severi, Frans, and Sylvia, the last being his youngest, who just turned seven and is agitating for violin lessons.

At Yamase, Saraste orders a platter of sashimi. He also seizes a bowl of cold spinach, meant for all three of us, and eats that, too. Having a minder present has been an in-house rule of the TSO ever since one of his predecessors made a couple of disastrous verbal slips. Saraste himself committed a Eurocentric gaffe soon after moving to Toronto. "It's a very great shame if we can't be among the first to perform a [Canadian] composition we think is very important ... but I haven't yet found a piece that I think will change the musical world," he said, sparking a firestorm of nationalist indignation.

As Saraste chews on a piece of raw tuna, he momentarily loses his hangdog demeanour. The side benefit of being a conductor, he says happily, is eating his way around the world. He tells me about a trip eleven years ago to China where he feasted on a succulent pigeon and a classic Peking duck, the latter crisply spherical and oozing fat. The fat, he sighs, "was the best part."

Saraste spends his summers fishing, boating, and chopping wood in Finland. In Toronto, he coaches kids' soccer. He loves jogging—without a Walkman. After work, he never turns on the stereo. There's already too much music, he explains, in his head. Saraste yearns for his own kids to play music the way it's supposed to be played. Unlike TSO musicians, however, the boys ask why. "I tell them that otherwise it sounds stupid. Nobody can dance [to it]. Nobody can sing."

I mention that my dad always wondered what a conductor did besides waving his arms. "It's the most puzzling profession in a way," Saraste agrees. "People don't understand what the hell the guy is doing. A conductor is somewhere between a traffic warden and somebody who inspires them to play in a certain way. But basically they're really like traffic wardens." Several hundred years ago, orchestras played without conductors, he notes. One of the first famous conductors, Jean-Baptiste Lully, at the court of Louis XIV, kept time by pounding a stave. One day, he smashed his foot. He contracted blood poisoning and died. I burst out laughing. Saraste looks pained.

I ask what's his favourite piece of music. He names a Strauss waltz. I write that down. The next day, his publicist calls to say that was a joke. I don't burst out laughing. Classical-musician humour and my own, I guess, just don't intersect.

In a letter to the editor, Kelly Rossiter wrote that my comments on Saraste's appearance were "shallow and mean-spirited" and my questions "unbelievably banal." Rossiter added, "By the way, I thought Mr. Saraste's joke about the Strauss waltz was quite funny—I burst out laughing."

The TSO's publicist called my editor to complain that I had made Jukka-Pekka Saraste's children cry. (Other kids had teased them at school about tearful piano practices.) So I was dismayed— and I'm sure the feeling was mutual—to discover a year later that Saraste's daughter and my son Ben ended up in the same class. Luckily, we never crossed paths at parent-teacher meetings.

In April 2000, after seven years as TSO conductor, Saraste announced he would quit in July 2001. He was tired, he said, of the poor acoustics in Roy Thomson Hall and the dearth of financing. He was also bruised by an eleven-week musicians' strike. And, he said a bit tactlessly, he wanted to raise his children to be Europeans, not Canadians.

The personality cult hadn't worked. The average capacity audience for symphony concerts was only 74 per cent. "When Mr. Saraste arrived in Toronto, he seemed like a fresh young tonic," wrote Robert Everett-Green, The Globe's *music critic, in reporting Saraste's departure. "As the seasons passed, however, his limitations became more apparent. Youthful energy couldn't hide a lack of depth in some important repertoires. The conductor, who had been promoted as the new face of symphonic cool, turned out to be a rather distant personality."*

Saraste himself told Everett-Green that he felt uneasy with the way the TSO had marketed him, confessing, "I think the campaign went overboard."

All I can say is, when someone insists on going all the way to Finland for a haircut, worry about how long they're planning to stay in Canada.

eartha kitt

DOWN TO EARTH

June 4, 1998

Eartha Kitt removes her sunglasses and glares. Twice, she asked her publicist to fetch her cigarettes from the limo. Now the waiter at Biagio is annoyingly vague about which vegetables come with the halibut. This minor Earthaquake comes at the end of five television interviews promoting *The Wizard of Oz*, which opens in Toronto tomorrow. Kitt, who plays the Wicked Witch of the West, had to let rip her spine-chilling cackle again and again. As Batman's original Catwoman, she also had to growl for the TV interviews ad nauseam. Now her stomach's growling, too.

"I carry food with me just in case. I have to keep my sanity," she snaps when asked if she's hungry. She lights a Marlboro Ultralight, takes a puff, and stubs it out. Kitt is tiny, muscled, and strong, like a sex kitten on steroids. At seventy-one, she still jitterbugs. She does handstands on talk shows. And for all her diva airs, she's a star who's, well, down to earth. "I scrub my floors and wash my windows and I clean my bathrooms," she says. "It's therapeutic."

Her café-au-lait skin is gently wrinkled. Asked whether she considers herself black or white, she arches her back like an angry cat. "I have no colour," she says. "I have no race. I was given away because I was mulatto." Rejection has scarred her life. Cosmetics tycoon Charles Revson loved her, but feared narrow-minded shareholders would dump his stock. Cinema-chain heir Arthur Loew Jr. loved her too, but couldn't defy his mother. He married Tyrone Power's widow instead. In 1968, even her country rejected her. Kitt was blackballed after criticizing the Vietnam War at a White House luncheon given by Lady Bird Johnson. Work dried up at home for the next twelve years.

"Those hurts never go away. That's why I'm so grateful to the public. Because they became my family. And they make me feel wanted. Going on stage, I'm a nervous wreck, because I never want to be rejected again." She relaxes when her salad arrives. At home in Bedford, New York, Kitt eats her own produce—garlic, tomatoes, squash, collard greens. Her only hired help is for her large garden.

The blacklisting hit as her five-year marriage to a Jewish-Irish Korean War veteran was crumbling. She took her only child, Kitt Shapiro, to Europe, South America, wherever there was work. She never took off her clothes, though. "I might be considered a sex symbol, but I was always a lady." At night she hired sitters to watch her slumbering child while she sang such hits as "C'est si bon." When her daughter turned five, she enrolled her in the French lycée system, which was always on the same page on the same day no matter what city they were in.

Kitt thinks her father might have been a plantation owner's son. When her mother, a Cherokee-black, wanted to marry another black, the man objected to Kitt's light skin. So her mother gave her away. She was maybe six. "Old enough to remember everything in detail," Kitt says.

She only recently discovered her actual age after a professor in her native South Carolina assigned students the project of unearthing her birth certificate. Kitt lived with a black family, but they weren't relatives. They abused her sexually and sent her to pick cotton for a penny a pound. She remembers hunger, too. "I'd follow the birds and snakes, the deer, and ate whatever they ate." She survived on wild grapes and scallions, dandelions, hickory nuts, and the soft inner leaf of cattails. She sucked the sour juice from a purple-flowering weed.

Two years later, she was sent to New York to live with someone else, who beat her. So did other kids at school. "Nobody wants you if you're a yella gal, because you don't fit in. And because you're illegitimate." She ran away repeatedly. She snagged loose change from under subway grates, using sticks primed with gum. She slept in subways and on rooftops. That's why today she supports Green Chimney, which teaches ghetto kids how to grow food. It's also why she went to South Africa before the end of apartheid and stood on the street, signing autographs for one rand each, eventually raising enough money to build two schools.

In New York, Kitt auditioned at the Katherine Dunham Dance Company on a dare and won a scholarship. In 1945, she toured Europe and later sang in a Paris cabaret. Orson Welles cast her as Helen of Troy in *Dr. Faust*. Although he called her "the most exciting woman in the world," he didn't like being upstaged. "Crunch," says Kitt, recalling one stage kiss. "Right down into my bottom lip. He drew blood."

She stands up, setting off a tremor at the neighbouring table, where her two publicists and a make-up artist are enduring second-hand smoke. "I have to go to the ladies' room," Kitt announces. "Come with me." The make-up person meekly follows. Later, asked why she wanted an escort, Kitt stares through her false eyelashes. "Because somebody might ask me for an autograph and I'll go 'Aaiieee!' And she'll calm me down because I never like to refuse. That's my bread and butter."

Kitt once took the sheets from a movie she was shooting. Now she would like a little bottle of the olive oil on our table.

She orders a bowl of blackberries. She picks one up, musing, "I lived on these when the family I was with didn't have enough," she says as the waiter adds the olive oil to *The Globe*'s tab.

"Diamonds and fur are wonderful, but give me land. I know how to survive from dirt."

I still wonder what she did with the bottle of olive oil. I keep imagining it leaking in her luggage, all over her black cashmere pants.

yo-yo ma

BACH AND A BLT TO GO

November 27, 1997

I'd always assumed that Yo-Yo Ma was the greatest cellist in the world. But after consulting several critics, it turned out that he's among the greatest. So what makes Yo-Yo Ma seem like No. 1? As Lunch shows, he has a genius for marketing.

Yo-Yo Ma still has to pack. All morning, the world's best-publicized cellist has been shuttling between camera crews in two hotel suites. Now he's eighteen minutes late. "He says he can pack in one minute," his publicist says when I fret about how much time I'll actually get with him.

At forty-two, Ma is the superstar musician with the Midas-marketing touch. Perhaps ten cellists in the world play as wonderfully as he does. But no one sells like Ma. "Can I quickly use the bathroom?" he says, bursting into the hotel room. Through the washroom door, he shouts to the publicist: "Can you just look around my room?" As she leaves to check for stray socks and cellos, she says to me: "You have until twelve-fifteen." That's twenty-eight minutes, minus toilet time.

When Ma emerges, he beams at the Four Seasons' room-service bounty I'd ordered in advance to save time: fruit, cheese, mineral water, Coke, and a BLT with fries. He reaches for a French fry with his thin, muscular fingers and begins speaking in Chinese. Ma, who was born in Paris, is also fluent in French and English. His parents named him Ernest but always called him Yo-Yo, which means friendship. That caused trouble when he was seven and his family moved to New York. Classmates called him Yo^2. "Or, you know, what Sylvester Stallone says to his mother: Yo! Mama," says Ma, whose face has only recently shed its baby fat. Lately, he's inspired stupid-name jokes on *Seinfeld*. Fans constantly send him, yes, yo-yos. And recently a cartoon portrayed him and Boutros Boutros-Ghali having lunch. Waiter: How was your mahi-mahi? Ma: So-so.

"People constantly come up with new ways of torturing me with my name." In the end, he should be happy Yo-Yo Ma is such a catchy name. "I'd prefer Jan Wong," he says, switching to English.

Ma knows airtime sells CDs. That's why he hasn't slotted in bathroom breaks in Toronto while promoting a film series called *Yo-Yo Ma, Inspired by Bach*. To smash out of the classical-music ghetto, he's also appeared on late-night talk shows, played jazz with trumpeter Wynton Marsalis, and cut a tango album.

When he was four, Ma chose the cello because his older sister already played the violin. They didn't make cellos that

small, so his composer father stuck an endpin on a viola. By
five, Ma had memorized three Bach cello suites. In New York,
his music school's annual recital was held at Carnegie Hall, creating the legend that he debuted at nine. "I played one piece,"
he says, noting his real debut came six years later. As a prodigy,
Ma says he skipped grades, practised for hours every day, and
graduated from high school at fifteen. "It's torture. Give bright
kids enrichment, extra stimulation," he says, "but do not take
them out of their age group. I was hanging around with
twenty-one-year-olds, trying to be tougher." At college, he
went wild—wild, that is, for a Chinese kid. He drank beer,
went AWOL from rehearsals, left his cello out in the rain. At
Harvard, he earned a B.A. in humanities and, at twenty-two,
married Jill Hornor, a German-literature instructor. His parents weren't thrilled their only son had married out of the race.

"One of the things for immigrants like my family—they're
dealing with what's new and what's old. They fear losing the
old traditions," says Ma, chewing on the bacon-lettuce-tomato
sandwich. In Chinese culture, he notes, the new wife is supposed to be her in-laws' servant. "So they see it as a loss. Their
whole investment is skewed." Ma describes his father, who died
of a stroke five years ago, as a highly intelligent and thought-
ful man. "But decisions were handed down. As soon as I
entered second grade, people asked, 'What do you think?' I
didn't know what I thought."

Both Ma's children play the piano. Emily, twelve, also
plays violin, and Nicholas, fourteen, sings. The only reason
they are musical at all, he says, is because his wife has insisted.
"At the first sign of 'I don't want to practise,' I would have
said, 'Okay.'" He doesn't wish prodigy-level talent on either.
"Are you kidding? I don't want anyone to be like me," says Ma,
who is on the road six months a year but makes a point of being
home for birthdays and at least half the weekends.

His publicist reappears. "Five minutes," she warns. Asked if he earns more than any other classical musician, Ma frowns. He talks about all the free and badly paid concerts he gives. The publicist hisses: "One minute."

Ma ignores her. "Go to Israel ... you basically play for your plane fare. Other places can't afford to pay, like China. So therefore, you don't go there? No. You go." Now his publicist is pacing. "Yo-Yo," she whispers, reminding him he has to autograph CDs at a record store and play before the lunchtime crowd.

"I have to play?"

"In ten minutes," she says.

He grabs a handful of red grapes, drops one on the rug, picks it up, and eats it anyway without breaking his stride. Just before the door bangs shut, he shouts, "Thank you for lunch. Best lunch I've had in days."

I decide to follow him in a taxi. Ten minutes later, Ma is on a makeshift stage. No other classical musician of his stature has ever hustled at HMV on Yonge Street before. Phones ring, the ventilation system hisses, and cash registers purr. But more than a hundred people listen to him as he performs the first Bach suite he ever learned. Ma's face is rapt. Heartbreakingly beautiful music fills the store. As his fingers range over the eighteenth-century Venetian cello he's nicknamed Sweetie Pie, the thought occurs: He hasn't had a moment to wash the grease off his hands.

grace slick

THE VOICE THAT LAUNCHED A THOUSAND TRIPS

October 27, 1998

Lunch with Grace Slick, a cigarette-puffing, recovering-alcoholic vegan, is a communal fruit platter. But it's on the coffee table, an awkward stretch from the sofa in the enormous sunken living room of her King Edward Hotel suite. So let's eat psychedelic sixties-style, cross-legged on the floor. The rock 'n' roll diva, who turns sixty next year, sighs. Her knee cartilage is wrecked. And she never eats during interviews. Told she must because the column is called "Lunch With," Slick sinks to the floor with a groan.

"I don't do two things at the same time," she mutters, plucking a grape. "That's why I didn't do orgies in the sixties." Slick did do almost everything else. As the female vocalist for Jefferson Airplane, she slept with every member of the band but one. She took every drug but heroin. And she was arrested more times than she can remember.

If you can remember the sixties, of course, you weren't there. In her new memoir, *Somebody to Love*, Slick forgets in what country in Europe it was that she slipped into bed with Jim Morrison, the Doors lead singer. (She does remember he was "larger than average.") She also forgets in what city she stood naked on a window ledge, howling at a storm. "I can't really blame it on drugs," says Slick, who carries file cards in her purse reminding her of airline flights. "I was sober all during the eighties and my memory was the same."

Unlike Janis Joplin and Mama Cass, two other rock 'n' roll

mamas, Slick survives. "Jefferson Airplane is the only group I
think that has nobody dead," says the voice that launched a
thousand trips. "Isn't that amazing?" At lunch, she's in all-
black. Her size-six vinyl platform sandals cost $9 (U.S.) at
Payless ShoeSource, her $16 top is from a catalogue, and her
"nobody jacket" is from Macy's, eight years ago. She's not poor,
but in her current life of buying vegetables in Malibu,
California, she needn't dress fancy any more. Unlike many
rockers, Slick didn't blow her fortune or allow record companies to rip her off. Her investment-banker father always told
her to buy low, sell high, avoid the stock market, and concen-
trate on California real estate.

"I never spent more than half of what I earned. I never
bounced a cheque," says Slick, dutifully munching another
grape. A former model, she's still beautiful, with flowing sixties-
style chestnut hair and startling cobalt blue eyes that lock on
to yours like radar. "Contacts." She leans forward, widens her
eyes, and, with a white-polished fingernail, helpfully slides a
blue disc around.

All her life, she kvetched about being flat-chested. Then, in
her fifties, she shot up to a 36D. She was so alarmed she saw her
gynecologist, who credited hormones. Slick swears she didn't
"have boobs implanted, because nobody cares in your fifties."
Her new breasts annoy her because she can no longer sleep on
her stomach. Alas, the newly voluptuous author of *Somebody to
Love* has nobody to love. The erstwhile goddess of free love is
celibate. "Heterosexual men don't like screwing old things."

Slick, who's had two husbands and umpteen serious relationships, dumped her last boyfriend in 1994. He was a manic
depressive who set her bed on fire when she was still in it. One
evening, he shoved her around, then called 911. Slick, who was
very drunk, ordered the fuzz off her property. "They said,
'Grace, put the shotgun down,'" she recalls. "But I was ready

to go out on that. I thought I had had a really good life." An officer knocked her over and disarmed her. Some $77,000 in lawyers' fees reduced a felony charge to a misdemeanor. She was sentenced to eight months of delivering meals to AIDS patients. It's hard not to note that, in her day, there was a cure for every sexually transmitted disease.

"Good timing, huh?" she says, sipping ice water. I ask which bedmate provided the best sex. "Initially, everyone's fabulous," she says. Endurance matters, she says. But in the end, "nobody's good. Now I'd much rather go to bed alone and fart."

It was that mouth that alienated Grace Wing's classmates. On her fourteenth birthday, twenty girls phoned to say they hated her. She began drinking. Her Mayflower-descendant mother sent her to Finch, a New York finishing school. In 1961, she dutifully married Jerry Slick, the son of her mother's best friend. Bored with housework, she modelled at I. Magnin's, an upscale department store. One night, she watched Jefferson Airplane play a San Francisco club. "They only have to stand up two hours a night" compared to modelling, which was eight. So she joined them.

"I am not a serious musician," she says. "I didn't join a rock 'n' roll band for any revolution. I joined a rock 'n' roll band because it looked like fun." Once, though, she plotted to slip LSD into Richard Nixon's teacup. Slick was on the Finch guest list at a reunion hosted by Tricia Nixon. But White House security blocked her and her escort, Abbie Hoffman, at the gate.

Slick last tripped twenty-two years ago, when her favourite hypnotic, Quaaludes, was taken off the market. She has no acid flashbacks. Today, her demon of choice is alcohol, which constantly gets her into trouble. "Without alcohol," she writes in her memoir, "I'd be richer by two million dollars that went to pay lawyers' fees." Her last bender was a year ago. She went into rehab, with her daughter China Kantner, whom she and fellow Airplaner Paul Kantner had originally named "god." Slick smiles and eats another grape. "They'd never had a mother and daughter at the same time."

Slick smiles a lot—to avoid alcoholic facial sag. Otherwise, she fears she looks mad. She chucks her chin wattle, pokes her belly roll, slaps her underarm flab. If it weren't for the pain, she'd love a little liposuction. "The only painkiller I can take is alcohol," she says, "and we don't want to do that, do we?"

Everyone later scoffed that I had bought Grace Slick's explanation that her bosom had suddenly blossomed late in life. I believed her. Hope springs eternal in the human, um, breast.

liona boyd

BLONDE AMBITION

October 20, 1998

Liona Boyd filled concert halls in the 1970s, famous as much for her guitar strumming as for her looks. Then, in 1998, she came out with her tell-all autobiography, recounting in particular her affair with Prime Minister Pierre Elliott Trudeau. As part of my research, I asked several music critics to rank her talent. They all said she was okay but hardly great. That led me to focus on exactly how Liona Boyd had managed her career.

Liona Boyd checks out the Formica tables at Fran's. Thirty years ago, she came to this restaurant with her mother for hot chocolate after Toronto Guitar Society concerts. The Unitarian church is just down the street. "I got $11 a shot playing there," says Canada's first lady of guitar. Boyd, forty-nine, now lives in Beverly Hills. She and her husband, a California millionaire old enough to be her father, call their 8,000-square-foot mansion Peach House. Their Sri Lankan manservant calls her Madam. He offers honeyed tea and morning massages. Once, when Boyd's cat went AWOL, he even slept in the garden in case the cat came back.

At breakfast, Boyd orders pancakes and coffee with steamed milk. She weighs 112 pounds, the same as in high school, and has an amazing twenty-four-inch waist. "I do not have breast implants, although everybody has them in L.A.," volunteers the 36C, with a toss of her cascading blonde hair. (L'Oréal, every three weeks, at home.) Whether or not she's a great guitarist is beside the point. Once upon a time, audiences loved her blonde beauty. "I was a good package," says Boyd. "I was on more magazine covers. If I was ugly and weighed three hundred pounds, maybe I wouldn't have gotten the same attention."

She's promoting her new autobiography, but you don't have to read between the lines to know she's always been terrific at self-promotion. When she played for the sequestered O.J. Simpson jury, she took a picture of herself in Judge Ito's chair and then called her agent, who phoned CNN. *In My Own Key* recounts her brilliant career. When she was twenty-two, a virgin, and an unknown University of Toronto music major, she met Alexandre Lagoya, the guitar virtuoso, at Toronto's Park Plaza Hotel. She ended up going to bed with him. He ended up teaching her for two years. ("Surprising," mused a 1978 *Globe* article, "since he normally takes no private students.")

Boyd began recording and touring, but until the midseventies she was known mainly as a warm-up act for Gordon Lightfoot. Then, in 1976, she began an eight-year affair with

Trudeau. Soon, Boyd was photographed strumming for the Queen, Ronald Reagan, and Margaret Thatcher. Afterward, Trudeau's driver would deliver Boyd to 24 Sussex Drive.

Of all the musicians in Canada, why was Boyd the artist of choice at G7 summits? "The guitar was the ideal instrument after a state banquet, a very elegant, classy touch," she says. "Besides, it was a lot easier than booking a string quartet or a whole orchestra." In 1982, a year before she and Trudeau stopped seeing each other, Boyd was awarded the Order of Canada.

Does she think she slept her way to the top? Boyd's smile doesn't waver. "I was attracted to these particular people, not just for career success." Her husband, Jack, seventy-two, didn't help her career in any way, she adds. But he's a millionaire. "So am I," says Boyd, who's sold a million albums.

She unwraps a billiard-ball-sized clump of tinfoil and selects eight vitamin pills. "It worked well for both of us," says Boyd of her career as state strummer. "He [Trudeau] got me to come to Ottawa more than I normally would. And I met a lot of interesting world leaders." As the prime minister's wife frolicked with the Rolling Stones, *People* magazine noted: "Margaret's Fave Guitarist May Be Keith, But Pierre Trudeau Digs Liona Boyd." When Trudeau and Boyd weren't skinny-dipping at Harrington Lake, the prime-ministerial retreat, he sometimes lent Boyd his wife's clothes. "Somebody said the other day Margaret was not looking too good, that she was kind of heavy now," says Boyd, swallowing a capsule of black-currant-seed oil (for strong fingernails). "I said, 'Goodness, she's had five kids. I'd look like that, too.'"

Boyd, who never wanted children, takes a tiny bite of pancake. She and Margaret aren't friends (surprise), but they agree on one thing: "Pierre was stingy," says Boyd. At Christmas, he gave her leftover chachkas. Once, when they were dining out, he slapped his pants pocket and announced he'd forgotten his credit card. "I forgot mine, too," Boyd sweetly told him. The restaurant sent the bill to Trudeau's office. She has sent him her book, but hasn't heard his reaction. "It's a bit of an invasion of privacy," she agrees, swallowing a calcium pill, "but I kept my mouth shut for twenty-two years."

In the early eighties, Boyd tried to break into Hollywood. She took a room at the Beverly Hills Hotel and tried to meet people. She soon gave up. Back in Toronto, she moved in with Joel Bell, a former Trudeau aide. By the late eighties, after a disastrous foray into pop music, Boyd's career was on the rocks. In 1991, she gave California another shot. Three days after her arrival, she met Jack Simon and began dating him almost immediately. A year later, they married, and he razed the house he had lived in with his late wife. The new mansion, down the street from Merv Griffin, has a gym, a domed conservatory, and a guest wing.

Boyd's career hasn't exactly flourished since her marriage, either. That may be why we're getting the kiss-and-tell book. Over breakfast, she makes a point of mentioning a forty-five-city tour of Canada, which she starts next month. Breakfast over, she airkisses me. Her coral lipstick is intact. Her meal is barely touched. By weight, she's eaten more vitamin pills than pancakes.

My sister sent me a clipping from a monthly called Forever Young Montreal *with a full-page Q & A, headlined: "Liona Fights Back!" According to* Forever Young, *Boyd had called them up and "volunteered to be interviewed in an attempt to respond to her critics."*

Sample hard-hitting question: "Many would describe you presently as glamorous and sexy. Are you comfortable with that?"

Answer: "Thank you, I always thought I had a very natural image ..."

Boyd was also asked: "What's it like being interviewed by The Globe and Mail's *columnist Jan Wong?"*

Answer: "Jan Wong was out to prove I slept my way to the top. That's ridiculous. Trudeau did not help my career, except for inviting me to play for a few heads of state. If I wanted to further my career, I should have slept with record producers and top managers."

denny doherty

CALIFORNIA DREAMIN' LEADS HIM HOME

March 26, 1998

Denny Doherty doesn't normally do lunch. His show-biz bedtime of 4 a.m. means he hates rising before noon. Never mind that his hit of the moment is a preschool TV show called *Theodore Tugboat*. At fifty-seven, the former member of the Mamas and the Papas has jowls. His reddish beard is shot with white. He drives a minivan. In the swinging sixties, he travelled by private jet. That was back when he was still California dreamin' in a psychedelic haze of drugs and alcohol.

"It all happened so quick. Bam! Pow!" says Doherty of his rise to fame and fortune. Over a table of spicy Swatow food in Toronto's old Chinatown, he talks about growing up in Halifax's north end, the youngest of five children in a staunch Catholic household. His father, a dockyard worker, would stumble home drunk every Friday night, he says. Doherty dropped out in Grade 9, too ashamed to continue. "I needed clothes, shoes," he says, eating a chunk of stir-fried chicken.

At nineteen, he moved to Montreal, where he played

nightclubs for a year. A year-long stint in Toronto followed before he moved to Greenwich Village in 1963, joining Bill Cosby, Joan Rivers, and Woody Allen on the coffeehouse circuit. "Bob Dylan was dropping off sheets of his song 'Blowing in the Wind,' " recalls Doherty, wearing black jeans and boa-constrictor cowboy boots.

Along with Cass Elliott, John Phillips, and Phillips's eighteen-year-old model wife, Michelle, Doherty formed the Mamas and the Papas in 1964. Before they hit the big time, the group dropped acid, smoked dope, and drank. After they hit the big time, the group dropped acid, smoked dope, and drank. Doherty's liquid intake was a quart a day of rum or vodka. "I never performed loaded, but I would stop and buy a jug of rum and put it in the trunk for after."

The group soon moved to Los Angeles, where Doherty bought a Cadillac, John and Michelle bought matching Jaguars, and Cass bought Rudy Vallee's mansion. Doherty bought Mary Astor's, complete with contents, including some Sèvres vases. (He sold a spare one to Bing Crosby.)

Then Mama Cass fell in love with Doherty. Doherty began to sleep with John's wife, Michelle. It was around this time that the group signed their first recording contract, but the seeds of their destruction were sown.

"To all intents and purposes it was over before it started," sighed Doherty, biting into a whole chili. "Cass had the hots for me. But I was stupid, drunk, vain, and in love with somebody else's wife. Cass weighed three hundred pounds, and I wasn't man enough to get past that and realize there was a human being inside who wanted to get married and settle down and have kids."

When John found out about Michelle's affair with Doherty, he kicked her out of the band. But before the four-part vocal group completely self-destructed in 1968, they produced a string of enormous hits, beginning in 1966. They included "Monday, Monday," "Got a Feelin'," "I Saw Her Again," and "Dream a Little Dream."

Through it all, Doherty remained true to his roots. He'd duck into church to pray, "freaking out my L.A. friends." He returned each Christmas to Halifax, where his folks were underwhelmed. "My father would say, 'Get yourself a trade, something you can put in your arse pocket.'" Wisely, Doherty put himself on a $500-a-week (U.S.) allowance. Stupidly, he hired the record company's attorneys as his attorneys. He never did find out how many records they actually sold. In the 1980s, after the group's catalogue had been tossed around during several corporate mergers, he made a claim of $8 million in royalties from MCA, which had ended up with the rights.

"I should have said $80 million," he says, finishing off his steamed rice. "But I swear if I got the money when I was young and crazy, I would have killed myself and ten other people." When he turned thirty-nine, Doherty tried in vain to quit drinking. "It's so insidious, so built in to our culture. I had a wonderful time when I was drinking, but I was poisoning myself," he says, sipping a Coke. When his second wife, Jeanette, became pregnant in the early eighties, Doherty went into rehab. He dried out in twenty-eight days. "I started getting information that you don't get from Seagram's on the bottle. The doctor said, 'Alcohol's a drug, stupid.' I never considered it."

His daughter from his first marriage lives in Florida and has one child. Doherty currently lives with Jeanette and their two teenagers near Lake Ontario, in suburban Mississauga. "It's been seventeen years," he says. "Neither of my children has seen me take a drink." Emberly, sixteen, attends an arts high school and studies piano at the Royal Conservatory of Music. John, fifteen, also in high school, is a drummer with green hair.

Any tattoos or pierced belly buttons? Drugs? Alcohol? "No, no, no," says Doherty, horrified.

Have his views on free love also changed? "Making love was never deadly before. It's too dangerous now, even with condoms. You're not talking about just getting somebody pregnant or getting VD."

"California Dreamin'" has recently become a cult hit in Britain and the Far East. The royalties, now properly recorded, are pouring in again. Doherty, who doesn't need to work, gets a kick out of playing the benign harbour master in *Theodore Tugboat*. It airs in seventy countries and is filmed in Halifax. "The strangest thing is doing it in my old high school," he says, explaining how the miniature boats ply a "harbour" created by flooding the gymnasium floor.

Mama Cass died, alone, of a heart attack in 1974. Michelle became a soap-opera star. John Phillips has had a liver transplant and two hip replacements. He has also served time in prison for drugs. "People say to me: 'Your life is so exciting, you've been all over.'" Doherty sips some jasmine tea. "Yeah, I'm back in my Grade 5 classroom playing with tub toys."

In keeping with the Theodore Tugboat *theme, I had originally booked Denny Doherty for lunch at a fish-and-chips joint in North Toronto. To my embarrassment, the restaurant had closed that day. But Doherty was cool. After he posed for a few photos in a windy doorway, we jumped in his garnet minivan and drove to Chinatown. He paid for parking, and even dropped me back off at* The Globe.

FOODIES

jean paré

COMPANY'S COMING

December 11, 1997

As a foodie myself, I'd never heard of Jean Paré. But she's famous within the canned-soup segment of the eating public. This one-woman wonder has sold more cookbooks than any other Canadian. Since our Lunch, I've started using her cookbooks. At ten, my son Ben loves whipping up her recipe for lemon squares.

Jean Paré shrieks and burrows, eyes squeezed shut, into the safe, dark centre of the glassed-in elevator. Sixty-one seconds later we've shot to the top of Toronto's CN Tower. At the world's highest revolving restaurant, the maitre d' blinks. No window seat? "Sorry," apologizes Paré, who turned seventy on Sunday. "I'm afraid of heights."

You'd think someone who has sold 13 million *Company's Coming* cookbooks might be a bit less apologetic. Or that an acrophobic who also runs a multimillion-dollar food empire with three hundred food outlets, including Domino's Pizza, Grabbajabba, Manhattan, and Pastels, might be a bit more assertive about vetoing the choice of restaurant. Not Paré (pronounced parry). But beneath her unassuming demeanour—five foot four, honey-coloured perm, delicate glasses, purple suit, and flowered briefcase—there beats a true-grit Prairie heart.

Indeed, she pulled it all together when her alcoholic, gambling husband walked out half a lifetime ago, leaving her with four children and a repossessed house in Vermilion, Alberta (pop. 4,000, "rounded up").

Paré's outsized lack of ego has struck a golden chord—$100 million in sales over sixteen years for her hostess-survival manuals. Fans devour the terrible puns—"a tall pile of toads could be called a toad-em pole"—that pepper her recipes. And with company coming this holiday season, they lap up her homespun advice: "Start your next dinner by asking everyone to compliment someone at the table."

Unlike the Martha Stewarts of the world, Canada's most popular cookbook author thoughtfully includes pronunciation guides for such exotica as caffe latte (ka-fay LAH-tay). Canadian Tire outlets sell her plastic-ring-bound books from $4.99 to $15.99. And no one seems to mind that she uses canned tomato soup in cake. "I'd make a bad food critic. I even like airplane food."

The menu at 360, as the revolving restaurant is called, trumpets its executive chef's philosophy: "If I have to go to Sweden for something special, I will." Paré rarely goes farther than Vermilion. Her recipe for Tuna Supper could be whipped up in a survival bunker: canned mushroom soup, canned mushrooms, canned tuna, canned French-fried onions, frozen peas and carrots, dried onion flakes, and chow mein noodles.

What with fresh vegetables, 360's menu is a bit too haute for Paré, who settles for a bowl of tomato soup. She also orders a cranberry soda. "At least it'll look pretty," says Paré, who just finished *Beverages*, her thirty-fourth cookbook. Her titles are as unintimidating as her recipes—*Casseroles*, *Salads*, *Cookies*, *Pies*. But don't assume she isn't fussy. Paré won't even try an oyster, an escargot, or sushi. She forced herself to taste lobster once. On a recent trip to Hong Kong, she was so cautious she sampled her

Chinese food at a pizza parlour. And she didn't eat her first shrimp until she was forty. "It looked like a cutworm," she says with a shudder. Nowadays, she sometimes dares to eat clam chowder. "But if I see a little frilly edge, I have to set it aside."

She blames her abattoir upbringing. In Irma, Alberta (pop. 250), her father owned the slaughterhouse and the general store where, at eleven, she worked the counter after school. It grossed her out. "I had to put a cloth over the liver in order to slice it for a customer." In the Depression, Paré learned cooking on a wood stove. She grew up without running water or a refrigerator, which may explain the appeal of canned goods. During the long Prairie winters, the only fruits available were oranges and the occasional lemon. Even now, her favourite snack is a hard-boiled egg. She always munches them during the two-hour drive to Comac Food Group Inc., her Edmonton corporate headquarters, where her parking space is marked "Mom."

She became one at nineteen. When her husband, a cattle auctioneer, walked out, she was thirty-eight and had four children. She moved with them to Edmonton and found a clerical job. But she couldn't afford a babysitter. And her kids missed Vermilion. Steeling herself against the small-town gossips, she moved back, took out a loan, and started catering. Two years later, she married Larry Paré, who worked for an oil company.

Everyone kept asking for her squares recipes. So in 1980, at fifty-four, she published a cookbook, *150 Delicious Squares*. No one told her she was supposed to find a publisher first. No one told her you don't distribute books yourself, either. Paré and her children sold them to hairdressers, hardware stores, lumber yards, and ice-cream parlours. That first year, she sold 64,500 copies. No one told her Canadian cookbooks usually sell a couple of thousand.

Paré samples 360's soup and pronounces it okay. A diamond band flashes on her finger. Her kids gave it to her in 1986 to mark her millionth sale. When she hit three million, they hired a plane to drag a "Congratulations" sign over Edmonton. Paré, who appears on a weekly television show, also puts in eleven hours a day at her test kitchen in Vermilion. With her thirty-fifth book, *Breakfast and Brunches*, due out in April, Paré arrives at work no later than six-fifteen every morning. She breaks only to drive two minutes home in her Oldsmobile Regency (vanity plate: COOKBKS) to make lunch for her retired husband.

And what does she serve her husband? "Soup and a sandwich. Canned soup."

marion warhaft

REVILED FOOD CRITIC NOT COMPLETELY OUT TO LUNCH

April 23, 1998

Marion Warhaft, long-time food critic of the Winnipeg Free Press, *was in hot water. Fed up with her lukewarm reviews, sixty restaurant owners banded together and tried to get her fired. They also banned her from their restaurants. As the daughter of a restaurateur, I was intrigued. I left it up to Warhaft to pick a place for Lunch.*

Marion Warhaft drives past Winnipeg's Tap & Grill. "That's the guy who said that if there was a hell, he hoped I'd roast in it. And I didn't even give him that bad a review."

She slows down at Nibbler's Nosh, a restaurant she said had flunked "the greasy-spoon standard." It hasn't yet opened for lunch. A man is sitting by the window. Could that be the owner, Ernie Walter? He stares back. "That's him!" she cries. We both duck, and she guns the motor.

For the past twenty years, Warhaft has reviewed restaurants for the *Winnipeg Free Press*. In that time, she's been refused service, chefs have phoned to weep, and she's been sued—unsuccessfully. In March, a group claiming to represent sixty restaurants, including Nibbler's Nosh, trooped into the *Free Press* offices. They accused Warhaft of "abusing the power of the press" and demanded her firing. They also vowed to ban her from their premises. "They don't know, but it isn't me they don't like," says Warhaft mildly. "They just don't want a restaurant critic."

Selecting a safe place for lunch is tricky, considering the Gang of Sixty's membership list is secret. (They said they're afraid she'll retaliate.) So Warhaft drives to Green Gates Country House & Restaurant, where she's known and liked—and where they'll still feed her. Most restaurateurs have no idea what she looks like. And Warhaft needs to keep it that way. Let's just say she's a widow, calories are a minor occupational hazard, and she wasn't born yesterday.

"Come to think of it, this is not my first scandal," she says. In 1987, the local restaurant association took out a quarter-page ad to review her reviews. "Her pen leaks ink spots that look like congealed grey sludge," the association carped.

The truth is, Warhaft looks for the positive. Seven out of eight reviews are enthusiastic. She samples my house-smoked fish, which I consider a bit dry. "Not bad," she says. "Moister than most."

When Warhaft dislikes the food, she often returns a punishing three times more just to make sure. She also advises the photographer to take an outdoor shot. "It's too cruel to have the owner smiling over a bad review." But some restaurants are steamed even when Warhaft dishes out praise. She awarded Cin Cin four stars out of a possible five and called the Italian restaurant "charming," with "big portions" and "good" food, "some of it well above average." Still, Cin Cin is among the eateries clamouring for her head, perhaps because she rapped it for hiking prices on Valentine's Day. She also called a 50-cent surcharge for decaf "petty."

"Winnipeg's a good eating city," says Warhaft, sighing contentedly over an appetizer of braised chicken livers. Her city, she notes, is second only to Vancouver in the number of restaurants per capita. Growing up in Winnipeg, she knew nothing about food. But then she moved to New York. After marrying a university professor, she lived in Los Angeles, London, Paris, and on the French Riviera. Along the way she learned the secrets of French cooking, including how to preserve a goose in its own fat for cassoulet. (Her only son is a caterer today.)

She was happy staying home. But then her husband dropped dead in 1978, at age forty-nine, of a heart attack while playing tennis. Warhaft, who had worked as a secretary before her marriage, heard that the freelance job of restaurant critic was coming open at the *Free Press*. She interviewed for it, and has never looked back.

Her critics accuse her of improprieties such as accepting free meals in exchange for good reviews. Warhaft scoffs as she dips into a bowl of mussels in white wine. "It's a measure of their naiveté that they don't know I have an expense account. So the last thing I need is another free meal." For her part, Warhaft suspects that her photo is posted in some kitchens and staff win rewards for recognizing her. But perhaps she's not completely out to lunch. Once, when a waiter took a long time to bring out the food and something splendid arrived, she joked, "What happened? You threw the first three out?"

"Yes," he said.

Some accuse Warhaft of being a food snob. Others say she writes only about "ethnic" restaurants. Some fellow Jews think she shouldn't eat pork. Warhaft, who can't imagine doing her job without eating pork, has reviewed truck stops. She's sized up the buns at Hooters (where she was the only female, apart from the scantily clad waitresses). And, at the request of the sports editor, she compared food at the local stadium to McDonald's. Which was better? "McDonald's. Especially the fries."

The ongoing food fight is making headlines as far away as the Cayman Islands and Germany. Warhaft has fielded calls from a radio station in Colombia (with a Spanish translator at the other end). During "all that fuss," as she calls it, she developed a stomach ache. Still, she soldiers on with a positive review of a Thai restaurant appearing tomorrow. Meanwhile, the Gang of Sixty is organizing a petition of even more restaurateurs. But the *Free Press* is standing by Warhaft. It stuck orange flyers on vending boxes promoting her Friday column. And it has threatened to print the name of any restaurant refusing to serve her.

So has she asked for a raise? "I thought of it," says Warhaft, sipping red wine. "But I don't want to push my luck."

Flight schedules and Marion Warhaft's disarming hospitality meant we spent eight hours together. She told me her strategy had been to count to fifteen before answering a question, but that soon fell by the wayside. For my part, I worried that she might write a column about her lunch with me. Thankfully, she never turned the tables. Like I said, she's a nice lady.

michel montignac

FRENCH DIET GURU GETS HIS JUST DESSERTS

August 4, 1999

The Michel Montignac diet had gained a lot of attention in France and later Quebec. It was an easy sell: all the red wine and dark chocolate you could consume. In 1999, Montignac set out to convince the rest of the Western world with an English edition of his diet book. I decided to Lunch him at Just Desserts, a downmarket chain that was struggling in the wake of a 1994 shooting that left one young female customer dead.

Just Desserts is just deserted. Are people deterred by the ongoing murder trial? Or is it the lacklustre food? Michel Montignac, fifty-four, has never heard of the chain or the murder trial. At lunch, the French diet guru—or charlatan, depending on your point of view—grabs the so-called wine list.

"What about your merlot?" says Montignac, in fluent, French-accented English, pointing to a small card stuck in Plexiglas. "Is it okay merlot? Which one has a high content of tannin?" Clearly, it's been some time since a customer engaged a Just Desserts waiter in a discussion of vintages. He unconvincingly suggests a Mission Hill "select cabernet" from British Columbia. Montignac wrinkles his nose.

"Is that a local wine?" he says. "I prefer wine from Chile." B.C. is too cold, he explains to both the waiter and me, which means the roots will produce grapes low in polyphenol, an antioxidant that ... oh, never mind. White wine, he continues, contains lots of sulphites to stabilize fermentation, which result in hangovers, especially in women because ... oh, never mind. We settle on something red and Chilean at $4.50 a glass.

The Montignac Method declares that you can lose weight by gorging on foie gras, chocolate, cheese, and high-polyphenol red wine. No wonder Montignac has sold 15 million diet books. He has also opened a string of diet centres, including nine in Quebec, a chain of food shops, a mail-order firm selling Montignac chocolate, a publishing house, an after-sales medical service, a seminar company, a restaurant near the Paris stock exchange, and a vineyard producing high-polyphenol "Michel Montignac Bordeaux." "Many people think I sell for the money," he says, flipping through the lurid photos of cakes on the menu. "But I have invested so much in research, it will be thirty years before I get it back."

Although the Just Desserts menu looks unpromising, Montignac is unfazed. After all, he launched his empire back in 1986 with a book for chubby executives called *Comment maigrir en faisant des repas d'affaires* (Dine Out and Lose Weight). "If we were at McDonald's, it would be more difficult," says Montignac, who was in Toronto to launch *Eat Yourself Slim*, the English version of *Je mange donc je maigris*, a huge bestseller in Quebec and France.

According to the Montignac diet, bacon and eggs are fine for breakfast. But water with meals is a no-no, because he thinks it interferes with digestive juices. Fresh fruit is another no-no, unless eaten three hours after a meal. At lunch, we follow the Montignac diet: red wine, but no water. We also need to order two entrées each, doubling the cost of lunch. Montignac tells our now-thoroughly confused waiter that we both want the tuna bagel without the bagel and the Caesar salad without the croutons and the fake bacon bits.

In his summery olive suit, which matches his eyes,

Montignac is a trim 170 pounds. He claims he was obese as a kid growing up in Angoulême, about a hundred kilometres northeast of Bordeaux. As personnel manager for an American pharmaceutical company in France, he packed more pounds on his five-foot-nine frame through expense-account restaurant meals. When he lost his job in 1986—the company closed its European headquarters—Montignac weighed two hundred pounds. He spent his time reading three hundred diet books, then wrote one of his own. Divorced by then, with custody of his three children, Montignac married his publicist, a thirty-three-year-old Minnesotan. They now have two little boys.

"You were right to come here!" he exclaims, when our bagel-less tuna and our crouton-less salads arrive. "This is perfect." As he expounds on his high-fat, low-carbohydrate diet—avoid bananas, rice, and cooked carrots; feast on rib steaks—a heretical thought occurs. If rice makes you fat, how come there are so many scrawny Asians?

"It's not the same rice," Montignac says. "The starch is different." In fact, I tell him, China imports rice seed from the West. And Canadians can buy Thai rice in any Asian supermarket. China is facing an obesity problem for the first time in history only as people switch from rice to Big Macs.

"Exercise is just burning calories," Montignac says. "I'm saying it's wrong to focus on the quantity of food on a plate instead of the quality of food on a plate." His own plate is littered with our uninspired Caesar salad. Will the Montignac diet permit us to have one of those gooey cakes pictured on the menu? Mais, oui.

The dessert recipes in his books call for non-fat cream cheese or quark, which is either a subatomic particle or a central European cheese. "I'm looking for a cake with soluble fibre: agar-agar, pectin, seaweed," he murmurs, scanning the photographs. Don't ask the waiter, I advise.

Montignac's eyes alight on the strawberry cheesecake. He assures me we can eat it, even the fresh strawberries, despite the ban on fresh fruit with meals. But when his dessert arrives, Montignac decides we can't have our cake and eat it, too. He pushes off the unnaturally red goop with his fork. "I'm going to eat this only," he declares, poking at the cream cheese interior. He tastes it. "Yes, I think there is seaweed there."

He stops eating after one bite. We ask for the cheque. Another heretical thought dawns. So that is the Montignac Method. Go to a bad restaurant. Order something inedible. Eat one bite. Ask for the bill.

suzanne somers

THREE'S A CROWD

September 1, 1999

Nobody at Brasserie Zola gives Suzanne Somers a second glance. In Toronto's overpriced Yorkville, who cares about big hair—even honey-coloured and teased—or a mauve pinstriped bell-bottomed pantsuit with matching five-inch slingbacks? Somers's husband-manager disagrees. "People are going to disturb Suzanne too much," Alan Hamel says, looking gravely at the courtyard table beside which only a soft-drink delivery man is loitering. "We need to be inside more."

But inside is too dark. A star needs exposure. So we're back to the courtyard, at another table. Then Hamel decrees the wrought-iron chairs are too low. The waiter brings out three upholstered ones from the dark dining room.

Phew. Now we can eat. But not just anything. Somers is flogging her bestselling diet book, *Get Skinny on Fabulous Food*. She's another of those combo nuts. We can't have carbohydrates with protein. We can have dark chocolate, but not carrots. We can't have alcohol or caffeine, though the occasional glass of red wine is okay. But not water. We can't have any water with our lunch, decrees the former star of *Three's Company*, former Las Vegas headliner, current cohost of *Candid Camera,* and owner of a bluntly named line of fitness products known as Thighmaster and Buttmaster.

"Sugar's the enemy. Fat's your friend," she says, reciting the combo-nut mantra. Her edicts sound a lot like those of that French diet guru, Michel Montignac. "Only I have to think my food is better," says Somers, who admits to first hearing about food combos in France, at her stepson's wedding.

Somers, fifty-two, orders a salad and an entrecôte with Roquefort sauce. "My metabolism betrayed me when I turned forty," she says. "Suddenly I became zaftig. It was not attractive." Her combo method, which she says helped her drop fourteen pounds, has propelled her onto *The New York Times* bestseller list. It has also transformed her from blonde bimbo to blonde diet guru. Now, five feet five inches and 116 pounds, Somers says she eats what she wants, as long as she never has, say, meat with potatoes.

She was the third of four children born to an alcoholic Irish-American labourer. He loaded beer cases and was drunk the day she was born. In her 1988 autobiography, *Keeping Secrets*, she says she was the only one of her siblings who abstained from alcohol. "But I shopped," says Somers, who has written two bestsellers about her dysfunctional family. "I would go buy something to distract myself from feeling blue, and I usually couldn't afford it."

She wet her bed until she was fourteen. At seventeen, she

had a baby, married the father, then divorced him a year later when she was caught having an affair with her forty-seven-year-old high-school drama teacher. In 1970, Somers, a single mother, was arrested in San Francisco for writing rubber cheques. She worked as a film extra, often bringing her toddler, Bruce. "It would be a way for us to both get lunch and $32 a day, and I would get to spend the day with him."

At nineteen, she met Hamel at a game show he was hosting in Los Angeles. Somers was hired to point at the prizes, but was fired after her first day because she kept looking at the wrong camera. Hamel was married, with two children, but they began an affair that would last eleven years and culminate in marriage in 1977. Hamel, now sixty-three, grew up in a Toronto boarding house at Spadina and College. At lunch, he wears Hollywood black leather. He keeps his sunglasses on throughout the meal. He eats steadily and talks little.

She and Hamel bought 100 per cent of Thighmaster Corp. in 1987. It has reportedly grossed $200 million (U.S.), especially since becoming the butt of a running David Letterman joke. Somers never minded. "I prayed that he would. Every time he did that we sold Thighmasters."

Somers says she hasn't had a facelift. "I don't love the look. But I looked in the mirror and was thinking: Maybe I should." She segues into a product description of Facemaster ($199.99 on the Shopping Channel), her latest product. When she rolls it over her face, microcurrents supposedly plump up her facial muscles.

"I think it's arrested the aging in me," she says. Somers's lime blouse is buttoned high at the neck. It only partially hides creeping crepe-neck syndrome. Hmm. Maybe what she really needs is a Neckmaster.

Somers sips some of our $11.90 Evian water. Isn't water a no-no, too?

"I know, but I'm choking," says Somers. But why is she sneaking a few of the crispy fries that come with her steak? "They're so good," she says, looking guilty.

Stardom came to Somers overnight, and left as quickly. In 1977, she was cast in *Three's Company* as the giggly, jiggly Chrissy Snow. The show soon became the No. 1 sitcom. So when her contract expired in 1981, Somers instructed her agent to ask for more, a lot more. She was getting $30,000 an episode; she wanted $150,000. "I just wanted to be paid what the men were being paid in the industry."

Instead, she was fired, labelled a troublemaker, and black-balled by the industry. She spent her decade in exile in Las Vegas, learning to sing and dance and crack jokes. Hamel slyly advised her to close her shows with "God Bless America," which guaranteed her nightly standing ovations.

Funny, that stardom. Few remember Somers's latest sitcom, *Step by Step*, which ran for seven years in the 1990s. At lunch, no one stops by our table, let alone stares briefly in that polite Canadian way. No one, it seems, even recognizes Somers. Not even the waiter.

Suzanne Somers was quite cheerful at lunch, in contrast to her husband, Alan Hamel. Afterwards, I realized he is the same Alan Hamel who, along with Howard the Turtle, cohosted the CBC kids television show Razzle Dazzle *in the 1960s. Given Hamel's dourness, it was hard to imagine him making kids laugh.*

In a letter to the editor, Kaye Hayes said that my "jealous, sarcastic diatribe on Suzanne Somers exposes Ms. Wong's naked, juvenile lack of respect for another woman. Poking fun at Ms. Somers's 'creeping crepe-neck syndrome' is offensive to those of us women who are over the age of forty-five. Ms. Wong will, if she is very fortunate indeed, have the opportunity to develop the 'creeping crepe-neck syndrome,' along with deep facial lines and age spots, while retaining a youthful countenance similar to Ms. Somers's."

Dear Ms. Hayes: I am *over forty-five myself. But I am definitely juvenile.*

Hugh Garber wrote: "Meow! Firstly, perhaps renaming the column Lynch with Jan Wong *would be more appropriate."*

Dear Mr. Garber: Hmm. Sounds like a good idea. Are you free next Wednesday?

jubal brown

THE PRIMARY COLOURS BARFER DOESN'T TOSS HIS COOKIES

December 26, 1996

Jubal Brown, a Toronto art student, had already puked on art in Toronto and New York. What better place to Lunch him than the Art Gallery of Ontario? Alas, Agora, its elegant restaurant, was fully booked. So we headed for the basement cafeteria.

Jubal Brown, a vegetarian, frowned at the sandwich selection. "I hate egg salad," said the Primary Colours Barfer, who made headlines recently by vomiting in red and blue on modern art. Earlier, he had threatened to complete the trilogy—with yellow.

"Egg salad is yellow," I joked.

"Ha. Ha. Ha," said Brown, twenty-four, glaring in the way adolescents reserve for unhip parents. He chose a lunch of cookies and latte. We were near the scene of his red crime, the basement cafeteria of the Art Gallery of Ontario. I admit I proposed the place, but I first asked if he was persona non grata. He assured me he had been there the previous day without incident.

Vomiting colour-coordinated food on modern art is Brown's idea of "invisible performance art" or, as he explained, "art disguised as incidents in everyday life." Performance art, invisible or otherwise, has always perplexed me. But then so did a Picasso painting titled *A Sailor or A Woman*. So I asked my six-year-old's opinion of the artistic merits of performance vomiting. "I think it's art," said the first-grader, "as long as you let it dry."

Inspired by Dadaism, which violently satirized all previous art, Brown, a student at the Ontario College of Art and Design, targeted paintings by Raoul Dufy and Piet Mondrian. He said he didn't stick a finger down his throat, but induced vomiting merely by gazing at modern art. "It's not just the one painting. It's the entire gallery. I work up my nauseous feeling by the time I get there."

As the mother of two small boys, puking guys don't especially faze me. I knew better than to wear my best suit, or shoes, to this lunch, but I also imagined the cleanup had involved little more than a damp sponge. News reports said neither work had been damaged. "That's one of the reasons I chose oil paintings," said Brown, who works part-time at a Toronto gallery. "They're very durable. If I wanted to destroy them, I would have used a razor blade or India ink."

For red, he ate raspberries, ketchup, cherries, and beets washed down with tomato juice. Why not just drink a vial of food colouring? "That would be too easy. This is art. It requires work," said Brown, who has wanted to be an artist since kindergarten.

For blue, he ate blue cheese, blueberries, blue ice cream, blue candies, blue cake icing, and blue Jell-O. If I fed my sons that combination, I told him, they'd probably throw up, too. "I did eat a lot of disgusting things," he acknowledged.

With a jaundiced eye, I examined his beige lunch. I was happy to feed a starving artist, but wondered aloud if he planned to toss his cookies. He gave me another withering "Oh, Mom" glance. He said he had decided to stop spewing primary colours ad nauseam. "I'm not a one-trick pony," he said. Currently, he is signing urinals all over Toronto, a tribute to Marcel Duchamp, the French artist who in 1917 wowed art lovers with The Fountain, a mass-produced ceramic urinal bought from a plumbing-fixtures store.

Six feet tall, with paper-white skin and greased black hair, Brown wore black eyeliner, a tartan tie, and black pants with a ripped knee. A bubblegum-machine "emerald" glittered on his left pinky. A black metal ring pierced his lower lip. The eldest of three boys, Brown grew up in Toronto and nearby Ajax, and says he never threw up as a child. His father, a factory worker, and his mother, a health-care aide and charwoman, worry about him, but they also retain a sense of humour. After all, this is a son, who, when asked how he transforms everyday life into art, says: "I clean the house as performance art."

Last year, Brown drew skulls over billboard faces, which he exhibited in a show called Ad Death that closed last Saturday. I confessed that as a teenaged feminist, I once branded panty-hose ads with a stamp that said, "This exploits women."

"That's a good idea," said Brown, looking at me with new respect. I changed the subject. Had anyone vandalized his Ad Death exhibit, say, by vomiting? "Someone pasted pink heart-shaped cutouts all over them," he said. An AGO employee spotted us in the cafeteria. "You're not going to throw up on anything, are you?" the staffer said pleasantly. Brown looked sheepish. "I'll tell you, when the kids come in on March break, it's much worse," the employee confided. "Or those special functions when advertising companies book a room. You find underwear on sculpture afterward."

New York's Museum of Modern Art, which took the blue hit in November, played it down, telling *The New York Times* the puke was a "fluke." Actually, the museum's chief of security and two policemen interrogated Brown for seven hours and variously threatened to toss him in jail, get him expelled from school, and shoot him.

Shoot him?

"One of the cops said, 'If you throw up on me, I'm going to shoot you.' The cop behind me said in my ear, 'He's not joking.'"

Unlike my six-year-old, AGO curators didn't realize that May's red mess had been performance art until *The Globe* ran a story in which Brown confessed to both art attacks. Since then, he has received angry calls, including at least one death threat. The Museum of Modern Art tried in vain to get him expelled from school.

After gulping a second latte, Brown excused himself to fetch something from the coat check. I waited, and waited. Suddenly a policeman loomed over me. Brown, he said, had been "formally barred" and taken outside. I felt a flash of déjà vu from my China reporting days—police cracking down on dissident artists.

It turned out an AGO official had nabbed Brown in the lobby and served him with a trespassing notice. Two police officers then escorted him onto the sidewalk. He went peacefully, so they radioed to say a backup cruiser wasn't needed. In the lobby, Karen Craig, AGO manager of protection services, was still fuming. "Should he return," she said, brandishing some legal documents, "he will be arrested."

I walked with Brown past the police van outside. "I'm depressed," he said. "From time to time, something moderately interesting is there." Then he cheered up. "This interview," he said, "is performance art, too. Naturally."

In a letter to the editor, Paul Ranalli asked an interesting question: "As the allotted fifteen minutes of fame draw to a close for vomiting performance-art student Jubal Brown, if one was to administer Gravol to Mr. Brown, would this constitute censorship?"

A year and a half later, Jubal Brown shaved his long, long legs, donned a pointy black-lace bra, and slipped into a thrift-shop outfit and a pair of black satin pumps. Then he sneaked back into the Art Gallery of Ontario to see an exhibit entitled Victorian Fairy Paintings. *In a scathing review published in* The Globe, *Brown decreed it to be "mostly Disneyesque" and "sappy, superficial, and decorative." He added that he hadn't suffered in exile. "It just means that if I go ... I have to go in disguise," he wrote. The AGO was not amused.*

susan powter

CHEWING THE FAT WITH THE FITNESS FREAK

January 9, 1997

Susan Powter, strutting fitness freak of infomercial fame, plunks down a Styrofoam cup and a brown paper bag. The author of the bestselling *Stop the Insanity!* diet book suggested we meet for breakfast at her hotel. Not expecting to brown-bag it, I had already decided on Eggs Benedict with Canadian Bacon and Chive Hollandaise. But because of Powter ("fat makes you fat"), I'm having just one egg instead of two.

"I would not order what you're eating. That's why I'm not eating here." Hey, I thought the hotel restaurant was her idea. She chews on a low-fat muffin bought next door and gulps her custom latte, made with her own soy milk. I compromise again. I'll just have orange juice for now. I put my egg order on hold. I'll eat it in peace later, after she rushes off to a radio interview.

Esquire magazine once voted her Scariest White Person of the Year. They are right. Food fascism aside, her right nostril is pierced with a ring. A super-model mole above her lip ... glints occasionally. I can't help asking. "It's a stud," she says. Using her tongue, she pushes out the stud. Oooh, that is scary.

Powter still hasn't sat down. "What's this?" she demands, pointing to the comfy brocade wing chair, with its tiny cushion for the small of the back. "Can I change my chair?" she demands loudly. A waitress quickly pushes the offending chair face-first against the wall like a naughty child and brings over a hard wooden one. I sink deeper into my wing chair and hope Powter doesn't notice. I also hope the restaurant doesn't notice that neither of us is ordering breakfast.

At thirty-eight, she looks like a white Grace Jones on speed. She is wearing chain-link jewellery, jeans, cowboy boots, and a charcoal-grey sweater unbuttoned to the base of her bra to reveal surgically perfect breasts. Although it is 8:30 a.m. and she has just flown in on the red-eye from L.A., she is fully made up—brown lipstick, black mascara, and pencilled arched brows. Her hair—still an unreal platinum that pool chlorine sometimes turns green—is less scary since she's grown out her trademark buzzcut. At least the top is now fluffy.

The nose ring, she admits, hurt terribly when she had it done recently. She says she did it to look "pretty." What about when she has a bad cold? "It's not a booger-catcher, you know."

A convent-educated former topless dancer who readily admits to facelifts, a tummy tuck, a surgically pinned ear, and the aforementioned breast surgery, Powter will give her height (five foot six) and dress size (two or four) but not her weight. "I don't believe in scales." She does, however, show me her rock-hard biceps and, in a move that turns heads among the staid breakfast crowd at Toronto's Sutton Place Hotel, yanks up her sweater to show me her washboard stomach. (No, her navel isn't pierced.)

Powter gulps the last of her latte and orders an espresso. I jot that down. "Are you writing about what I eat?" she demands. "I never speak about what I eat. Otherwise, everyone would copy me." Somehow I can't envision soy-milk lattes catching on, but I smile lamely. Jabbing a stubby, black-lacquered nail at me, she tells me she doesn't like print media. "You write this any way you want. If I don't like it, I'll never talk to you again."

Just as long as she doesn't sue me. Powter is currently embroiled in multimillion-dollar lawsuits with Nutri/System, a U.S. diet company. Two years ago she declared bankruptcy in the midst of another lawsuit with her partners, Dallas brothers Gerald and Richard Frankel. She recently settled, paying them $2.8 million (U.S.) and an additional $1.5 million to lawyers. Referring to one of her erstwhile partners, she says, "The man's a hemorrhoid."

Speaking of which, Powter is in Toronto armed with props of shellacked gobs of yellow fat to promote *Stop the Insanity, the Sequel*. Her gig includes a motivational seminar and hour-long shows on the Shopping Channel. *The Sequel* is not a book but a $99.99 self-help "package": audiotapes, exercise video, cookbook, "program guide," measuring tape, and journal for "personal thoughts."

Powter, who emigrated from Australia when she was ten, dropped out of high school and later obtained an equivalency diploma. Her white-picket-fence marriage to a restaurant manager in Garland, Texas, soured while she was pregnant with her second son. In her unhappiness, Powter says she ballooned to 260 pounds. (Her younger brother, Mark, told the tabloids that she was never that big. Powter says Mark is an alcoholic and was paid $16,000 to say that.) She says she woke up from her "fat coma" one day, lost 133 pounds, and began working as a $13,000-a-year aerobics instructor.

Then Powter discovered women loved her manic monologues about her ex-husband's girlfriend. Sample: "I'm thinner, prettier, and richer than she is, so who cares?" At her motivational seminars, she stalks up and down the stage like a Texas drill sergeant, dumping on her ex, by name, for his faithlessness, stupidity, taste in girlfriends, and prowess, or lack thereof, in bed. Without her weird hair, Powter might be just another former fatty. But since 1993 she has made a ton of money selling books and tapes to late-night couch potatoes and New-Year's-resolution dieters. Her common-sense message: eat healthy food and move your body. I tell her that millions of Chinese peasants have done that for centuries. Powter, now twice-divorced, frowns at the comparison. "It's a luxury to live the way I live."

She gets up to leave. I wave goodbye, explaining I need a moment to recover. She has left her brown paper bag on the table, and I briefly consider finishing off the remains of her low-fat muffin. Instead, I drain my juice, cancel the single egg Benedict, and pay the bill. Then inspired, or maybe frightened, I walk the four kilometres to my office.

Susan Powter never did talk to me again, but then, I never requested another interview either. And she never did sue me. Eventually, we ended up together at an authors' reception at Chapters' flagship store in Toronto, where I spent most of the evening hiding behind bookshelves.

PERFORMERS

sable

August 11, 1999

The mammary glands of Rena Mero, the wrestler formerly known as Sable, cantilever over the table at lunch. Restrained only by a black Mossimo tank top—and no bra—they look like two balloons, defying gravity and nature. "It makes me feel better about myself," says Mero, thirty-one, of her saline implants inserted three years ago, before she became queen of the World Wrestling Federation.

Now dethroned, she was also the first female wrestler to sue the WWF, for $110 million (U.S.). Mero alleged sexual harassment. She also alleged that the WWF wanted her to expose her breasts in rip-it-off evening-gown matches, participate in a lesbian story line, and jump off the ropes in spike heels, not necessarily in that order. She was also afraid of falling on those implants. "They're very durable, but you want to be careful," she says, ordering a plate of spaghetti with marinara sauce and a well-done tuna steak.

But Mero has landed on her stiletto-shod feet. The WWF, which plans an initial public stock offering and can't be eager for bad publicity, recently settled. "Let's just say I'm extremely happy with the settlement," says Mero over lunch at Joso's restaurant, an expensive midtown Toronto eatery famous for its breast-fetish artwork. Her husband, the WWF wrestler formerly known as Marvellous Marc Mero, joins us. Adding to her joy is the $1 million *Playboy* paid her to pose for its September issue, even if she did have to dye her pubic hair blonde to match her dyed blonde mane (her hair is actually brown).

The settlement bars her from using her wrestling moniker. But *Playboy*, which had already gone to press, blares: "Sable II, The Rematch, 14 Great All-New Pages." Translation: Mero had already appeared on April's cover, which sold out so quickly *Playboy* booked her again, the first time anyone has graced two covers in one year.

She sees no contradiction in posing naked while declining to expose herself in the ring. "Children go to matches," says Mero, who stopped taking her daughter, now eleven, to fights. It's nice to know someone has standards.

Clad in skin-tight pants, a navel ring, false eyelashes, fake nails, and a dense cloud of Estée Lauder's Beautiful, Mero carefully forks her pasta past her lips and teeth to avoid smearing her lipstick. When she accidentally flicks some marinara sauce on herself, she just wipes herself clean. That's the handy thing about exposing so much cleavage. Asked how the implants feel, husband and wife both answer.

"Very natural," she says.

"Marvellous," he says.

But do they feel, um …

"Fake?" she interjects.

"Not at all," says her husband. "Want a squeeze?"

She and I both recoil. The breast operation, she says, was very painful because she opted to implant the saline sacs underneath the muscle for a more natural look. Because she was unconscious, her husband approved the final product in the operating room. "I was very supportive," agrees Marc, thirty-nine, who looks like a cartoon villain with his biceps, moustache, and curly brown hair cascading down his thick neck. "She wanted them. I thought she was very beautiful before."

"Then quit looking at these boobies," Mero mutters, referring to his interest in the artwork. She was a 38C before—and after. Although she didn't breastfeed, she sagged after giving birth at age nineteen. The implants reshaped her breasts and, apparently, relocated her nipples north.

A high-school dropout in Florida, Mero was widowed at twenty-three when her first husband killed himself and three others in a drunk-driving accident. After she met Marc, she accompanied him to matches. Vince McMahon, the WWF's flamboyant chairman, soon hired her as a bikini-clad "ring girl," escorting wrestlers to centre stage. Encouraged by Marc—but without any training—Mero began wrestling. Stunts included dropping a three-hundred-pound man on his head. Within a year, she "won" the WWF women's world championship. "All wins in the wrestling industry are scripted," she notes.

Mero has an unbroken nose (unlike her husband) and all her own teeth (unlike her husband). But she has injured her ribs, hurt her neck, and broken a toe. Once, when she forgot to remove her earrings, the right one was ripped out. She leans over to show me the tear. Ouch. For that, Mero earned $150,000 a year, plus a cut of Sable merchandise and pay-per-view revenues. Her lawsuit alleged that females were paid less than males. Her husband, for instance, vastly out-earned her. "And she was a lot more popular in wrestling than I ever was," says Marc, a former title winner.

The WWF loves perky women, but not uppity ones. After Mero complained, her script was rewritten so she'd lose. On Mother's Day, her last match, she was introduced as "horizontally accessible." Later, someone filled her gym bag with feces.

At five foot six and 127 pounds, Mero looks like a Barbie doll. Her biceps are no bigger than mine. Unlike her husband, she says, she has never done steroids. "I want to be feminine. Muscle is the last thing I want." But does her secret WWF settlement preclude her from wrestling? There's only one way to find out.

"I'd never live it down if you beat me," says Mero when I challenge her to an arm-wrestling match in lieu of dessert. "You might be setting me up. Maybe you take some Chinese herbal stuff." With Marc offering to referee, she gives in. We clear the table. We lock hands. She beats me, fast. Both arms. "I have to say you're extremely strong," she says kindly. "I thought you'd be a pushover."

"Lunch With" thought *she'd* be a pushover. As I write this, my back is killing me.

Rena Mero later guest-starred on a television-action series, Relic Hunter. *Critics noted that the episode confirmed that her stunts for the WWF were no act. "That's because, on the available evidence of Saturday's* Relic Hunter, *Mero cannot act, period," declared a critic for the* New York Daily News. *Mero, who has also played an alien terminator, was considering a television show with National Basketball Association star Dennis Rodman. In 2000, Mero began shopping for a book publisher. She already had a title:* Busting Out: My Life as Sable and Beyond.

rosemary altea

HER HOTLINE TO THE DEAD HAS A FUZZY CONNECTION

October 30, 1997

*Rosemary Altea was a psychic who wrote bestsellers and who
claimed, among other talents, to be able to make contact with the
dead. My research included an overwrought article by a* New York
Times *reporter who actually believed that Altea had communed with
her late husband. When I phoned the* Times *reporter, she refused
point blank to discuss Altea. Still, it gave me a few ideas of my own
for Lunch. My husband gave me his blessing to use his late mother as
bait, and my editor allowed me to use her dead dog. The column ran
the day before Halloween.*

Rosemary Altea, fifty-one, has forgotten her glasses and can't
read the menu. But surely, the clairvoyant already "knows"
what's for lunch? "Fish," she says. Congratulations. There's fish
on the menu.

Altea is a psychic, a faith healer, and a medium. She's
"clairaudient" and "claircognizant," too, which means she hears
and knows things you and I can't. She also claims to astral-
travel and communicate with the dead—and not just at
Halloween. Her 1995 autobiography, *The Eagle and the Rose*,
was a bestseller. In Toronto recently, 750 people paid $29 to
hear her speak. In Vancouver, 300 did the same.

Her constant companion is Grey Eagle, an ancient Apache
"spirit guide." He's a New Age kind of guy, despite being several hundred years old. When Altea cooks, he's in the kitchen,

reminding her—in fluent English—when to take out the roast. You can't see him, but he's standing beside us right now, bare chest and all, in Scarborough's Old Scott House Restaurant. I should have booked a table for three. "Oh, that's all right," says Altea, a slim English brunette dressed in black pants, a long white jacket, chunky gold jewellery, and mock-croc boots with four-inch heels. She's done Oprah. She stunned Larry King, who is easily stunned, by describing his dead parents. And she reduced a sympathetic *New York Times* reporter to tears by supposedly communing with the journalist's late husband.

Altea's original surname was Edwards. She invented Altea when she got into the supernatural business. Previously, her parents just assumed she was crazy. They threatened to commit her to a mental asylum, for instance, when she had visions. Rosemary Edwards dropped out of school at fifteen, married at nineteen, and by thirty-five was divorced and broke. Then she discovered that many people, especially bereaved parents, would pay cash to contact dead loved ones. Struggling to raise her daughter, Altea charged £3.50 a session back in 1981. That paid the grocery bills. Her current rate is $200 (U.S.), and conveniently for everyone, a session can be done over the phone. These fees and her bestselling book have boosted her way beyond broomsticks. Altea now drives a silver BMW and a blue Mercedes roadster. She has homes in Vermont and northern Lincolnshire, England.

Vanity Fair magazine once asked her to make predictions about the stock market. "I really don't do it for Jim," she sniffs, referring to her live-in stockbroker boyfriend, "and I certainly won't do it for *Vanity Fair*." You'd think, though, she'd play a few stocks to fund her five free faith-healing centres in England. Instead, she says, she relies on old-fashioned bake sales. Nor has she communed with the late Princess of Wales. "I'm too busy. I have a waiting list of thousands of people," says

Altea, who is here to promote *Proud Spirit*, her latest book, and *Give the Gift of Healing*, a motivational tape.

Luckily, she's fast. I mention my mother-in-law, Lillian, who died a few years ago at the age of eighty-three. "Actually, I've seen two people while I've been talking to you," Altea says quietly, putting down her salad fork. Her voice soothes. Her hazel eyes radiate sincerity. She stares over my shoulder and describes a short, plump woman. "She was sick before dying. In the hospital. Hating every minute of it. Great trouble breathing."

Lillian wasn't plump. But she died in a hospital, as do most people in North America these days.

"She keeps talking about Sam," Altea says. That's a no-brainer. Altea has just met my four-year-old, who, as a result of a child-care snafu, is inhaling fettuccine Alfredo at a separate table with Altea's editor, a book publicist, and an amused publishing executive.

"She's stroking your cheek as she's talking to you," Altea continues. "She wants you to know she's fine now. She's apologizing for being a terrible patient. She knows you didn't mind."

Mind? I wasn't even there. Lillian passed away while I was working overseas.

Now Altea hears my mother-in-law talking about my old glasses. "She says they slipped off your nose," she reports triumphantly. "You know, it's the small things that can tell you they're real." I think, show me an Asian nose without the sliding-spectacle problem; my new glasses slip, too. But maybe Altea *can* read minds. "I should stick with the safe stuff because you're a journalist," she blurts, taking a bite of her fish. But she can't stop psyching me out. "She says she misses you. You have a great relationship, you two." That's the safe stuff? Lillian and I, to put it delicately, never bonded.

"She's talking about how hard it was to walk. 'Just tell her I'm on my feet again.' " I finally interrupt to say my mother-in-law was a ballroom dancer, right up until the end. "Really?" says Altea, looking off into the distance. She drops Lillian.

Now Altea says I'm surrounded by dead people. The waiters don't seem to mind. She describes someone on my right. "A man who suffered with his heart.... It was very sudden. He's small. Very slim. Greying hair. He tells me when you were a small girl, you sat on his knee."

What race is he? "I would say Far Eastern," says Altea, looking at me expectantly. I inform her that both my grandfathers died before I was born. She looks disappointed, and drops the Far Eastern man, too.

I ask for one last communication—with Cyrano, my editor's dead dog. Altea hesitates. "The only dog I can see is a black one." Yes! Cyrano was indeed black! Encouraged, Altea continues: "He looks a bit like a Labrador. Very healthy and sleek. Tell her the dog is safe."

Cyrano, alas, was a poodle.

After the column ran, I was crushed when a reader called to ask for Altea's phone number. She wanted to pay her to find a lost wristwatch. Can it be, is it possible, that "Lunch With" is too subtle? Say it ain't so.

valerie pringle

A Morning Host Who Really Knows How to Percolate

September 15, 1998

Uh-oh. The waitress at Pangaea brings a bottle of Evian. Last time Valerie Pringle encountered French mineral water, Paris was conducting nuclear tests in the South Pacific. In protest, the cohost of CTV's *Canada AM* tossed the bottle over her shoulder. On camera. Will she or won't she today?

"Oh, honey, they've stopped nuking, so I'm back. My boycott ended." Fresh from her daily postshow workout, Pringle is a flash of Technicolor: red-blonde hair, blue-green eyes, trillions of freckles, white jeans, and a navy and fuchsia Chinese jacket with matching fuchsia loafers.

"So," she says, opening the menu, "you get one good meal a week?" The cohost of Canada's most popular morning show, who later this month also begins hosting *W5*, CTV's current-events show, orders a cold tomato soup. She confesses she's slightly nervous. Why?

"Because you write vicious and mean columns. That's why." I'm nervous too, because Pringle is a problem, journalistically speaking. What can you say about a baby boomer who never dropped out, never inhaled, and admits that the only man she's ever slept with is her husband? Pringle's so wholesome, she's perky. "I never understood that 'perky.' You never hear it about a man. For morning television—hello? Do you want someone glowering at you? Perhaps it's a slight job requirement."

Pringle, who turned forty-five this month, never even left home until the day she married. She still golfs with her mom and fly-fishes with her dad. She met Andy Pringle when she was sixteen and he was at the University of Western Ontario. He dumped her once, during a four-year courtship. "I was heartbroken. I cried my eyes out." Pringle cries on air, too. "Where does it say in broadcasting the range of emotion is from A to B with a pickle up your behind?"

Viewers love her. Now in its twenty-fifth year, *Canada AM* is decimating the competition. Last spring it had 370,000 viewers, almost ten times that of *CBC Morning News* on the main CBC network. (The CBC has just revamped its morning show, now called *CBC Morning*.)

Andy Pringle eventually saw the light. They married the day she finished her program in radio and television arts at Ryerson Polytechnical Institute (now Ryerson Polytechnic University). She was twenty. He was twenty-three. "For a long time, I was quite embarrassed by that, getting married so young, like white trash," she says, digging into a salad of Jerusalem artichokes. "I didn't go to my graduation because I was busy getting hitched, like Loretta Lynn."

It didn't occur to Pringle, even in those feminist seventies, to keep her own name, which was Whittingham. "I am an anachronism," she says, turning to ask the waitress if she's going to keep her name when she marries. (She will.) Pringle has always been home for Andy, a director at RBC Dominion Securities, and their three children, now twelve, fifteen, and seventeen. Although she never stopped working, including twelve years in radio and eight at CBC-TV, she didn't travel, do investigative reporting, or anchor evening shows. The sacrifice, she says, "was worth it. I like my kids."

Despite her weird hours, she and Andy share a bed, though they're rarely in it at the same time. "He's a complete night owl.

He's often coming to bed as I'm getting up." Weekdays, she rises at 4:30 a.m., showers, and throws on whatever she's going to wear on camera—unless she taped interviews the previous day and forgot those clothes at work. "Then I just wear my coat." Just her coat? "I don't do it all the time," she says. "I don't want stalkers."

A CTV driver picks her up, with a pit stop for take-out café au lait. After the show, there's a post-mortem and a planning meeting. That's when Pringle vents about boring guests.

"I'm not trying to hurt the producer. It's an item. If it sucks, it sucks." Later, the limo drops her at the gym. After a quick lunch, she's at home, napping. Then she picks up her youngest son from school. At 9:30 p.m. she's in bed, reading research. It's lights-out by ten. She unplugs the phone. Then she tries to sleep, not always successfully. "The kids talk to me all the time—no point being hysterical. One thing is I don't fear sleeplessness. You can do this job on one hour's sleep."

When *W5* starts, however, she'll skip the Tuesday-morning *Canada AM* broadcasts. Still, the horrid hours haven't taken their toll. She doesn't have bags. Monthly facials keep her skin fresh. And, as she edges into the bifocal age, she recently had laser surgery in her right eye. That's so she can read the TelePrompTer while using her unzapped left eye for reading notes.

On her own time, Pringle also reads every article on menopause (she's not there yet), liposuction (she orders fresh berries for dessert), and plastic surgery. Not that she would ever have a facelift. "I don't care that much. I'm not pretty. But I'm okay with make-up on a good day. At one point, I thought maybe I should go back to radio, that I'd have a longer career." She rattles off names of female colleagues, including Pamela Wallin and Hana Gartner. "We're basically all the same age. No one's in her fifties or sixties that's ahead of us on a daily show. One of us has got to last. Baby boomers are aging, so they're going to like looking at us all wrinkly."

It's 2 p.m. Pringle says she isn't tired. I tell her she seems quite perky. "Fuck off," she says.

I wonder aloud if that's printable in Canada's National Newspaper. "I doubt it," she says happily as she sweeps out of Pangaea. "Besides, my parents would be very annoyed with me."

Valerie Pringle heard from her deeply unhappy parents—and all kinds of disapproving fans. But when you're that perky, disgrace can only be a badge of honour.

The day the story ran, F-word and all, Roger Parkinson, then The Globe's *publisher, wagged his finger at me in the company cafeteria. I thought he was kidding. He wasn't. He imposed a complete ban on swear words in the paper that lasted, um, 24 hours. The very next day, the F-word was back in the paper. In a letter to the editor, Barry W. Cook wrote: "Thank you for letting the term 'fuck off' enter* The Globe and Mail's *lexicon and not replacing it with 'Oh, you!' 'Fudge' or, coyly, 'F**k off.'"*

Sorry, Mr. Parkinson.

alan thicke

INSECURITY ON THE CELEBRITY GRAVY TRAIN

April 16, 1998

Alan Thicke double-parks his rental, rushes into the Rosewater Supper Club, and orders lunch. He rushes out again to find a parking lot. Thirty minutes and three downtown parking lots later (the first two were full), the *Pictionary* game-show host returns fuming. "In L.A., you plan a certain part of your day around parking, stalling, and drive-by shootings. But you don't expect that here."

He butters a roll, shakes salt on it, and takes a bite. He showers salt over his salad, too. Ditto for the duck risotto. Thicke, fifty-one, eats like he never left Kirkland Lake, Ontario. This was his "diet" to slim down for his role in the musical *Chicago*, now playing in Toronto: batter-fried coconut shrimp, buffalo wings, fries, nachos, and barbecued ribs. He says he lost twelve pounds in three weeks by pigging out on this stuff—and limiting himself to one meal a day. After today's lunch, he won't eat again except for an apple.

Thicke isn't thin. But he's a nice 177 pounds on a six-foot frame thanks to teetotalling and playing Sunday-night hockey with Tom Cruise, Jason Priestley, and Cuba Gooding Jr. He's also a name-dropper, having once suffered in social Siberia. After a meteoric career, he flamed out when his 1984 talk show *The Thicke of the Night* went up against *The Tonight Show* with Johnny Carson. The very day the show was cancelled, his wife served him with divorce papers. He instantly disappeared from party A-lists.

"I was the joke that year," he says. "I was the entertainment industry's whipping boy, the poster boy for failure."

These days, he hosts celebrity softball games and Miss World contests. And he jealously guards his perks, insisting on a limo, even at charity events. He's flattered that his two grown sons have followed him into show business—film school and songwriting. "If I had a vote, they'd both be dentists because show business is fickle, but gum disease is forever."

Thicke wears his insecurity on his sleeve. He locks eyes with anyone passing our table, as if willing them to stop. One diner on his way out pauses to say he's seen Thicke on television, but can't remember on what. Midway through his risotto,

Thicke looks longingly at the cholesterol on my plate. I offer him half my fries, which he dots with butter. Butter? "It's not nearly as outrageous when you consider how poutine is made," he says. "I love poutine. That, and butter tarts."

Several times a year, he visits his eighty-seven-year-old grandmother, Issie, in her old-age home in Kirkland Lake, an eight-hour drive north of Toronto. "Nine if you include poutine and butter tarts," he says. "I stop the limo at the first chip wagon." When he was little, his parents divorced. Thicke adopted the surname of his stepfather, an airforce doctor. In six years, he lived in four cities and skipped two grades. By fourteen, he was in high school in Elliot Lake, Ontario.

"It wasn't exactly fat-girl or ugly-duckling, but it was my version of it," says Thicke, adding that he was always too young to get a date. Instead, he became emcee at high-school events. His high-school principal, Ernie Dixon, drove him to public-speaking competitions all over Northern Ontario. One memorable year—until someone noticed—Thicke was simultaneously head of both the local United Church and Catholic youth groups. "The Protestants had better picnics," he says.

He eyes my club sandwich. I give him half. "You're a great date!" he says. "I'll just have a bite." He salts it heavily. Soon there is nothing left but a crust. After graduating in arts from the University of Western Ontario, he worked at the CBC, then made his way to California. Earlier, he had contacted some hole-in-the-wall talent agents in New York.

"They all had the same advice: Get a couple of girls with big tits who sing and dance," he recalls. "So I left New York thinking, now I've got to find girls with big tits—not that it hadn't occurred to me before socially."

In 1994, Thicke married Gina Tolleson, a former Miss World, whom he met while hosting the 1992 contest. He's happy she's twenty-two years younger. "Someone my age would likely have her own ex-husband, a couple of kids, her own emotional scars, and a mortgage. I already have my own baggage," Thicke says. "Of course, we share the Louis Vuitton as well." She planned the wedding, inviting Wayne Gretzky, Sharon Stone, and Mr. Dixon, Thicke's old high-school principal. Robin Leach (*Lifestyles of the Rich and Famous*) "narrated." Brian Mulroney (famous for his own rich lifestyle) crooned "When Irish Eyes Are Smiling."

Thicke hands over a photo of their nine-month-old son, Carter. "I shudder to think what the kid's first birthday party in July is going to be like." Recently, *Time, People,* and *TV Guide* called. Alas, they only wanted to discuss a certain kid actor on *Growing Pains,* Thicke's 1980s hit sitcom. He sighs. Ever since Leonardo DiCaprio starred in *Titanic,* he says, "there's a minor industry in Leonardo quotes. I'm going to start making up quotes. Like walking into his dressing room and catching him with Monica Lewinsky."

As Thicke gets up to leave, two women at the next table call over, "You're not leaving without saying goodbye, are you?"

Thicke beams. He's been recognized.

I still mourn the loss of half my club sandwich, a succulent combination of rare tuna steak, smoked bacon, and sliced avocado. Alas, the Rosewater Supper Club has since deleted that particular $9.99 sandwich (with Yukon Gold fries) from its menu.

mickey rooney

LIFE'S TOO SHORT

June 25, 1998

Mickey Rooney orders shrimp cocktail and makes a bet. "Twenty dollars on Horse Five," he says, handing an American $20 bill to his adult son, Chris, who heads to the off-track betting wicket. We're lunching at Bigliardi's, a Toronto restaurant that offers steaks and stakes. Rooney's eyes are glued to two television screens above our table. The right shows horse racing at Fort Erie racetrack near Niagara Falls. The left shows harness racing at Rideau Carleton Raceway near Ottawa.

"Where's Ottawa?" Rooney says. Actually, he doesn't care. He gambles wherever and whenever he can, currently between his twelve shows weekly at Toronto's Hummingbird Centre, where he is the wizard in *The Wizard of Oz*.

"Hey, I have nothing to drink," shouts Rooney, who is as round and bouncy as a beach ball. A waiter rushes over with a ginger ale. No. 5 loses. We can talk—for a minute—until the next race starts. At seventy-seven, Rooney is marking his seventy-fifth year in show business. He made his debut at eighteen months of age in his parents' vaudeville act as a tuxedoed midget, waving a rubber cigar. By the time he was five, his parents had split. In Hollywood, his mother got him more film roles playing midgets. Maybe child labour stunted his growth. Rooney insists he's five foot three. But as one of those myself, let's just say we don't exactly see eye to eye.

"You look like a midget next to some of the ladies I've worked with," retorts Rooney, who's dressed in baseball cap, olive golf shirt, and hiking boots. When I suggest he's five-one or less, Rooney swallows a shrimp and glares. "It isn't how big you are. It's what you do with it." He reels off a list: "Four foot six, Attila the Hun; four foot eight, Alexander the Great; five feet, Napoleon." Are you shrinking? I persist.

"No, I'm thinking," he snaps. He sizes me up and snarls, "Oh, you're just tall as hell."

Let's talk about something less touchy, such as his eight marriages. But life's too short. Rooney wants to tell me his second wife was five foot eight, and produced two sons, one six feet, the other six foot two. Neither of them was Chris, who is of medium height and is lunching at another table with two publicists. Rooney peels off another $20, summons his son, and mutters the name of another horse. "Do you know what that's worth?" he demands, showing me his wad of greenbacks. He means the metal money clip, not the cash. It's engraved: "Frank Sinatra Celebrity Invitational, 10th anniversary, Palm Springs, Mickey Rooney."

Did he also attend the recent Frank Sinatra Celebrity Invitational funeral? "Dear God, no," Rooney snaps. "I'm doing twelve shows a week. Frank wouldn't have wanted me to go. I think they made a fiasco out of it. Everybody came who wasn't invited." His stage voice booms through the restaurant. But aside from his entourage, the only other diners are three lone men who seem more interested in gambling than star-gazing. His horse loses again. Rooney momentarily concentrates on his grilled Dover sole and mashed potatoes. When the waiter hovers with a pepper grinder the size of a baseball bat, Rooney brusquely waves him away. He prefers the ready-to-shake stuff on the table.

Sixty years ago, Rooney was the Tom Cruise of his day, the world's No. 1 box-office draw, more popular than Clark Gable or Spencer Tracy. But he flamed out by age thirty. In 1962, he filed personal bankruptcy. By his late forties, until he made his comeback in 1979 with the Broadway show *Sugar Babies*, Rooney lived in Florida and charged fees for appearing at private parties.

His eight wives produced ten children. After his first wedding, to Ava Gardner in 1942, MGM sent its press agent on the honeymoon. The couple divorced after seventeen months. Wife Two was the tall one, a Miss Birmingham. Then came Wife Three and Wife Four. Wife Five was murdered by her lover. That didn't deter him from Wife Six or Wife Seven. "The last time I got married, I said, 'I do, I do.' The minister said, 'I know, I know.' "

Rooney finally got the hang of marriage with Wife Eight, a singer named Jan Chamberlain, with whom he marks his twenty-fifth wedding anniversary next month. These days, he's even prepared to dispense marital advice. "You don't marry anyone you love. That lasts for two years. Out the window. It falls apart if you do the awful thing of 'I love you' every twenty minutes. You marry someone you like. If you marry your best friend, it grows into a lasting love."

He places another bet, orders raspberry sherbet, and loses again. Undeterred, he bets another $20. "We'll win this one. Ya hear me?"

Where were we? Oh, yes. Marriage. So does he have to pay a lot of alimony? Is that why he keeps working? Rooney is only half listening. He always paid child support, he says. "But I never paid one centime of alimony to any of my wives. You know what alimony is? It's like pumping gas in another guy's car."

Finally, his horse wins. He lets out a small yelp. How much has he won? "For crissakes," he scowls. "That's why I never take a woman to the racetrack." His son delivers the winnings, which I can't help noticing is $105. That puts Rooney $45 ahead. He peels off another $20 bill and bets again. His horse loses. He's now just $25 ahead, but I keep that observation to myself, merely jotting it down in my notebook.

"Why, you son of a bitch!"

I look up, startled, but he's only talking to the television monitor. "This guy was the worst rider in the world! You schmuck!"

Later, I saw The Wizard of Oz *with my boys. But after meeting Mickey Rooney, I just didn't find the wizard was very magical. Maybe it's because I didn't have to wait for the curtain to be pulled.*

In rereading the column, I feel that I harped too much on Rooney's height. Still, no readers complained. One did call to congratulate me. She and her child waited outside the performers' entrance after one show to ask Rooney for an autograph. He brushed them off, she said. "He was very rude."

alex trebek

KING OF *Jeopardy!*

February 6, 1997

After living in the U.S. for decades, how much did Trebek remember about the motherland? I prepared for Lunch by obtaining the official list of Canada's citizenship questions.

It's bad enough Alex Trebek can't get through an airport without some fan tossing him a trivia question. Now I want to test him, over lunch. But the know-it-all host of *Jeopardy!*, the A & Q television game show, brightens when told the questions are supplied by the Department of Citizenship and Immigration. "Let me see that," he says, his professional interest piqued. He glances at Section 2 of the two-hundred-question booklet, *A Look at Canada*. It warns prospective citizens: "You should be able to answer these questions about the region in which you live."

"Oh, geez," says Trebek, fifty-six, the son of a Ukrainian immigrant and a French-Canadian mother, who grew up in Sudbury. " 'What is the most valuable manufacturing industry in your region today?' " I snatch the booklet back. Trebek sighs and takes a bite of Caesar salad. We are lunching at Toronto's Sutton Place Hotel, where he is spending a weekend auditioning wannabe *Jeopardy!* contestants. He looks faintly professorial, with his neatly trimmed moustache, silver hair, and half-rim glasses suspended from a chain around his neck.

Canada supplies the United States with a disproportionate number of game-show hosts, including Monty Hall and Art Linkletter, according to *Mondo Canuck*, a new book by Geoff Pevere and Greig Dymond. To his 15 to 20 million viewers, Trebek may be the brainiest of them all. When he tries out the questions in advance, he routinely scores 84 to 90 per cent.

How good is that? Let's put it this way: To make the first cut, applicants must score at least 88 per cent on a written test—and that's before producers look you over to see if you're perky, telegenic, and a good loser. Later that afternoon I take the written audition with seventy-five hopefuls, and promptly join seventy-three of them in flunking out.

As Trebek tries to eat his lentil soup, I pepper him with government-approved questions. Question: What are the three main groups of aboriginals? "Eskimos, er, they're called Inuit now, ah, Indians and ..." Trebek looks puzzled.

Métis, I tell him, according to the booklet.

"They're a mix of European and Indian blood, so that's not accurate," he splutters.

Question: In which parts of Canada did the aboriginal peoples first live? "It's a dumb question," grumbles Trebek, who plays on celebrity Hollywood hockey teams whenever he can. "They first came over the Bering Strait, and they first lived in Alaska, and moved south. Then you had the Plains Indians ..."

I shake my head. "Every part," according to the Citizenship and Immigration Department.

"*Jeopardy!* writers would never write that," he erupts. He grabs the booklet back. "Look at this," he snorts. " 'Who do Canadians vote for in a federal election?' What does that mean? These things are not pinned the way we like seeing them."

To placate him, I toss him a couple of no-brainers. Question: Which animal is an official symbol of Canada? "The beaver," he says triumphantly.

He also knows the United Empire Loyalists came to Canada in the late 1700s and that the face on the $10 bill is Sir John A. Macdonald's. ("A lucky guess," he admits.) And he knows *Canada* derives from the Indian word *kanata*. But when I ask Trebek to name Canada's capitals—an actual *Jeopardy!* category—he confuses Whitehorse with Yellowknife. And he doesn't know the capital of New Brunswick.

To be fair, he has lived in California since 1973. That has insulated him, he says, from all the "weird and crazy things" up here. He means separatism. "It's naive of Quebec to think that by forcing everybody to speak French, they're going to protect their language. Xenophobia never works. It hasn't worked throughout history and it isn't going to work here," says Trebek, who grew up speaking English at home and French at school.

In 1981, Trebek divorced his first wife after a childless seven-year marriage. His mother, Lucille, now seventy-five, moved in with him. On a subsequent show, after a contestant correctly guessed that flamingos mate just once a year, Trebek ad-libbed, "Flamingos and I have a great deal in common." His mother now lives in a guest house on his two-acre Hollywood estate. She moved out, sort of, after his 1989 marriage to Jean Currivan, an American property manager twenty-four years his junior. Trebek, who once hosted *Reach for the Top*, CBC's high-school quiz show, retains his Canadian citizenship. But last fall he also became an American. He hopes his two Californian-born children, Matthew, five, and Emily, three, will also become Canadian.

"I think Canadians sometimes fail to realize the wonderful things they have, including bilingualism and biculturalism. Being familiar with two cultures enriches you," says Trebek, a 1960 philosophy graduate from the University of Ottawa, where he studied in English, French, and Latin. He blames both sides for Canada's language crisis. "There are stupid, narrow-minded people everywhere. Being able to speak two languages is a good thing." To anglophones, he says: "Instead of treating it as an adversary, let French culture enrich your life."

At the same time, he doubts Quebec could maintain itself as a French nation. "Forget about the 25 million [Canadians]. Think about the 300 million south of the border. I'm just hoping reason and common sense will prevail and Canada will find a way to work itself through this problem," he says. "But it's very serious. Look at East and West Pakistan."

In the hotel ballroom an hour later, Trebek meets the seventy-five *Jeopardy!* hopefuls, one of four batches randomly selected from twelve thousand Ontarians who applied by fax and mail. "Most of you will fail this test," Trebek warns. Few care. They're just happy to have a chance to rub shoulders with their idol, who, somehow, looks elegant in a windbreaker and black slacks. They're shocked when he confesses to muffing a bunch of questions from the Canadian citizenship test. As seventy-five tongues cluck, Trebek sighs.

"It made me realize," he tells them, "the easiest way to become a Canadian is to be born here."

Since that Lunch, Who Wants to Be a Millionaire? *has hammered the quiz-show competition. But Alex Trebek insists* Jeopardy!'s *questions are way tougher. "You have to wonder about some of the contestants on that program," Trebek told a reporter, launching into an imitation of* Millionaire *host Regis Philbin and an imaginary player.*

"What's the usual colour of Post-its?"

"Uhhhhh …"

Trebek noted that Philbin, a friend, has been on Jeopardy! *twice. "And he finished third both times."*

By the way, I think Trebek manages to look elegant in a windbreaker and slacks because he starves himself. At Lunch, he had only lentil soup and half a Caesar salad.

paul burrell

PRINCESS DIANA'S BUTLER

December 1, 1999

Princess Diana's butler remained singularly discreet, even after he was dumped from his job on her charity. But in an effort to make a living, Paul Burrell finally cashed in on his connection. In Toronto to promote his new book on entertaining, Burrell walked the fine line between remembering Diana and exploiting her. To his credit, he never once crossed over.

Paul Burrell is twenty minutes late for lunch at Hiro Sushi. "Ten minutes is okay, but twenty minutes ..." The butler to the late Diana, Princess of Wales, simultaneously apologizes profusely and imparts a protocol lesson. He shakes my hand with a two-handed clasp. "I'm so pleased to meet you," he murmurs, bowing almost imperceptibly at the waist. He turns to our Japanese waitress. "And your name is?" he says, giving her the same two-handed clasp and slight bow.

The super-polite treatment goes over big in this restaurant, and ensures the loan of a tray, a pink rose, and a teapot so *The Globe* can photograph him standing on the sidewalk. Even when a panhandler approaches, Burrell, forty-one, retains his butler's poise. "I'm so sorry. All I have is tea." The panhandler shrugs and moves on.

Back at the table, Burrell rushes to pull out my chair. He'd be great to have around the house. The only problem is, you wouldn't be able to lounge in torn stretch pants, not when he's a Tom Hanks lookalike in silver cufflinks. The cufflinks are a Diana gift, emblazoned with a "D" and the coronet of a princess. He's also wearing another Diana gift, a neon pink tie of giraffes and palm trees. "The Princess bought all my ties from Hermès. This was the very first one she gave me. It's my lucky tie. When I wear it, good things happen to me."

You can see why Diana Spencer bought him ties, why she famously called him "my rock." He's pleasant and unpretentious but never familiar. "Is that proper?" he murmurs, when asked the brand of his four-button pinstriped suit with three-quarter-length jacket. (It's Versace.) Burrell was there for the whole ride and worked directly for Diana for ten years. They met in 1980 when he was twenty-two. She was nineteen and lost in the maze of hallways during her first visit to Balmoral Castle. When she and Charles split, Diana put her butler at the top of the list of everything she wanted to take to Kensington Palace.

Burrell was there, too, in death. As soon as he heard, he packed two bags—one for her—and flew to Paris. He dressed her, fixed her hair, and held her hand until her family arrived. At the burial, Burrell was the only non–family member present.

At lunch, and in his new book on entertaining, *In the Royal Manner*, he is as discreet as, well, a butler. Ask about Di's famous attempt to slash her wrists with a lemon zester. "I have no knowledge of that," he says. Ask whether he went around the palace hiding all the sharp objects, he simply smiles. Repeat the question and he says: "I don't understand the question." He smiles again.

To be sure, Diana was a high-maintenance princess. Alone one Christmas Day, she lit too many scented candles and set off the smoke detector. She didn't know what to do, so she called him. Midway through his Christmas dinner, he rushed over to turn off the alarms—and help her entertain five truckloads of firemen. Burrell drops Diana's name with every breath. But his book rarely mentions her, except to note that she really liked pears in port wine. "The book is my calling card. The Princess is there only when it's appropriate for her to be there. I won't give anyone the satisfaction of pointing the finger at me and saying: 'He let her down.'"

At lunch, he confesses he has never tasted sushi, although he once accompanied Diana to Tokyo for the coronation of the Japanese emperor. "We stayed at the British Embassy," he says. We approach the sushi bar to watch Hiro Yoshida, the owner, making rolls of vinegared rice wrapped around strips of deep red raw tuna. "Now you steam it?" Burrell asks hopefully.

Everyone at the sushi bar recoils. "Sushi is not my usual fare," he adds hastily. With an unbutler-like lack of tact, he explains he must board a plane later and would like something actually cooked.

That would be miso soup. When it arrives without a spoon, he's told to slurp it right out of the bowl. "I've seen the Queen often presented with drinks and brews in bowls," he murmurs, gamely taking a sip. His deep-fried shrimp tempura is just fine. But he's unnerved by the disposable chopsticks that you have to snap apart. The waitress brings him a fork.

The son of a truck driver in a Derbyshire mining village, Burrell grew up in a house with no indoor toilet. At sixteen, he attended hotel school. In 1976, at eighteen, he won an interview—and a job—at Buckingham Palace. "It was such an honour, I would have worked for free," he says. He practically did, with a starting salary of £1,200 (about $2,500) a year, plus room and board. After a year, he became a personal footman to Queen Elizabeth. When he wanted to marry Maria, the Duke of Edinburgh's maid, the Queen waived the rule forbidding married couples to work at the palace. (Maria left to have the first of their two sons.)

Later, he worked for Charles and Diana, and was the first to know when the royal marriage had unravelled. "We knew the split was coming. The Princess warned us." And when Diana put Burrell at the top of her divorce wish list, Charles objected. "He said, 'You can't have Paul because Paul came from Mummy.' She said, 'You said I could have whatever I wanted.'"

When Diana moved alone into Kensington Palace, Burrell uprooted his family from Highgrove, Charles's country residence, and moved them there, too. She pulled strings to get his two boys into the same state-run school that Tony Blair's children attended. And she doubled Burrell's wage to about £35,000. "She said, 'I'm so sorry, but the only thing I can promise you is I'll always take care of you.'"

When she died, Burrell lost everything—his job, his home, his medical insurance. There was no pension. For a year, he worked as fundraising manager for her charity, the Diana, Princess of Wales Memorial Fund. Last December, he was fired by the trustees, who included the Archbishop of Canterbury, Diana's divorce lawyer, and Diana's sister. Asked why, Burrell says: "Think about it. I'm a servant."

He got offers from rich people around the world but turned them down. "I didn't want to become a trophy," he says. Nor could he return to Buckingham Palace. "Because I became a known person, it was impossible to work for the Queen. A butler is an invisible pair of hands around the house." At the moment, he has no job. His dream is to write a magazine column and have his own television show. "Martha Stewart started somewhere, didn't she? I'd like a little slice of her pie."

After we finish, Yoshida sends over a California roll, beginner's sushi for the squeamish. "For you, and only you, sir, I will try it," says Burrell. Asked how he liked the vinegared rice with avocado and cooked processed fish, he whispers: "It is an acquired taste."

As we leave, he strides over to the sushi bar to shake Yoshida's hand. Alas, the owner is finger-deep in raw fish. He proffers a bare elbow. Burrell doesn't bat an eye. He shakes Yoshida's elbow.

In April 2000, Paul Burrell launched "Etiquette 101," a column in Flare *magazine, giving his "golden rules" for attending parties. Among them, he advised arriving ten to twenty minutes late (just like at our lunch). Burrell also discouraged airkissing. "It's not appropriate to kiss … unless you are actually acquainted. If you are close, then offer the left cheek first." In addition, he began writing a weekly "Social Graces" etiquette column in the* Daily Mail.

After Diana's death, Burrell and another palace butler, Harold Brown, had helped a team of experts carry out a Kensington Palace audit of Diana's possessions. In January 2001, seven police officers raided Burrell's home before dawn. As he wept, the police tore up floorboards in his red brick Victorian house in the village of Farndon, in Cheshire. Police arrested Burrell in connection with the disappearance of some of Diana's possessions. He was held overnight in a cell before being released on bail. His lawyer has said Burrell is maintaining "a dignified silence."

michael enright

THE MARTINI-SWILLING, COWBOY-BOOT-WEARING, GUN-SHOOTING, BIKER REBEL OF THE CBC

May 27, 2000

Michael Enright is a rebel, sometimes with a cause, sometimes without. Except for tan cowboy boots, he's dressed all in black.

He has a moustache and goatee. But when it comes to martinis, he's a traditionalist: Blue Sapphire, ice cold, two olives.

As usual, the host of *This Morning*, CBC Radio's flagship show, has been up since 4:15 a.m. He hates that. Even more, he hates going to bed before his youngest son, Gabriel, who is four. Enright is sick, literally, of the grind of daily radio. As he speed-reads the menu at La Fenice, he yawns, then explodes in a spectacular cough. Ten days of antibiotics haven't cured his bronchitis.

And so, at fifty-seven, Enright is rebelling. Next fall, he is quitting one of the best jobs in Canadian journalism, downsizing to the Sunday edition of *This Morning*, plus six specials a year. In addition, he might become a weekly quizmaster, if the CBC approves a new radio show.

"We sent up a proposal and haven't heard anything," he says. "I think it would be fabulous."

Enright has spent his career doing as he pleases. In 1968, as *The Globe and Mail*'s Washington correspondent, he ignored the business editor's repeated pleas for auto-pact stories, writing instead about Martin Luther King, the Vietnam War, and Bobby Kennedy. Enright was yanked back to Toronto after one glorious year.

On air last year, he famously declared his bias in favour of gun control, at the start of a CBC panel discussion on, yes, gun control. Listener complaints poured in. But Enright isn't only unrepentant, he doesn't think he was particularly brave.

"It's the majority opinion. The gutsy thing to do would be to say: 'Everybody should own a gun from age seven on.' Do you think they would have let me keep my job if I'd said that?"

Enright actually adores guns. At thirteen, he owned a Cooey single-shot .22. Later, he had a Remington rifle. "I love firing guns," he says, draining his martini.

In 1997, he called the Catholic Church "the greatest criminal organization outside the Mafia." Compliment him on the eloquence of his subsequent apology and he says, "Which one was that? I write a lot of letters of apology."

At age seven, he once caved in to authority. Under pressure from his parochial-school nuns, he switched to writing with his right hand. But that was partly because he had just put his left hand through the wringer of a washing machine.

"I was dared. I was double-dared," recalls Enright. Infection set in. He nearly lost his hand. The doctors mentioned amputation. His handwriting, to put it mildly, suffered. Today, he blames his right-handedness on a playmate named Jimmy Hotchkins. "I believe he later went to work for Pol Pot," says Enright, showing off the angry white scar on his left wrist.

He may be the only broadcaster without a television. Two years ago, he hurled his last set out the front door when he had to call his teenaged son, A.J., one too many times to dinner. "I was cooking. I ran upstairs. I had the strength of ten."

No wonder he's in favour of CBC's plans—since cancelled—to kill fourteen local supper-hour television shows. "No one watches except for St. John's, Halifax, Charlottetown, and Winnipeg. The rest is borscht."

After a non-borscht soup, Enright orders lobster spaghettini and a glass of red wine. Besides hand-wringing and television-tossing, he's asked what other stupid things he does. He admits to owning a Kawasaki Vulcan 1500. "It's the biggest motorcycle on the road. It beats the crap out of those sissy Harleys," he says happily. "But I'm really careful. I didn't break my arm on my motorcycle."

He broke that horseback riding. Last year, while tracing the original path of the Northwest Mounted Police, his horse threw him in the middle of Nowheresville, Saskatchewan. It took two excruciating hours for the ambulance to reach him, and even longer, counting a mechanical breakdown, to get him to Regina.

Last fall, Enright joined a health club to strengthen his injured arm. At six-two and 216 pounds, he also wants to burn the fat off his belly. But when his spaghettini arrives, he asks for some grated Parmesan.

"Are you sure you want to do this?" the waiter says, frowning. "It's a seafood sauce. You don't put cheese on seafood. On mushrooms, on sausage, yes. But not on seafood."

"Oh, really?" says Enright, as archly as when he's interviewing someone about cucumber-chutney recipes.

Encouraged, the waiter continues. "In the south of Italy, we don't put cheese on our seafood. It's the wrong flavour. Cheese doesn't go with fish."

"I'm learning something!" says Enright, sounding oh-so-sincere.

He still wants cheese. After the waiter grates some over his pasta and leaves, Enright mutters, "Well, *that's* embarrassing, isn't it. Let's put *that* in the newspaper."

The lobster pasta tastes acrid. The waiter was right; cheese doesn't help. Or maybe Enright is just a picky eater. He says he avoids all Chinese and Japanese food and "anything that looks like bait." He asks about a beige disc on my plate. He yelps in disgust when told it's grilled eggplant.

"Ooh," he gasps. "I even hate the name."

Enright grew up in downtown Toronto, the only child of a teetotalling civil servant who was the chief investigator of the Liquor Control Board of Ontario. As a kid, he joined a neighbourhood gang, an experience that left him with a souvenir scar on his left temple. He was also, he adds, "a hell of a good altar boy." At St. Michael's College, he flunked Grade 12, twice, flummoxed by math and science. To this day, he can't add double digits. Nor can he handle e-mail or surf the Net. He keeps his passwords stuck to his computer.

At nineteen, eager to change the world, he entered a

Passionist seminary in Dunkirk, New York. "I wanted to save my soul," says Enright, who combs his thinning hair forward, like a monk. Back home that Christmas, he saw his pals having a good time. He also saw a couple of girls he was crazy about. He returned to the seminary, wracked with indecision. "I didn't think I could take the vow of chastity," he says, adding that he was making dentist appointments just to go into town. Six months later, he dropped out of the seminary.

For years, he avoided churches, except to attend funerals. Three years ago, for reasons still unclear to himself, he went to an early-morning mass.

"But it was all in English," he says in a hurt tone. "I didn't know where I was."

He lets rip another astounding cough. He's off cigarettes at the moment, but misses them deeply. To change the subject, he removes his circular tortoise-shell glasses and peers at the ceiling. "I'm going blind," he announces. "I've got cataracts. *Cataracts*. You have to be eighty-five to have cataracts."

Enright has four children, three from his first marriage. In two weeks, he'll take A.J. to a ranch in Montana to cowherd and brand. He also wants to spend more time with his daughter, Nancy, seventeen, who is severely retarded and lives away during the week. "I've been doing daily radio for fifteen years. I want a smaller life, thank you very much."

His wife, Janet, died in 1990 of a rare bone cancer. She was forty-two. "She could have lived another year. But it meant removing part of her pelvis and one leg. She refused the operation. I agreed with whatever she said."

He remembers the date of her death, of course, even the day of the week. Daniel was twelve, A.J. was nine, and Nancy was six. Enright's eloquence vanishes as he talks about the aftermath. It was, he says haltingly, "not great. Not great for a while. Thank God Karen came into my life."

Karen Levine was his boss, the executive producer of *As It Happens*; Enright was then the host. They haven't married, but he wears two rings on his right pinky, his plain wedding band from Janet, and a thicker, curvaceous ring from Levine.

They're raising Gabriel Enright Levine in the Jewish faith. "I like that: a Catholic having a Jewish kid," he says, adding, "Look, I'm not in early rebellion with the Holy Mother Church. I'll probably cry out on my deathbed: Get me a priest!"

Speaking of death, he suddenly remembers he has to take his medicine. But you're not supposed to mix antibiotics with alcohol, right?

"Well," says Enright, tossing back a pill, "that martini was a long time ago."

jeanne beker

A FASHIONISTA UNCLOTHED

November 2000

This "Lunch With" column never ran in The Globe and Mail. *Four days before its publication date, Jeanne Beker surprised me by writing her own version in Southam newspapers across Canada and in* The National Post, *our direct competitor.*

At lunch, Jeanne Beker is head-to-toe in designer clothes. "It's one of the pitfalls of the job," says the host of *Fashion Television*, a never-ending infomercial in which designers get free ads and Beker gets free clothes. Frankly fulsome *Fashion Television*, surprisingly, is now in its fifteenth year. It draws huge audiences, split equally between women and, yes, men. It's also rumoured to be the most popular show in Canadian prisons.

"Glad to be of service," chortles Beker, forty-eight. For those too cheap or too incarcerated to subscribe to the *Playboy Channel*, her weekly half-hour show offers a reliable dose of soft porn. Under the guise of fashion, *Fashion Television* lets it all hang out, including nipples, bums and breasts. "But that's what they're showing on the runway," says Beker, over a tiny bottle of designer water at Toronto's Kit Kat Bar and Café. "It's all about creating a stir. A lot of that stuff never gets worn by ordinary people, never gets into production. It's all about making you watch." And watch it they do. Gay men love it. So do straight men. "It's like the *National Geographic* of its time," says Beker.

She chose Kit Kat, a noisy sliver of a restaurant where the food is bad and the tables are tiny. Still, it's her hangout, which turns out to be helpful. When I phoned for a reservation and asked for a booth (for note-taking elbow room), I was told in no uncertain terms that booths were reserved for parties of three or more. But when I arrive, Beker is already ensconced in a booth. She's wearing a belt by Kieselstein-Cord, poured-on indigo jeans by Parasuco and a spidery knit sweater by Misura, the latter a designer freebie. "I don't like to say 'gift' because they got a credit at the end of the show."

While *Fashion Television* reaches more than one hundred countries via satellite—clearly enough to merit a Kit Kat booth—it doesn't translate into megabucks. "I work at *Citytv*, remember?" she says. "Everyone thinks I own part of the show. I wish. If I earned that much, why would I be holding down five gigs?"

Beker, who lives in Rosedale, is driven. Each year, in addition to a grueling thirty-nine episodes of *Fashion Television*, she makes several full-length television specials. She also writes a monthly column for *Flare* magazine, a weekly column for the Southam newspaper chain and the occasional report for the *New York Daily News*. And she's just finished *Jeanne Unbottled*, her tell-all memoir that recounts everything from date rape to life as a single mom.

Consumer advisory: don't expect deathless prose—Beker wrote her book on airplanes and in hotel rooms. That's because every second week, she's in New York on assignment. This fall, she skipped London, but made the shows in New York, Paris and Milan. On average, she spends over one hundred days a year on the road. "Much as I complain about the travel, the minute I stop, I think I'm missing out on something."

She may indeed be missing out on something. Her daughters, eleven and thirteen, wish she'd stay home more. (For her older daughter's twelfth birthday, she gave her a weekend in New York. "I had to go anyway, for a Bill Blass fashion show.")

Her second husband, morning-radio host Bob Magee, walked out in 1998. "He didn't explain," says Beker, who says she was devastated and swears she didn't see it coming. Now she tries to be home with her girls three nights a week. It's hard because she's asked to host so many galas. "I'm lucky to be asked," she says. "I hate to say no."

Our soup arrives, a pumpkin purée so peppery it's nearly inedible. Beker, who doesn't want to behave like a diva at Lunch, gamely spoons it down. But our waiter overhears us complaining, and swoops down with replacement bowls. Alas, they are equally inedible.

Beker's parents, both Holocaust survivors, arrived penniless from Poland after the Second World War. Her father worked in Toronto's garment district making children's slippers. She had other dreams. At twelve, in an attempt at being classy, Beker dropped the "i" from "Jeannie," but kept the pronunciation. After a couple of semesters at York University, she quit to get married and moved to Newfoundland where she found work as a mime. "Now," she notes, gulping her third tiny bottle of designer water, "I never shut up."

That marriage, to a high-school sweetheart, lasted three years. In Toronto, while working as CHUM radio's "Good News Girl," she met Magee. In 1979, she jumped to *Citytv* to cover rock 'n' roll, movie stars and eventually, fashion—after a fashion. "There's no question there's T and A," says Beker. "But it's not all T and A. It's nice that we squeeze in stories on architecture, photography, the visual arts, design in general."

Ah, yes, the arty stuff. A recent segment on performance art focused on a gaggle of nude models posing at a New York museum. Another segment on computer doctoring of photographs used a sample photo that just happened to be of a beautiful naked model. Beker, who is not above flashing a little cleavage herself beneath the mesh Misura, says supermodels don't intimidate her. Still, at lunch she avoids the bread and butter. She proclaims her farfalle pasta with pesto shrimp delicious, but leaves two-thirds of it on her plate. And forget about dessert.

Beker has blow-dried black hair, huge dark eyes and a wide mobile mouth. When she turned forty, she had her eyes lifted. She declined the plastic surgeon's offer to do her nose, too. But she has had botox, a kind of paralyzing bacteria, injected into her forehead, hoping to smooth out her wrinkles. She quit after the first few injections because they hurt too much—and left a bruise in the middle of her forehead that looked like a third eye.

Looks are important during *Fashion Television* interviews. Beker often sucks up to the designer by donning a borrowed outfit by said designer. If the chat goes swimmingly, she may end up getting to keep the clothes. Thanks to these freebies, her wardrobe occupies an entire room in her house.

If *Fashion Television* deals with cocaine addiction or racism in the industry, it's in the lightest possible way. Most of the time though, Beker lobs softball questions like this one to Miuccia Prada, an Italian designer: "One of the first things

people say about you is: 'She's such an intelligent designer.'"
Ms. Prada, surprise, agreed.

Even after some egomaniac designer has kept Beker waiting
for hours, her toughest question may be: how will fat ladies look
in this stuff? "Obviously, we're not *60 Minutes*," she says. "But
every once in a while, I like to ask that. On days when I feel especially bloated." Beker fears that if she doesn't stroke the designers, she won't get into their shows. Last year, despite sustained
sycophancy, she wasn't even given a seat at the Prada show. After
Beker threatened to leave, the designer's assistant gave her a seat
in the back row. This year, Beker says she's determined not to
cover Prada at all because Miuccia has declined to give her an
interview. "But do you think they give a shit?" she says gloomily.

She pulls out a Chanel compact to fish around her eye for
a lost contact lens. "We're in a totally neurotic business," she
says. "Those that survive are the ones that have learned to keep
their neuroses at bay." With Lunch over, she gets up to leave.
She dons a curvy red sheepskin jacket, keeping a wary eye out
for anti-fur protesters. Then she hoists a big black purse onto
her shoulders. It's by Prada.

But wait a minute. Isn't she boycotting them?

"They make the best purses," she says sheepishly. Then she
unleashes her wide, wide smile.

*Jeanne Beker never let on that she was going to write a column about
our lunch. She didn't take notes. She didn't even offer to split the bill.*

*My editors decided that Beker should be punished for scooping
The Globe. And the punishment, they decreed, would be to kill
my column.*

*Beker's column, entitled, "Jan Wong and me," ran on
November 14, 2000. In it she revealed that she had spent the
previous weekend fretting about what to wear, what to say and
how much makeup to apply. Although she called me "a dragon*

lady," "mean-spirited" and "sneaky" (who me?), the column was immensely flattering. How can I dislike someone who was so scared of having lunch with me, she hoped she'd "get lucky, and get run over —just so I could miss lunch, and have Jan Wong feel sorry for me."

At the end of her column, Beker confesses that she "sort of enjoyed" our lunch. "In the end Wong was—dare I say it—pretty sweet. Still I'm sure she'll crucify me in her column—make me sound stupid or insipid or vain or, at least, neurotic. And she'd certainly be right on the last count."

FELLOW SCRIBBLERS

michael bate

TO BE *Frank*, ALL GOSSIP MAKES GRIST FOR HIS RUMOUR MILL

March 6, 1997

Frank *magazine is notorious for its pranks, which feed on the vanity of the barely famous. After "Lunch With" had been around for a few months, I fell into* Frank's *crosshairs. Luckily, my years of living in China—six as a student and six as a foreign correspondent—meant I'm way more paranoid than your generic Canadian reporter. So when someone called asking if I'd like to make a cameo appearance on a hit CBC show called* The Newsroom, *my antennae went up.*

Straining to say absolutely nothing quotable, I said I'd never seen it (which was true) and asked if the caller would send me a couple of tapes. I promised to call her *back. Her number, as I expected, didn't start with 205, the CBC exchange. Next I hunted down an actual producer on* The Newsroom, *who confirmed my hunch that it was a hoax. Then I called* Frank *in Ottawa. I told a staffer that* The Newsroom *was looking for media types to appear on the show. I had recommended, I said, Michael Bate,* Frank's *editor-in-chief.*

There was a pause, then an embarrassed laugh.

I paused. "And could you please tell Michael Bate I'd like to take him to lunch."

Michael Bate feels sick. Or is this a ploy to avoid Lunch? The editor of Ottawa-based *Frank*, a low-brow satirical magazine, says he meant to cancel. He has a fever. He may have the flu. He just took a Dimetapp. I'm on Contac C, I say. The interview goes on.

It's hard to feel sympathy for someone who makes a living printing scurrilous rumours about the rich and famous, or even the slightly well known. Modelled after Britain's *Private Eye*, *Frank* magazine's humour is sophomoric, sweaty-palmed, and nasty. Ministerial aides are "fartcatchers." Anyone rumoured to be having an extramarital affair is a "horizontal jogger." *Frank* magazine has heaped scorn on everyone from Hilary Weston to Peter Mansbridge—not always accurately. (It has a 60 per cent accuracy rate, an abysmal record.) If an item has what Bate calls "the ring of truth," meaning it could be true, then *Frank* prints it. "It was a sad day for satire when Brian Mulroney left the government," Bate sighs.

Still, the thirty-two-page biweekly rag scores genuine scoops. It disclosed Ovide Mercredi's amnesia over child-support payments. It broke new ground on the 1994 Just Desserts shooting in Toronto, reporting that undercover police had been present but failed to intervene. And unlike mainstream papers that require solid sources, *Frank* was the first to report rumours that seventy-one-year-old Pierre Trudeau had fathered a daughter. (It was right.)

But *Frank* also won infamy for dreaming up a "young Tory" contest to "deflower" Mulroney's teenaged daughter. "Once in a while we go over the line," says Bate. "It's like pornography. Everyone has their own definition of what's too much." Even *Frank* thought it went too far when it published a joke involving the 1992 Westray mining disaster, in which twenty-six died. It was the only time *Frank* ever pulled an issue from the newsstands.

At the Plaza Café on Ottawa's Sparks Street Mall, a nervous Bate orders exactly what I order. Although he wears his grey hair long and plays in a rock band, at fifty-two, he is firmly middle class. He drives a used gold Volvo wagon, is on his second marriage, took his family to Europe last year—and says he owns 25 per cent of *Frank*.

"Canadians, god, are so easily offended," says Bate, a Canadian. "There's no such thing as kindly humour. Doing humour like we're doing is an angry business." The Mulroney-deflowering article sparked a visit from police and a death threat—*Frank*'s first. The former prime minister said he'd like to "take a gun and go down there and do serious damage to these people."

A few years back, a man also burst into their offices brandishing a starter pistol. "It looked like a real gun," says Bate. "It scared the daylights out of Glen [McGregor] and Steve [Collins]," the two Ottawa staffers. The man, a disgruntled source, hadn't been paid for his tips. Bate said *Frank* had never used any of them.

As for disgruntled victims, *Frank* doesn't have libel insurance—"who'd take us?"—although it retains high-priced legal help, McCarthy Tétrault. When anyone threatens a lawsuit, which happens all the time, *Frank* prints an apology, which is sometimes worse than the original. Ontario provincial court Judge Mary Hogan sued after *Frank* detailed her impending divorce and child-support payments. She eventually accepted an apology and three subscriptions to *Frank*, says Bate, adding, "They originally wanted five." (Hogan's lawyer, Harvey Strosberg, says the terms are confidential, but confirms he personally got a subscription. "I wanted to be sure he didn't do any further damage to my client, and I didn't want to be embarrassed by being seen buying their rag at the newsstand.")

For lack of real celebrities in Canada, *Frank* ends up targeting the media, lambasting everyone from the CBC ("The Corpse") to the "Ottawa Senior Citizen." In return, at least half of the people who sue *Frank* are journalists, including CTV's Mike Duffy, whom it calls the "Puffster," and *Toronto Sun* columnist Heather Bird. *Frank* had to run an apology drafted by her lawyer, not once but twice, make a donation to a charity of her choice, and pay her legal costs. "Media people take themselves very seriously," says Bate. "We're trying to deflate pomposity."

The original *Frank* was founded in Halifax in 1987 and still focuses on local issues. Bate's Ottawa offshoot began in 1989, concentrates on central Canada, and has only three full-time employees, not including himself. On the newsstand, *Frank* actually outsells *Maclean's* magazine, which has many more subscribers. Bate says nearly 80 per cent of *Frank*'s eighteen-thousand circulation is single-copy newsstand sales.

But didn't I read somewhere circulation is twenty thousand? "Eighteen thousand is the honest number," he says, looking sheepish. "We were rounding it off for our nonexistent advertisers."

It's time to be *Frank*. (After all, *Frank* ran a parody last week of me having lunch with myself.) I had heard Bate once did drugs. Using *Frank*'s trademark "ring of truth," I ask: "So are you still a drug dealer?"

Bate chokes on his ice water. He says he never sold drugs. "I smoked dope when I was a musician."

"Did you inhale?" I ask.

"Yes, but I didn't exhale."

"Are you still doing drugs?" I ask.

"Jeez," he says. "No, I haven't. Honestly. Guess after you have kids you sort of get a bit responsible." Speaking of kids, why did he leave his first wife when his twin daughters were only seven? "I don't think ... It would be hurtful." His voice trails off.

I lob another "ring-of-truth" question. "Did you keep up with child support?"

"What?! Who's feeding you this?"

I smile.

"So this is what it's like," he says, "to be on the other side."

Bate has worked at the *Nelson Daily News* and the now-defunct *Kamloops Sentinel* in B.C. He also worked at Canadian Press, designed computer games, and chose the music for a CBC drive-home show in Ottawa. "A pathetic résumé," he concedes. The last song he allowed through was "Show Me the Length," about a male beauty contest. The incident still holds the record for most irate-listener calls, he says, adding, "I just didn't listen closely enough."

"So the CBC fired you," I say. It's not a question.

He protests mightily, but concedes, "I left soon afterward."

The son of a British radio officer, Bate grew up on "grim" military bases all over Canada. "We were never in the same house two Christmases in a row." In May, he will accompany his seventy-seven-year-old father back to some old bases in England. "I'm dreading it," he says. I jot that down. "No, don't write that," he begs.

There is no mercy when it comes to *Frank*.

In keeping with Frank's *pathetic accuracy rate of 60 per cent, I wrongly reported the number of times Michael Bate has been married. Several readers called to say he is actually on his third marriage. Bate later confirmed this. He also said that* Frank's *oft-quoted 60 per cent accuracy rate is no different from that of the mainstream press.*

At lunch, Bate told me that he had planned to stand me up. Instead, he had intended to send a photographer to snap me sitting, alone and forlorn, in the restaurant. But I foiled that by showing up at the Frank *office to escort him to lunch. After the interview, I held off, awaiting the inevitable parody in* Frank. *(I do enjoy having the last word.) The week after* Frank *ran its parody of me, I wrote my column.*

Frank *regularly lampoons me as* The Globe and Mail's *"restaurant critic." But I'm one of its many closet cheerleaders. The magazine keeps the mainstream media honest, not only by routinely scooping us but also by giving us a well-aimed kick in the pants whenever we deserve it—and sometimes when we don't.*

mordecai richler

HIS RULES FOR DRINKING AND THRIVING

September 25, 1997

"I don't drink nearly as much as people think," Mordecai Richler says. "But I enjoy the reputation." At sixty-six, he has a bulbous red nose, glowering eyes, and grey hair that flops over his forehead like a damp mop. His melon-shaped belly bulges over his chinos. Like the characters that populate his novels, he's sardonic, contrary, grouchy. For lunch, he picked Prego, an old Toronto haunt he doesn't even like any more. And he could care less that the smoke from his Davidoff cigarillo, which he puffs throughout his clam chowder, might bother others.

"I'm a very agreeable fellow," he sulks. "Nothing you've read about me is true." For the record, the man whose excerpt of his latest novel, *Barney's Version*, was typeset around the shape of an Absolut vodka bottle says he downs two scotches an afternoon at a tavern near his Eastern Townships cottage. Once a week, he has wine and cognac during an all-afternoon lunch with friends in Montreal. "Then I go home and have a nap. Of course I drive. I certainly think you can drive after three drinks."

He orders a glass of red wine. "I couldn't be a drunk and write every day."

A junk dealer's son, Richler grew up on Montreal's St. Urbain Street. His Hassidic grandfather whipped him with a leather belt for minor infractions of religious laws. At thirteen, Richler declared himself an atheist, which got him into a fistfight with his father. They didn't speak for two years. The worst break was with his mother, Leah, a Polish immigrant. She was angry about Richler's harsh portrayal of a Jewish mother in *St. Urbain's Horseman* (1971), his most autobiographical novel. "Of course I worried about my mother. But she was a very difficult and distressed lady."

Leah retaliated a decade later with *her* memoirs, *The Errand Runner: Reflections of a Rabbi's Daughter*. She wrote: "Always when I am greeted with the exclamation, 'I read about your famous son,' my retort is invariably, 'Which one?'" Her elder son is an optometrist in St. John's.

When Mordecai was thirteen, she secured a *get*, a religious divorce. Richler eventually reconciled with his father, who died in 1967. But he and Leah didn't speak for two decades. When his mother died eight months ago, at age ninety-two, he didn't go to her funeral.

Richler scraped out of Baron Byng High School, then dropped out of the only university that would have him, Montreal's Sir George Williams, now Concordia. At nineteen, he fled to Paris. "I wanted to write." Four years later, he moved to London, where he married Catherine Boudreau, from St. Catharines, Ontario. After their divorce, he married Florence Wood, another Canadian in London, in 1960. Their five children include her son, Daniel, from a previous marriage. They went to Seders at Passover and Richler has taken them all to synagogue at least once. But, he says, the children had a secular upbringing. "I had to break the news to them that I was Jewish."

Neither wife is. "I'm not developing a policy on it," he snorts. "Sure, I've had Jewish girlfriends, when I was a teenager, in Paris." But what about his acid portraits of Jewish women? He eats a mouthful of fettuccine bolognese. "I'm a satirical novelist. You want nice? Read Leon Uris."

Richler erupts at the next question. "What do you mean, how tall am I? I've never been asked that before." He recovers. "I don't know ... five-seven?" He really isn't short, nasty, and brutish, just a grumpy old man. Questions about his second wife (model, actress, book editor) provoke sarcasm. "I suppose you want to know how tall she is." Now that he mentions it, I do. Turns out she's taller. Annoyed, Richler manages to quip, "She usually sits down when we're together."

Oddly, for a writer, he hardly ever read to his children, even *Jacob Two-Two Meets the Hooded Fang*, his prize-winning children's book about his youngest son, Jacob. He had Florence read them the draft, then inquired about their response.

In 1972, Richler came home to Montreal. He felt ignorant of ordinary life in London, where he hung out with the literati (and still spends five months each year). "If you're a novelist, you have to know all sorts of banal things. If you have to research it, you're dead in the water." In Quebec, he notes, he drinks with lawyers and manufacturers, farmers and snowplow operators. To Richler, writing is rewriting and rewriting. *Barney's Version*, about an unruly film producer, is his first novel in eight years. "I haven't got the imagination to go from one novel to another, so I do other things in between."

That includes venomous commentary on Quebec separatists. He was perversely pleased by Jacques Parizeau's vengeful speech blaming "money and the ethnic vote" on referendum night. "I'd always said it was tribal and ethnic, and there was the proof for everyone to see." In gratitude, Richler created the Prix Parizeau, an annual $3,000 award, open to "ethnics," for Quebec fiction published in English.

At Prego, the waiter is perplexed when Richler orders an espresso allongé. "Is that a single or a double?"

"A single, with extra hot water," murmurs Richler.

The waiter brings a single. No hot water. Such indignities are why, despite everything, Richler's a Montrealer who wouldn't dream of moving to Toronto. He meekly sips the non-allongé brew. His wineglass is still half full. A little self-conscious, perhaps? The meekness fades as he reverts to type. "I've got a flask in my jacket. I'm going to have a drink in an alleyway," he says sarcastically. He looks at his watch. His next appointment isn't for twenty-five minutes. "We could go somewhere," he says, "and shoot up drugs."

In a letter to the editor, Sarah Reynolds suggested The Globe *give me "something more to do and let her eat lunch alone." Reynolds wrote: "Snarking at Mordecai Richler, trading inanities with the voice of Sleeping Beauty—it's depressing to read such drivel from a gifted writer and sharp political observer."*

The danger of writing about writers, of course, is that they retaliate. In Belling the Cat: Essays, Reports and Opinions, *Richler bemoans what he calls the "ordeal" of the book tour, including Lunch with me. The funny thing is, in his version of our Lunch, he makes himself one inch taller.*

In 1997, Richler won the $25,000 Giller Prize for Literature for Barney's Version, *his novel about a thrice-married man who is a drunk and, maybe, a murderer, too. In 1998,* Barney's Version *won the Stephen Leacock Award for Humour.*

evelyn lau

GETS PERFECT GRADES IN THE SCHOOL OF HARD KNOCKS

April 3, 1997

Evelyn Lau is wearing a baggy oatmeal sweater. So it's not immediately apparent that she is one of the few surgically unassisted Chinese women in the world to require a DD-cup bra. "My bosom has been the bane of my existence," she sighs. In her first and most famous book, *Runaway: Diary of a Street Kid*, she graphically describes how, as a drugged-out teenaged prostitute, johns were forever doing unmentionable things to her breasts.

"People are a lot more civilized now," she remarks over a dinner of raw oysters at Vancouver's Century Grill, a sleek Yaletown bistro with nineteen wines by the glass and an exceptionally tall coat-check personette.

Of course, it's Lau's world that is more civilized now, not the johns. At twenty-five, she is one of Canada's most successful young authors, with six books of poetry and prose published to date. She owns a condo in pricey downtown Vancouver. And she is in what she calls her "first serious relationship"—with author W.P. Kinsella, who, at sixty-one, is thirty-six years older.

But back to Lau's past. Now, I left my comfortable Montreal home at nineteen to voluntarily haul pig manure in China during the Cultural Revolution. But I have trouble understanding why someone so smart would drop out of school and run away from home at fourteen and end up as a junkie-whore. Yes, it's hard to be the dutiful daughter of immigrants from China and

Hong Kong, the kind who consider friends a frivolity and an 89 per cent exam mark a failure. Yes, it's hard to have parents who speak the language of the old country when you speak that of the new. And yes, it's hard when a sister suddenly displaces your entrenched nine-year status as an only child.

But I'm a parent now. Millions of Canadians have overcome such traumas, if that is the word, without self-indulgent meltdowns. When Vancouver-born Lau was in Grade 4, her father, the sole breadwinner, lost his job as a structural engineer. Her uneducated mother became obsessed with ensuring Eldest Daughter was on track for medical school. But Lau wanted to write. At twelve, her poetry was published in literary journals. At thirteen, she won a *Vancouver Sun* essay contest—"What would you like to ask the Pope?"—and met John Paul II. Her uncomprehending, unimpressed parents considered her scribblings a waste of time.

"Someone else in my circumstances might have thrived, but I just couldn't stand it. I don't want to whine or assign blame, but I couldn't live there," says Lau, who contemplated suicide in Grade 5 after getting the imperfect 89. Overnight, she went from being an A student to a drug addict. On the streets at fourteen, she dropped into a free-fall of pot, hash, methadone, cocaine, LSD, and a potpourri of downers and uppers. To support her habit, she donned Lycra and spike heels and tottered over to strange men's cars. She was raped. At the time she left home, her parents had not even told her the facts of life.

"I used to think I could get pregnant from oral sex," says Lau, who worked as a prostitute off and on for five years. She attempted suicide. She became bulimic. "When I was hooking, that was a way for me to feel clean. I would shower, but that would only clean the outside. By vomiting, I could clean the inside, too." She says she was never beaten while hooking. "I was compliant. I would rather do what the person told me to do than resist and get hurt, which is also why I would go home and throw up."

Lau has a heart-shaped face, bee-stung lips, and perfect even, white teeth. Her clear skin seems unravaged by drugs and alcohol. Nor can you tell that repeated vomiting has ruined the enamel on her teeth. It was a hole in her esophagus, burned through by stomach acid, that ended eight years of bulimia. "It simply became so painful to throw up."

Sex hurt, too. As a teenaged hooker, Lau took painkillers before she went to work. "I never knew why people did it voluntarily if they weren't going to get paid for it."

I ask whether, after dropping out in eighth grade, she plans to go to university. (She doesn't.) "Now you sound like my mother," she says. "I like men who are paternal, but I don't like women who are maternal." Lau has always dated older men, including married ones. But a sexagenarian sex toy? One of his grandchildren is practically her age. For a year and a half, she has been with Kinsella, a prolific thrice-married writer whose first novel, *Shoeless Joe*, was made into the film *Field of Dreams*. They don't live together—she wants her sixty-square-metre condo to herself—but he relocated from White Rock, B.C., to a place just four blocks away.

Unlike most other writers of Chinese descent, Lau doesn't write about her heritage. Instead, her subjects are sadomasochism, extramarital affairs, and the loneliness of the sex trade. After spending a year on a novel that "hasn't gone anywhere," she is writing poetry again. That worries her, because it doesn't pay the mortgage.

Lau has quit smoking, renounced drugs, overcome an addiction to tranquillizers, and stopped seeing her psychiatrist. To relax, she watches violent movies. "I love violence. The more people dead, the better." But she doesn't like sex and violence. "I'm very touchy about sex. I'm very puritanical now."

She wouldn't see *Leaving Las Vegas*, she says, because of the scene of the gang-rape of a prostitute.

When *Runaway* was published, Lau, then eighteen, eagerly called home. "Somehow I thought my parents would be very happy that I had published a book." Instead, her father yelled at her for bringing disgrace on the family. The subsequent made-for-television movie didn't help. For the past decade, Lau has had no contact with her sister or parents. She didn't call when she became, at twenty-one, the youngest Canadian poet to be nominated for a Governor-General's Award, or when, at twenty-four, her first novel, *Other Women*, was published.

Lau still dreams about her family. Her mother must be in her fifties by now, she thinks, her father in his sixties. "If one of them gets sick and dies without the relationship being healed," she says, "that would be devastating." She muses that her baby sister must be just about the age Lau was when she left home. "I live in fear that she's going to turn up on my doorstep and say, 'I've run away from home.'" Lau sips her chardonnay. "That would be a great payback."

I never heard from Evelyn Lau after the story ran, but I did receive a note from W.P. Kinsella. On remarkable letterhead that listed all his books, all three movies made from his books (with an asterisk for the one that won an Academy Award, Lieberman in Love*), and all his other awards and decorations, including the Order of Canada, he wrote:*

> Dear Jan Wong:
>
> While I could go on for pages, I won't. I'll just say, "What a cruel, mean-spirited column you wrote about Evelyn Lau."
> Bill Kinsella

Lau and Kinsella broke up three months later. Within weeks, Lau was describing her disgust for his teeth, his skin, his clothes, his sexual performance, and his diabetes in an article in Vancouver *magazine entitled "Me & W.P." This is how she describes their first meeting, at a Christmas party at the home of Kinsella and his third wife: "For a while, I thought he was staring at my chest, but this was only an effort to escape meeting my eyes."*

Kinsella sued, citing invasion of privacy. They settled in March 1999. Vancouver *agreed to print an apology. There was no cash settlement, and neither side covered the other's legal costs. In Lau's statement of defence, she maintained that she had a written agreement with Kinsella in which either was free to write about their two-year relationship. Lau also wrote a novella based on their relationship, but it was rejected by all her publishers. In 1999, she published* Choose Me, *a collection of short stories about needy young women who chase after older men and ultimately see them for the self-absorbed geezers they are.*

lynn johnston

FOR BETTER OR FOR WORSE, DON'T GET SURLY WITH THIS CARTOONIST

November 17, 1999

For better or for worse, lunch with Lynn Johnston is at Toronto's Old Spaghetti Factory. As it turns out, it's for the worse, at least as far as the waitress is concerned. But more on that later.

The cartoonist, who has to create 365 strips on deadline a year, shows up on time. She may even be a minute early. When asked the secret of her success, she intones: "Show up on time."

It must work. Her annual income exceeds $1 million (U.S.). *For Better or for Worse* runs in two thousand newspapers. In 1999, it beat out *Garfield*, *Dilbert*, *Peanuts,* and *Doonesbury* as North America's most popular comic strip, according to an annual survey of *Editor & Publisher*, a trade magazine. Johnston (the "t" is pronounced) even persuaded a young woman, who drew for *Dennis the Menace* and *The Flintstones*, to move last year from Carmel, California, to North Bay, Ontario, 320 kilometres north of Toronto. The young woman now does all the colouring and lettering for the strip. She's one of five hired hands, including a publicist, a business assistant, a Web-site designer, and an intellectual-properties manager.

"I can't believe how easy it is to be successful," says Johnston, fifty-two, who lives in Corbeil, twenty minutes' drive from North Bay. "There are millions of people who can draw like me. They just don't show up on time!" She said as much last month to graduates at the University of Western Ontario. "My parting words were: 'Show up on time; be good at what you do; charge a fair price; be honest; and be a pleasant person to work with.'" For this wisdom, UWO gave her an honorary degree—her third. She's always felt inadequate because she dropped out of the Vancouver School of Art. Still, she pooh-poohs the honour.

"It's an opportunity to get a free speaker and some publicity for the school." She says that twice in two minutes.

Like Johnston herself, *For Better* has an edge normally absent from the funny pages. In her strip, she killed off the family dog, Farley, named after Farley Mowat. She has also tackled child abuse, birth defects, and race relations. Her 1993 series on the coming-out of a gay man—his family reacts by kicking him out—won her a Pulitzer Prize nomination. But mostly, *For Better* is the warm and fuzzy story of the Pattersons, a Canadian family based largely on Johnston's own. Like her heroine, Elly, Johnston is married to a dentist. And like Elly, she has a son and a daughter. (When Johnston turned forty-five and longed for another baby, she added a third cartoon child.)

Unlike most cartoonists, Johnston never had to submit her strips for rejection slips. Not that she hasn't tasted rejection. Her first husband walked out when their son was six months old. As a single parent on welfare, Johnston offered to draw cartoons for the examination-room ceiling of her Hamilton obstetrician. They developed into a bestselling book, *David! We're Pregnant!* In 1979, her work caught the eye of Universal Press Syndicate, which signed her to a twenty-year contract. By then, she had married her second husband, the dentist.

"People are so jealous of success," says Johnston, who is marking her twenty years of cartooning with her twentieth book: *The Lives Behind the Lines*. "Success doesn't come to you. You have to generate it." She sometimes fails. An avid flier, she flunked her pilot's exam twice, first getting 70 per cent, then 71 per cent. The passing grade was 72. "I begged for the extra per cent, but they wouldn't give it to me," says Johnston, who was tripped up by the multiple-choice math. She was so depressed, she gave up trying, but not flying. (She's allowed to fly if accompanied by a licensed pilot.)

Johnston has brought along an old friend from Dundas, Ontario. She met Andie Parton, also fifty-two, years earlier at a La Leche League meeting on cracked nipples. "Andie took one look at these ladies in Fortrel and said, 'We're outta here!'" she recalls. Johnston isn't wearing Fortrel to lunch, but is dressed in a cartoon-purple sweater and suede pants that set off her blonde highlights. On her wrist is an old Caravelle watch, which she bought for the magnifying crystal. "My eyes are not that great any more. They're tired and out of focus," says Johnston, who wears bifocals. "There are times when I shouldn't drive. That's why I don't do all the drawing any more. I just partially finish the strips." She first writes the scripts, then inks in the characters. Rather than pay everything in taxes, she says, she prefers to invest in staff to colour in her cartoons and market her work. "I know it's going to come back to me in spades—green spades." Her staff works in the basement of her huge two-storey log house, set on fifty hectares of wooded lakeside property. She works upstairs. Her indoor pool, she says, is "the size of Westminster Abbey."

After a few mouthfuls of Caesar salad, Johnston puts down her fork. "I can't eat this," she says, grabbing a 'We'd-love-to-hear-from-you' card on the table. In her clear cartoonist's hand, she writes: "Too much sludge on the salad!!! Bleah!!!"

Later, our twentysomething waitress brings Johnston's minestrone and asks if she still wants her salad. (She doesn't.) After the waitress leaves, Johnston reaches for the card again. Under "service," she ticks off the box labelled "forgettable." Aloud, she says pleasantly, "I like to fill in these things because not enough people give you feedback."

Hmmm. That kind of feedback can get you fired. A moment later, Johnston decides "forgettable" isn't strong enough. "Surly. They need one more box," she says, writing the word down. "Surly. Yeah. Don't have lunch with Lynn."

It's mystifying. Our waitress may not be telling us to "have a nice day," but she doesn't seem particularly surly. "Andie and I have both been waitresses," Johnston explains. "It doesn't cost anything to be nice. It's an acting job. I don't care if your boyfriend dumps you and it's Monday morning and you look like hell. You still have to do it."

Yes, but what exactly has the waitress done wrong? "No eye contact. Mouth turned down," says Johnston.

Our waitress returns. "Dessert for you ladies?" she asks, devoid of hostility. Later, she brings the cheque, on which she's written, "Thank you!!"

"It's tip time," says Johnston dryly. (We're talking a tip of approximately $2.25 here.)

"I just don't think it was deliberate," says Parton gently, trying to moderate her famous friend. Parton suggests "medium surly?"

"Medium surly," Johnston agrees. Then she decides not to hand in the comment card after all. "Maybe she doesn't love her teeth." Johnston smiles. Her own teeth are a gift from her dentist husband, who bonded on new surfaces to give her a lovely smile. For better, or for worse.

The day the story ran, I called the Old Spaghetti Factory to tell the manager that, Lynn Johnston's comments notwithstanding, the service had been just fine. For her part, Johnston had a friend call Frank *magazine to report I had stiffed the waitress. She's right. My tip was short about 50 cents.*

Coming from a restaurant family, I automatically check the bill. At lunch, I noticed—and said so aloud—that the waitress hadn't charged for Johnston's minestrone. Perhaps the server had been confused by her celeb refusal to order off the menu. The set lunch, which everyone orders, includes soup and salad. But Johnston wanted only soup and salad, no main course. I humbly confess that by the time the waitress came back to pick up my credit card, I forgot to remind her about the soup. But then neither did Johnston.

A souvenir from this Lunch now graces my bulletin board. As Globe *photographer John Morstad snapped away, he coaxed Johnston into sketching my portrait on a napkin, which* The Globe *printed that week in lieu of my regular columnist's photo. Johnston gets the last laugh. She drew me with little dots floating around my head. In hindsight, I think that's supposed to be dandruff.*

jeffrey archer

THE INDISCREET CHARM OF THE NOVELIST AND LORD

October 16, 1997

At the Royal Ontario Museum, Jeffrey Archer lingers over a seventeenth-century Chinese figurine of a legendary scholar-official known as the God of Wealth. Lord Archer has the wealth—he's sold more than 120 million books, including *The Prodigal Daughter* and *Kane and Abel*. But calling him a scholar-official would be a stretch. Although the bestselling novelist sits in the House of Lords, critics deride his literary output as "mental bubblegum."

Upstairs at the awkwardly named restaurant Jamie Kennedy at the Museum, Archer orders mineral water, squash soup, and roasted monkfish. He has one more week to go in a weight-loss competition with his secretary. Not surprisingly, he's winning. Being Archer, he immediately hired a personal trainer and a dietitian. He's no dummy in the interview department, either. Two weeks earlier, he asked for my faxed résumé. He comes to lunch having read all my columns to date.

He's wary. So am I. A couple of years ago, publishing assistants at the American Booksellers Association voted him "Author from Hell." Book-tour escorts, who privately refer to him as "Lord Archole," gave him their "Golden Dartboard Award." (Past winners include Martha Stewart and Faye Dunaway.)

At this lunch, Archer is very charming. Has he changed? "I haven't changed at all," he says, the charm fading. "They wouldn't have given them to me if I was No. 3 on the bestseller list. What you find in life is, if you dare to be No. 1, they run you down."

At fifty-seven, Archer resembles an aging Dick Cavett, with wrinkles fanning across his tanned forehead. He takes a bite of fish and explains how he has to be so careful now. "I wouldn't have said in front of you to my driver, 'Now, Tom, have the car back on time, you pathetic object, because otherwise we will miss our flight at the airport.' He would know I'm joking, but you would misconstrue it." The charm vanishes completely when he's asked about some confusing items in his background. His father, who was sixty-four when Jeffrey was born, was a small-town printer who already had a colourful career as a bigamist and con-man. His mother, Lola, was twenty-seven and had already given away two children, one also called Jeffrey. Archer always assumed he was an only child. But soon after Jeffrey II was elevated to the House of Lords in 1993, Jeffrey I surfaced and sold his story to the tabloids.

"He made a quick buck out of it. Mother was very distressed," says Archer, his blue eyes turning to ice. Of his father, he snaps, "I never talk about it. If that's what you're going to write about, I'm sorry we met."

Lunch continues only because he's here to sell his latest novel, *The Fourth Estate,* about duelling press barons. His standard plot is about two men, one originally poor, now both rich, who clash over money, power, and women. Archer's only brush with university was a one-year teaching certificate at Brasenose, then a jock-oriented college at Oxford. After high school, he variously worked as a police trainee, P.R. man, and gym teacher. At one time, he put the mysterious initials FIFPC after his name. He hasn't since a biographer discovered they stand for "Fellow of the International Federation of Physical Culture," which turns out to be from a body-building correspondence course.

At twenty-nine, Archer was elected to the House of Commons. His standard book-jacket bio claims that made him the youngest member of the British Parliament. Actually, at least three others have been younger. "I meant youngest ... at ... that ... time." He spits out each word.

Archer's parliamentary career ended five years later when he lost all his money and then some. Based on a tip, he poured $560,000—his entire net worth—and another $560,000 of borrowed money into Aquablast, a Canadian company whose head office was a rented corner of a Scarborough, Ontario, gas station. Aquablast, which cleaned the outside of buildings, eventually went bust. The RCMP later charged four men with conspiracy to defraud investors.

"A stupid, arrogant mistake," Archer says. He was saved from bankruptcy because a friend's silk-stocking lawyer impressed the creditors enough to keep them at bay. Although Archer couldn't even type, he brashly decided to write his way out of his debts. His first novel, a semi-autobiographical account of his disastrous investment, was called *Not a Penny More, Not a Penny Less*. In Britain, it initially sold a respectable 3,000 in hardcover and 30,000 in paperback ("and 312 in Canada," he adds wryly).

The $6,700 advance didn't impress his wife, Mary, who was struggling to bring home a pay cheque as a chemistry professor. But his next book did better. And his third, *Kane and Abel*, earned him a $4.5-million advance. Although reviewers have blasted his writing as "airport literature," fans love it. His two most recent triple-book deals went for a total of $75 million, or $12.5 million a book.

Archer now confines his investments to property and a collection of eighty Impressionist paintings. In 1985, he was made deputy chairman of the Conservative Party. He resigned fourteen months later. The Department of Trade and Industry was investigating him for trading in Anglia Water shares, on whose board his wife sat. No charges were brought. About the same time as the Anglia scandal, a British tabloid reported that Archer paid a prostitute named Monica Coghlan $155 for services. He denied ever meeting her. Then the *Daily Star* learned that he subsequently sent her $4,475—through an intermediary—for a holiday in Tunisia to, literally, make her go away. Archer later sued the tabloid for libel and won $1.1 million in damages.

"I don't want to talk about it," he says sharply, "because I don't want to sue you either. Any reference to it, anywhere, and my solicitors get straight in touch with you."

Luckily, his diet precludes dessert.

The Globe *never heard back from the litigious lord. Perhaps he didn't dare focus any more attention on his links with the prostitute. It turns out that he had a lot to hide.*

In 1999, as Lord Archer was running for mayor of London under the Conservative Party banner, an erstwhile friend, Ted Francis, revealed that Archer had asked him to lie in the Daily Star *libel case. Francis had sworn an affidavit concocting an alibi for Archer on the date of his alleged encounter with the prostitute.*

As the scandal broke, Archer quit the mayoral race. He admitted to meeting the prostitute but denied having sex with her. He also admitted that he and Francis had agreed to lie about having dinner together on September 9, 1986, "when in fact I was having dinner with a close female friend at a restaurant in Chelsea." Ironically, the "friend" was not the prostitute. The British press identified her as Andrina Colquhoun, his personal assistant, who also acted as his London hostess while his wife and children were at home in Cambridge.

The Daily Star *demanded the return of the £500,000 libel award. The Conservative Party expelled him. And Scotland Yard arrested him over allegations that he had attempted to pervert the course of justice. When reporters sought comment from the Conservative Central Office, a spokesman harrumphed: "Lord Archer is not a member of the Conservative Party and has got nothing to do with us." Unbowed, Archer continued to show up in the House of Lords. The first day he took his seat on the Tory benches, he even had his assistant alert* The Guardian *ahead of time.*

After the perjury scandal, his latest book, To Cut a Long Story Short, *dominated the bestseller lists in Britain. The collection of fourteen short stories is helpfully marked with asterisks to show which ones are "based on true incidents." In one tale, the hero encounters a married woman whom he has admired from afar for years. He runs off with her to Paris for a day of torrid sex. Back in London, they do it in the back of his Mercedes, in the service lift at Harrods, and in a box in the dress circle at Covent Garden. Who knows how much, if any, of this is autobiographical?*

pierre berton

A HISTORIAN'S REMEMBRANCE OF THINGS PAST

September 4, 1997

Pierre Berton orders a glass of red wine. "Not a bottle," he cautions the waiter at the Royal Ontario Museum. He explains: "I used to drink a lot in the old days. Less now."

At seventy-seven, he looks not a day over, well, seventy. His trademark sideburns are gone. His Father-of-Confederation eyebrows are snow-white. Age spots dot his hands, which tremble slightly as he peruses the lunch menu. These days, he sometimes forgets the names of close friends, famous actors, or other authors, or misses a dose of pills. His secretary reminded him of this lunch at the last minute. As for his seven-year-old Lincoln Continental: "It's brown, or grey. I can't remember which."

He sighs. "I'm slowing down." Bertonian slow is another man's swift. His forty-third book is out next week: *1967: The Last Good Year*. His forty-fourth, a coffee-table book, *Sea Coasts*, will hit the shelves in a few months. Meanwhile, he's starring in a series for the new History Channel, recycling footage from his 1960s interviews with Alger Hiss, Jimmy Hoffa, and others.

In his prime, he churned out a book or two a year while working full time at *Maclean's* or *The Toronto Star*. He'd also appear on three weekly CBC shows and make eleven daily commentaries on a local radio station. "The kids were coming," he says. "That's why I worked so hard." There are eight. He and his wife, Janet, had six of their own: Penny, Pamela, Patsy, Peter, Paul, and Peggy Anne. Then Janet, a woman of matching energy, joined the Committee for the Adoption of Coloured Youngsters. "How can you be on this and not adopt?" he asked her.

"I was waiting for you to ask," she said. That's how Perri, a half-white, half-black baby, entered their lives. Later, a scoutmaster brought over Eric, fifteen, a part-Italian, part-Blackfoot Indian kid from Scarborough, Ontario. "He adopted us," says Berton.

They all lived in a stuffy basement apartment in suburban Toronto. Figuring the family could live as cheaply, and maybe better, in the country, he bought four hectares in Kleinburg, a forty-five-minute drive north. Initially, the tiny house was a hell, without doors, window glass, or even a stove. The floors were raw cement, the walls exposed asphalt sheathing. "I spray-painted the walls green. Pamela, the baby, had green paint all up her nose," says Berton, who was born and raised in the Yukon.

Luckily for future Berton babies, his prodigious output made him a millionaire by his forties. Still, he can't escape his Depression-era upbringing. "It's in the blood," says Berton, whose father was variously a gold miner, a cabinetmaker, a Mountie, and a mining recorder. Two years ago, partly to save on lawn-care costs, he instructed his gardener to let half the Kleinburg property go to seed. "Now it's a meadow and looks quite nice."

A two-finger typist, Berton sometimes pounds out first drafts in a month. When Smith-Corona went out of the type-writer business, he bemoaned the news on air. Fans sent him their old ones. Today, he has seven electric Smith-Coronas, always with one or two in the repair shop. His books—on the North, the Canadian Pacific Railway, the Klondike gold rush, the Great Depression, the Dionne Quintuplets—popularized Canadian history. But he says he didn't, and doesn't, have time to research his own books. (He pays his researcher one-third of gross.)

Nor does he read them once published. But his favourite is *The Secret World of Og*, illustrated by daughter Patsy, now a massage therapist and artist. Aimed at ten-year-olds, it's in print thirty-six years later, still eliciting letters from young fans.

"Just between me and you, I don't know what I'd do if I retired," says Berton, who is about to sign a new three-book contract. "I don't have any hobbies besides my kids." His friends are slowing down. Charles Templeton, the former preacher and journalist, has Alzheimer's, says Berton, who visits him once a week. His old publisher, Jack McClelland, is recovering from a stroke. After polishing off a salad and pheasant paté, Berton wistfully considers the crème brûlée. He opts for fruit salad. So I order crème brûlée and let him steal spoonfuls.

Is there anything in his life he regrets?

"God, yes, but I wouldn't tell you!"

Another spoonful.

It's time to ask about the Sordsmen, a swinging sixties men's club whose members included Berton, McClelland, author Arthur Hailey, architect John Parkin, and cartoonist George Feyer. The Sordsmen always played host to an equal number of women—not their wives—at monthly five-hour, wine-soaked lunches. Sometimes they were held in hotel restaurants, sparking rumours that lunchmates wandered upstairs afterward. Berton has hung up on reporters who dared ask about hanky-panky. Now he swallows a mouthful of crème brûlée. "It was aboveboard. If ever there was a public dalliance, we kicked the member out," he says, noting that two were expelled in his time.

"We only invited women who were fairly prominent and interesting," he adds, citing artist Dorothy Cameron, broadcaster Adrienne Clarkson, and author Barbara Moon. "They had to make speeches. The club provided transportation for women to get home because they'd drink." Berton blames McClelland for the club's wink-wink name. "I said, 'Jack, you shouldn't use a name like that. People will think the worst.' 'Well,' he said, 'we'll take the "w" out.'"

Berton sighs again. "If we had called it the Olympia Club, nobody would say a word."

Unlike some Lunch guests, Pierre Berton bore me no grudge. A year later, he even invited my family to a fundraiser in his town of Kleinburg, and later to his home. My boys romped through his meadow and clambered around an old caboose he had installed on his property. Despite failing health, Berton continued to be productive. His latest books include Pierre Berton's Canada: The Land and the People *and* Welcome to the 21st Century. *In 2001, his forty-eighth book is due out:* Marching As to War: Canada's Turbulent Years 1899–1953.

allan fotheringham

TAKING THE MEASURE OF THE MAN

December 22, 1999

After Mickey Rooney and Mordecai Richler, I decided it was time to start bringing a measuring tape to lunch.

Allan Fotheringham is waiting in a banquette at Biagio. The waiter walks by, does a double take, and exclaims: "What's this? White wine?"

"I gave you the script before she arrived," Fotheringham mutters, scowling. To me, he swears he drinks Scotch only after 5 p.m. and that he's off martinis entirely.

Canada's veteran back-page columnist lobs the first question. "So I hear you tried to take my job. I like ambition."

Whose lunch is this, anyway? I patiently explain the rules: when *The Globe* pays, *The Globe* calls the shots. But he may ask every fifth question. "I'll pay for lunch," Fotheringham, sixty-seven, says grandly.

I set my tape recorder next to his tape recorder. This is one lunch where there will be no awkward pauses while I scribble down quotes. Whenever I write, he writes. "Omigod," he says suddenly. "Here comes Anna Porter. She just published my book—and so we're not speaking to each other."

Last Page First, a collection of his *Maclean's* magazine columns, is his fifth book with Key Porter. He had words with Ms. Porter because a copy editor deleted an obscenity on page 130, inadvertently wrecking an anecdote about Jean Chrétien. Now, Fotheringham is going from book signing to book signing crossing out the mistake with his silver Cartier pen (which matches his Cartier watch) and writing in the obscenity.

It must be nice having a publisher like Ms. Porter mad at you. The waiter announces that she is sending over two glasses of champagne. "Put it in storage," says Fotheringham. "I'll order it next time." Suddenly, Ms. Porter is standing at our table. She stagily hands him a gift, a book called *Dealing with Difficult People*. He doesn't tell her the champagne is in storage, and he doesn't thank her either. He tells her it's the least she can do "because you owe me a lot." Ms. Porter smiles tolerantly.

Each week, Fotheringham writes two syndicated columns for *The Toronto Sun* and a back-page column for *Maclean's*. A good column takes him two hours, he says, a bad one four hours. He doesn't write drafts. He uses a computer—an ancient Tandy 200—like a typewriter. "Darling," he says, dipping a chunk of bread into a pool of olive oil, "after twenty-five years, if I don't know how to write a column …" He lets the unfinished sentence hang in mid-air, like a reproach to competitors like me who must rewrite.

He was born in Hearne, Saskatchewan (pop. 26). "It was a town," he says, demonstrating his columnist's flair, "twice the size of this restaurant." His mother, Edna, was widowed at twenty-four. He was just two years old, the third of four children. In high school, he dreamed of becoming a gym teacher. At the University of British Columbia, he worked on the newspaper. *The Vancouver Sun,* and later *Maclean's,* hired him.

Fotheringham's first marriage ended in divorce after seventeen years and three children. In 1998, after eighteen years of energetic bachelorhood, he married a Toronto gallery owner twenty years his junior. At their wedding in Bermuda, Anne Libby wore pink. He wore lemon yellow. Three weeks later, he learned he had prostate cancer. He lost twenty-five pounds after surgery and took three months off work. Now, he says, he is cancer-free and back to his normal weight of 170. He looks well. His hair is a mass of silvery curls, his face the same rich burgundy as his knit tie. Maybe it's the effect of his flashy wardrobe—glen-plaid suit, red silk hanky, and blue-and-red windowpane-checked shirt—but he seems shorter than his declared five feet seven.

Fotheringham takes out his driver's licence. But they don't measure you at Motor Vehicle Registration. Besides, people shrink. So I pull out a measuring tape. "I'll lie down on the floor," he jokes. He's told that standing up will be just fine. "You're not serious?" he harrumphs. "In the middle of Biagio's?"

No need to create a scene. "I'm going to get you for this," he mutters darkly as he follows me to the cloakroom. But he stands up straight against the wall while I mark the spot over his head. He's exactly five feet seven. Back at the table, he gulps his second glass of wine. "Does size matter?" he asks. His wit can't mask his annoyance.

"Accuracy matters," I reply.

That leads to a related topic. In 1986, and again in 1990, other writers accused him of plagiarism. The 1986 case concerned articles about John Magee, a Royal Canadian Air Force pilot whose Second World War poem "High Flight"—"Oh! I have slipped the surly bonds of earth"—was much quoted after the *Challenger* space shuttle exploded.

"You can't plagiarize facts," says Fotheringham. "Plagiarism is when you take another person's thoughts or creative writing and pass it off as your own."

Ah, but what about the amazing coincidences? The original article, by a British writer, ran in 1982 in a magazine called *This England*: "It [the poem] appears in numerous air training schools and flying museums in the U.S.A., Canada and Britain. It has also been set to music and as such has been used as a closing theme for several TV stations in America and even as a useful handout to nervous passengers on airlines."

Fotheringham's 1986 column said: "It appears in numerous air training schools and flying museums, has been set to music and used as a closing theme for TV stations—and is even used as a handout to nervous airline passengers."

Fotheringham stops eating his spinach ravioli. "I should have rewritten. That's not plagiarism. It's called laziness." Call it what you will, but he sometimes doesn't let work interfere with his parties. *Maclean's* sent him to London to cover Princess Diana's funeral. To the annoyance of his editors, he flew back early—the morning of the funeral—to attend his sixty-fifth-birthday party right here at Biagio.

He's asked if he's enjoying lunch. "I'm getting a column out of it," he says. The bill comes. We switch off our duelling tape recorders. Does Fotheringham follow through with his offer to pay for lunch? He does not. Good thing I only answered every fifth question. Let's see how he does with his column.

A few weeks later, Allan Fotheringham struck back with his own column in Maclean's, *entitled "Lunch with Jan Wong." In it, he accused me of "specializing in the shock personal." He wrote: "As a young girl she massaged the erect penis of an older man with Vaseline."*

Fotheringham omits to say I was about six or seven at the time, that the man was my babysitter, and that I disclosed this in an opinion piece during the rape trial of the Reform Party's justice critic. In 1999, Jack Ramsay was convicted of the attempted rape of a fourteen-year-old aboriginal girl when he was a Mountie in charge of an isolated Cree community in northern Saskatchewan. (In January 2001, the Saskatchewan Court of Appeal overturned the conviction after the Crown agreed with Ramsay's appeal that the trial judge made errors. Ramsay may face a second trial.)

In 1999, his supporters had wondered out loud why his accuser took years to come forward. Drawing on my own experience, I said it sometimes takes that long to speak up. I, for instance, had never told my father about the Vaseline encounter. He learned about it when he read my column in the newspaper. With trepidation that day, I called my sister to find out how he had reacted. She said he went for a long walk.

Aside from being accused of "specializing in the shock personal," I also object to being called cheap. "The proprietor {of Biagio} tells me that no one tips below 15 per cent here," Fotheringham wrote, noting that I left $8 on a $70 bill. I hate to break the news to him at this late date in his expense-account career, but you only tip on the pretax total. As Jerry Dykman pointed out in a letter published in Maclean's, that works out to 13.14 per cent.

In a letter to Maclean's, Elizabeth Bricknell wrote: "When Mr. Pot calls Miss Kettle a cheap tipper, I must point out I served Fotheringham a gutful of his favourite single-malt scotch on an authors' evening in Toronto's Coyote Grill in 1993, and he left me not one sou."

POLITICAL ANIMALS

sir john a. macdonald

WOULD YOU LIKE FRIES WITH THAT?

January 1, 2000

For a special New Year's Day 2000 issue, my editors asked me to "lunch" anyone from the previous millennium. I briefly considered Mao Zedong or Adolf Hitler. Colleagues suggested Susan B. Anthony, Martin Luther, and Johann Gutenberg. In the end, I chose Sir John A. Macdonald, Canada's first prime minister. Naturally, I took him to McDonald's.

Sir John A. Macdonald looks confused. "Where am I?" he asks, looking at the blacks, Asians, and East Indians lunching around us.

"McDonald's," I say. "In Toronto. Yonge Street."

"McDonald's?" he says. "What's that?" In eleven days, he turns 185. But he doesn't look a day over seventy-six, the age at which he died in office in 1891. Indeed, he looks exactly like his portrait on the $10 bill: the same unruly hair, the same thin lips, the same purple-veined bulbous nose. No one gives his Victorian frock coat and wing collar a second glance. We are, after all, on Yonge Street. Clearly, though, Canada's first prime minister is out of touch. He's surprised I'm from *The Globe and Mail*.

"Last I heard, it was just *The Globe*. George Brown was my good friend," he says, referring to a fellow Father of Confederation and *The Globe*'s founder, who died in 1880 after a disgruntled former employee shot him in the leg. Actually, Macdonald and Brown were hardly "friends." In the early 1860s, Brown, a leader of the Reformers, formed a cross-party coalition to work toward Confederation. Macdonald joined only when he realized that a political union would happen with or without him. In the process, Macdonald grabbed the glory for himself. Brown once noted that his rival's path to power was littered with the broken careers of erstwhile colleagues. By Confederation in 1867, Macdonald was prime minister—and Brown was out of the coalition.

"The public prefers John A. drunk to George Brown sober," Macdonald sneered at the time. At lunch, he is asked what he wants to drink. "Gin? Champagne? Whisky?" he says hopefully. He is unhappy to learn that McDonald's is dry. "I haven't had a drink in 109 years," he sighs.

He doesn't realize that McDonald's has no waiters. Out of deference to his age, I'll fetch lunch. "That's fast food," he exclaims when I return in two minutes with two Big Macs, medium fries, and Cokes. A picky eater, his normal fare is mutton chops with boiled vegetables. He requests a knife and fork for his burger. Now *that* turns heads.

"And you," he says, gamely tasting a fry dipped in ketchup, "where were you born?"

"Montreal."

"No, where were you really born?" he persists.

"The Montreal General Hospital."

Macdonald chokes on his Coke. In 1885, it was his Conservative government that imposed the first Chinese head tax. Both my grandmothers and one grandfather each paid $500 to enter Canada, more than $10,000 each in today's dollars. My other grandfather arrived even earlier, in the early 1880s. He was a nineteen-year-old peasant from south China, one of fifteen thousand Chinese coolies transported here to build the Canadian Pacific Railway.

"It was all your idea," I remind Macdonald.

Knowing that Confederation would be a mere "geographic expression" unless the new nation could be reinforced with steel from sea to sea, the prime minister had pushed for a transcontinental railroad. Chinese coolies were given dangerous jobs—placing nitroglycerin and lighting dynamite. Grandfather Chong was one of those who had helped blast tunnels through the Rockies. Andrew Onderdonk, a CPR contractor, estimated that three Chinese died for every kilometre of track laid. My own grandfather survived. But when the railroad was completed, another contractor reneged on a promise to ship him back to China. Grandfather Chong had the choice of spending his savings on passage home or staying on and working more. He found work as a dollar-a-month houseboy to Col. Josiah Greenwood Holmes, the deputy adjutant-general of the British base at Esquimalt, B.C. By coincidence, it is the same military base where Canada would detain the Chinese illegals who floated here on rusty ships in 1999.

Macdonald is upset to learn about the latest migrants. His plan was to keep us all out. That's why, when the CPR was completed in 1885 and coolie labour was no longer needed, his government imposed the head tax. I can't resist telling him that Grandfather Chong became a citizen in 1899.

"Isn't there anywhere I can get a drink?" Macdonald says. In his heyday, he was famous for his binges. He often showed up drunk in the House of Commons. The final pre-Confederation meeting in England was delayed for weeks, historians say, because Macdonald was on a bender in Ottawa. Once, he even vomited on stage during a debate with an opponent. Later, he asserted that the man's words had turned his stomach.

"And these other people," says Macdonald, gesturing to those eating around us. "Are they Canadians, too?" Why is he so surprised? After all, he was an immigrant himself, as were both his wives. His second wife was from a British slave-owning family in Jamaica. His first wife (and cousin) was an opium addict from Scotland. She died in 1857 from a Victorian disorder that today might be diagnosed as chronic fatigue syndrome. Macdonald himself was born in Glasgow in 1815. At five, he immigrated with his parents to Kingston. He became a lawyer there and, at twenty-eight, was elected a city alderman. The next year, he was elected to the legislature of what was then the Province of Canada.

Macdonald didn't believe in universal male suffrage. He did think that—as an experiment—single women with property might be given the vote. But his main interest in females used to be with ladies of the night. (Some historians say that may have accounted for his first wife's bedridden reclusiveness.) Macdonald reddens and changes the subject. "You speak English very well," he says.

"So do you," I say.

On a trip to England, Macdonald once witnessed a lady take a tumble as she alighted from her carriage, her hooped skirt flipping over her head. Macdonald couldn't stop laughing. When the lady finally got up and dusted herself off, she snapped, "Sir, I can see you are no gentleman!" Macdonald retorted, "And I can see, madam, that you are not one either."

After being reminded of this incident from the history books, the former prime minister peers under the table. "You're wearing trousers," he exclaims. Then he notices that so are most of the other women in McDonald's. "It is the dead of winter," I explain, before adding gently, "We can vote, too."

"I really need a drink," he says.

Unaware I've already paid for lunch, he gallantly offers to pick up the tab. He was never very good with money. I would ask for a $30,000 head-tax refund, adjusted for inflation and with interest, but he's broke. He frittered away his law practice, lost heavily on real estate speculation, and didn't even own the Kingston house he shared with his first wife. In 1868, a year after Confederation, he went bankrupt.

But it was the railroad that proved his undoing. While the CPR gave my family a chance at a new life, it led to Macdonald's political downfall. In 1872, when he was both prime minister and justice minister, he made a dark promise to Sir Hugh Allan, a leading Montreal capitalist. Macdonald would make Sir Hugh the president of the company building the transcontinental railroad. In return, he hit up Sir Hugh for $300,000 in campaign contributions, the equivalent of more than $6 million today.

The Pacific Scandal, as it was known, broke in 1873. The opposition unearthed a self-incriminating telegram from Macdonald to the businessman. "I must have another $10,000. Will be the last time of calling. Do not fail me. Answer today." Macdonald tried to save himself with an impassioned five-hour speech in the House of Commons. It was too late. On November 5, 1873, he resigned. He was the first and, so far, only Canadian prime minister to resign for ethical reasons. His only regret? "I should never have put it in writing," he says.

Four years later, Canadian voters returned him to power. His last hurrah was a campaign against free trade. Endearing himself to local manufacturers, he erected a wall of protectionist tariffs against U.S. imports. "How is the economy doing at the moment?" he asks.

"Great. Low inflation. Low unemployment. By the way," I tell him, "it was a Conservative government that signed a free-trade agreement with the United States."

Macdonald has lost his appetite. He hasn't finished his Big Mac. His fries are getting cold. Would he prefer a McDonald's personal pizza instead? "What's a pizza?" Macdonald asks.

He sighs heavily. "What I really need is a drink."

Some readers thought it unfair that I held Sir John A. to present-day standards. One pointed out that he had sent his daughter to a school run by a Métis headmistress as proof that he was racially tolerant for his time. But the point of the millennium piece was to show how far Canada had come. And that was exactly why I brought our first prime minister back to life and plunked him down in a Toronto fast-food outlet.

In a subsequent essay published in The Globe, *Donald Smith, a historian at the University of Calgary, lamented "the reduction of Sir John to a comic bit-player." He saw it as "yet another sign" that Canada is a country that does not know its past. In this column, I stuck to the facts. Macdonald's alcoholism, his fondness for mutton chops and prostitutes, his first wife's opium addiction—all came straight out of the history books. My cousin-in-law Colleen Parrish supplied the anecdote about the hooped skirt.*

stockwell day

"SORRY I NEVER WROTE"

May 13, 2000

In 1997, the Reform Party led by Preston Manning established itself as the Official Opposition in Parliament. After failing to win a single seat in Ontario, the party changed its name to the Canadian

Conservative Reform Alliance Party. Then someone noticed the
acronym. The party hastily renamed itself the Canadian Reform
Conservative Alliance. In 2000, Manning called a leadership vote.
Among his challengers were the beautiful Dr. Keith Martin and a
newcomer to federal politics—Alberta's provincial treasurer,
Stockwell Day.

Stockwell Day and I grew up one block apart in Montreal. His
birthday is the day after mine. We both have sons named Ben.
At Sir Arthur Currie Elementary School, we even had the same
kindergarten teachers. He was smitten by Mrs. Wharton, the
lovely blonde. I liked Miss Clark, the beautiful brunette.

Okay, so he's actually two years older. And his grandchildren are about the same age as my children. But—eew,
gross—we might have played with the same toys in the big
green cupboard at school. Then again, considering he's a hyper-
hetero, he probably played with guns.

Naturally, I was a model kindergartener. The principal had
to call *his* parents after he recited an indelicate poem at "show
and tell." At breakfast, Day rattles it off: *What will you have?*
said the waiter, as he rudely picked his nose. Give me a hard-boiled egg,
said the man. You can't put your finger in those. He grins, and continues eating his eggs (scrambled) at Ottawa's Westin Hotel. In
Montreal, his father worked at the local Zellers in the Côte-
Saint-Luc shopping centre. That's where my brother bought me
my first lipstick, Cleopatra Pink, when I was five, I tell him.
"I'm sure we hung out together," says Day, who switched to
another school after first grade. "Sorry I never wrote."

The media says he's telegenic, but he yearns to be taller.
Asked his height, he replies, "If I hang from an overhead chin-
up bar for thirty seconds to stretch my spine, then run to a
measuring stick, I'm just under six feet." At forty-nine, he
works hard to stay trim. So he jogs. He snowboards. And he

does karate kicks, at least for the cameras. Last year, as he rollerbladed into the provincial legislature to deliver the budget to Premier Ralph Klein.

This morning, though, he skipped his regular run. "This is exercise, too," he says, warily eyeing my notebook. A former auctioneer and Christian-school administrator, he was elected as a Conservative to the Alberta legislature in 1986. Outwardly, he's relaxed—jacket off, elbows on table. But he stiffens when asked about abortion. Suddenly, he's a Chatty Cathy doll. Pull his string, and a canned, oddly dispassionate message unfolds. Day opposes abortion, even in cases of rape. And he opposes funding for "medically unnecessary" abortions under the provincial health act. He would also deny gays equal protection under Alberta's human-rights law. "Marriage should be defined heterosexually," he says. Push him harder, and he retreats into that cowardly politician's defence: waiting for his constituents to come around. Not that he's a coward. In 1996, he chased an armed robber for blocks, then fingered him to a SWAT team.

His agnostic father raised him (and his five siblings) as Anglicans. At thirteen, Day prepared for confirmation. But from fourteen on, he adds, "God became increasingly irrelevant." At eighteen, he rebelled. Day chose drugs. I chose Maoism. In hindsight, it's unclear which caused more brain damage.

"Marijuana on and off, depending where the party was, for a couple of years," says Day, when asked what drugs he took. "I never got into needles, cocaine, heroin, the hard stuff. I don't have flashbacks." While I dropped out and dug ditches in China, he dropped out and worked on construction sites in Vancouver. Now, in his white polyester shirt and tie, it's hard to picture him as a hairy hippy. Or to think his longest-lasting job back then was hauling dead bodies for Vancouver Hearse Hire. Over breakfast, he describes his first corpse. "We slid the tray out of the refrigerator. It was a typical John Doe, complete with toe tag. He was stark naked. I picked up the feet. The skin moved liked the skin on a turkey. I put it down and gulped. The other guy said, 'Oh, it's just skin slip.'" Eew, gross.

Later, in Victoria, he raised three Leghorns for eggs in the back of a 1956 Plymouth. He pitied them all cooped up in the backseat, and fashioned little leashes out of bootlaces. "My undoing was walking the chickens," says Day. The neighbours complained. So he took an axe and a block of wood and chopped off their heads (the chickens', not the neighbours'). His breakfast conversation is a real appetite killer, what with nose-picking, "skin slip" and axe murders. I stop eating. Day, however, finishes off his cantaloupe and waxes rhapsodic about how he stuffed the chickens. "Bread—fresh, not dried— buttered, and orange slices—peeled—fresh pepper and spices."

He warned his roommate not to be late for supper that evening, but he was. "I actually ate the three chickens myself that night," Day admits. "It's still a sore point if I run into my roommate after all these years." *Three whole chickens?* "The drumsticks," he says, "were small." At nineteen, he succumbed to parental pressure and enrolled at the University of Victoria. He lasted six months. The following year, he met Valorie Suzanne. They married six weeks after his twenty-first birthday, and a month before hers. "To us, religion was a shrug," Day recalls. But, perhaps in rebellion against his agnostic father, he wanted to be married by a minister. The one he sought out was an evangelical Christian, who insisted on pre-marital coun- selling. That was the beginning, he says, of his fundamentalist beliefs. Asked if he now takes the Bible literally, Day nods. "The Bible is the written revelation of the ways of God," he says, his grey-blue eyes unwavering. He says he prays several times a day, and always when he boards a plane. It's hard to tell if he's pray- ing for this interview to end. If so, his prayers are answered. It's time for him to make a campaign speech to some underwriters.

He pays the bill and leaves. At my request, the waiter cancels his payment and puts it on my credit card. On my way out, it occurs to me that my tip might be less than Day's. "Don't worry," the waiter says. "He tipped the same."

Gee, maybe we did play with the same toys in kindergarten after all.

To my chagrin, Day's oldest son, Logan, called to say his dad really enjoyed the column. Stockwell Day won the race to become leader of the Canadian Alliance, but lost the 2000 federal election to the Liberals.

lise bissonnette

Her Quebec Doesn't Include Canada

January 30, 1997

Lise Bissonnette, a staunch separatist, usually ignores the Rest of Canada. But, like celebrities everywhere, she had something to sell— her newest novel, Affairs of Art. *In English, yet. For this she would hold her nose and venture into Toronto, the heart of anglo territory.*

Lise Bissonnette, hard-line separatist publisher of Montreal's *Le Devoir*, is—how to put this delicately in Canada's National Newspaper?—extremely likable. In 1974, when she was twenty-eight and trying to break into reporting, a secretary liked her so much she plotted to get Bissonnette a job. "Call at four," the secretary instructed. "I'll be out."

Claude Ryan, editor-in-chief, picked up the phone. After several more impeccably timed calls, Ryan, who hadn't hired a woman in ten years, gave Bissonnette a job. The first day, she wrote a page-one story. Ryan liked her so much he gave her a raise two weeks later. She rose to editor-in-chief within eight years, after Ryan left to head the Quebec Liberals. A subsequent publisher fired her, but the board liked her so much that in 1990 they asked her to replace him.

She is so likable that when the paper almost went bankrupt a few years ago, supporters raised nearly half a million dollars at an $800-a-plate dinner with—guess who?—as guest of honour. To save *Le Devoir*, Bissonnette restructured capital and talked the unions into concessions. Last month, the independent newspaper reported a tiny operating profit, its first in ten years.

Even I like her. *Le Devoir*'s first female publisher is my kind of person—a workaholic journalist who likes reading, shopping, and bossing people around. We are lunching at the bar at Toronto's Four Seasons Hotel on indifferent salad and pasta. With close-cropped brown hair, a leopard-print zipped sweater, and oval tortoise-shell glasses, Bissonnette, fifty-one, looks simultaneously chic and severe.

I'm curious about her first page-one story twenty-two years earlier. "It's the same story that could be written today," says Bissonnette, who has been known to clear the front page for her editorials. "Some francophone parents in Brossard [Quebec] wanted to send their kids to English schools." I tell her that I have met people in China who risked their lives to learn a foreign language during Mao's reign. Why not let French-Canadian children have a choice?

"It's not free choice. It's a semblance of free choice. Even if you had bilingual schools, the first thing is everyone would speak English," she says. "Most immigrants would learn English, which we would do if we were in their place." When I continue to advocate freedom of choice, adding that in Toronto I send my six-year-old to French school, she stares at me. "Asking for free choice is an extreme position nowadays," says Bissonnette.

Who's being extremist? After three generations in Montreal, my family has lost our ancestral language. It's not a disaster. A billion people already speak Chinese. I tell her French, too, is unlikely to die out any time soon in the world. Why should there be a special place in language heaven for francophone Quebeckers? If anyone has a legitimate worry, it's Canada's native peoples.

I try another tack. If Bissonnette is so anti-English, then why is she in Toronto plugging the translation of her second novel, *Affairs of Art,* about a bisexual art critic who dies of AIDS? "You don't resent English as a language," she says. "You resent it as difficult to deal with sociologically."

Bissonnette grew up in Rouyn, north of Montreal. The sixth of seven children of the owner of a second-hand shop, she remembers francophone girls from better-off families flaunting their English. "The status symbol was to go out with English-speaking guys," says Bissonnette, who could understand English but couldn't speak it. After graduating in education from the Université de Montréal, she was assigned to teach English. "They gave me the textbook and I went in. That's how I learned grammar," says Bissonnette, who is now fluent. No wonder bilingualism is in trouble in Quebec today. My French teachers came from France or Algeria, with the result that I still have trouble understanding Québécois French.

Unmarried and childless, Bissonnette wears a sculpted gold band on her ring finger. It's a gift from Godefroy Cardinal, a professor and former director of the Musée du Québec, with whom she shares a bungalow in suburban Ahuntsic. "It's a real love story," says Bissonnette, who began a relationship with him when she was young and he was still married. In her office, a special phone line is reserved for him.

During the 1980 referendum, Bissonnette cast the sole separatist vote in her poll in anglophone-dominated Montreal West, where she had impulsively bought her first house, oblivious to the neighbourhood. As a third-generation Montrealer, I pose this question: If Quebec can become a country, why can't Montreal's Chinatown secede, too? Bissonnette looks astonished. "I don't think it's the same thing. It would have to be viable." I assure her I could find a few million Chinese willing to move there.

As we sip cappuccino, I confess that, having lived abroad and seen true oppression, I just don't understand what she is so unhappy about. "People of my generation became sovereigntists because of our experience. We were insulted by people who said, 'Speak white,'" says Bissonnette. But I don't want to talk about the past. I want to know why there is no future. "It gets to the point where you feel the whole political structure isn't working any more," she says with finality.

I feel like the insensitive spouse who, after years of therapy, has finally changed, only to discover the marriage is really over. But shouldn't we stay together for the sake of the children? "Young people are less angry than we were, but they vote yes because Canada has become irrelevant," she says. "There is no sense of belonging. There was some sense of belonging in my generation."

That's tragic, I say.

"I don't find it very tragic, actually."

Almost pleadingly, I ask, "Don't you think Canada is a wonderful country?"

"No, I don't," she says, with a pleasant smile.

Lunch is over. I feel sad. Lise Bissonnette is a very likable person who doesn't want to share my home and native land.

After eight years at the helm of Le Devoir, *Lise Bissonnette was unable to push daily circulation beyond thirty thousand. In 1998,*

*she resigned to head the Quebec government's new mega-library, a
controversial project she had championed in countless editorials. The
$75-million institution, called the Grande bibliothèque du Québec,
paid her $130,000 a year for a five-year term.*

*Although we disagreed on everything, Bissonnette couldn't have
minded our lunch much. A year later, her publicist called, asking if
I wanted to interview her again. I declined.*

martin lee

CHAMPION OF A DEMOCRATIC
HONG KONG

April 10, 1997

*Martin Lee symbolized Hong Kong's pro-democracy movement.
Despite his wealth, social status, and conservative bent, he dared to
stand up to Beijing's Communist regime. I caught up with him as he
passed through Toronto on his last trip before the July 1, 1997,
handover of Hong Kong to China.*

On this Sunday in April, Hong Kong's most popular politician
has already been to early mass. Now Martin Lee is ready for
breakfast, dressed in a pinstriped suit, Pierre Cardin shirt, silk
tie, and wafer-thin gold Concord watch. He's staying at a
Bridle Path home, in Toronto's toniest neighbourhood. His
bags are by the door. In a few hours, he flies to Geneva to
address the UN Human Rights Commission.

This is dissent, Hong Kong–style. In a normal setting, Lee
would be a conservative. He's against unemployment insurance. He's for low taxes. He drives a blue Jaguar. He also tied

for first place in a "Top Ten Hunks of Hong Kong" competition staged by the *South China Morning Post,* the colony's largest English-language daily. "Sensual" and "attractive," readers sighed. Lee's response: "Absolutely stupid." (He is definitely not a hunk, which only goes to show his popularity.)

But within the repressive context of China, the chairman of Hong Kong's Democratic Party is a radical. He advocates democracy. Worse, he isn't leaving when the Chinese People's Liberation Army marches across the border this July 1. That is why he is the Hong Konger China fears most.

"You cannot sit back and do nothing," says Lee, fifty-eight, a rich lawyer who was chairman of the Hong Kong Bar Association from 1980 until 1983. His hostess offers platters of honeydew and English muffins and a pot of freshly brewed coffee. Lee eats sparingly and sips hot water. He hasn't touched coffee, or even Chinese tea, since swearing off caffeine in 1985. Hong Kong friends joke he is practising for a bread-and-water gulag diet. The pundits call him "Martyr Lee."

Lee may well be one of the first arrested. A scholarly-looking man with fine coal black hair and a slightly plummy British accent, he has been an unyielding advocate for the colony's six million people. In 1989, after the Tiananmen Massacre, Lee traded his pinstripes for a headband and protest T-shirt to lead Hong Kong's massive demonstrations.

Two years later, in the colony's first-ever democratic elections, Lee won his seat with 74 per cent of the vote, more than any other candidate. His tiny political party— Hong Kong's first—swept the election, winning twelve of eighteen seats.

In the 1995 elections, Lee won his seat with 80 per cent of the votes. Again, his party swept the elections. Beijing—surprise, surprise—vowed to scrap the elected legislature when it ends 150 years of British colonial rule in July.

"China is doing so many terrible things here. This is only the beginning. And what is the world doing? Nothing," says Lee. Many of Hong Kong's elite are acquiring foreign passports, shifting out assets and buying stately homes in Palo Alto, Vancouver, or Brisbane. Others hope to get even richer doing business with the mainland. Like the compradors in Shanghai a century ago who cast their lot with the imperialist powers, some of Hong Kong's biggest tycoons are cozying up to the Communists. "You don't have to be a communist in Hong Kong to tango with another communist, cheek to cheek," says Lee.

He could have done the same. As a British-trained barrister, Lee is one of Hong Kong's highest-paid lawyers. Ownership alone of his spacious Mid-levels flat and his centrally located offices makes him a millionaire many times over. Although he was born in Hong Kong—his mother happened to be there in 1938—Lee didn't live there until age twelve. That's when his father, a Kuomintang general and the first Chinese to obtain a doctorate in pharmacy from the Université de Lyons, fled the victorious Communists.

Now the victorious Communists are at the gates. In a normal place, people stuff pockets of popular politicians. But Big Brother is watching. Two years ago, Lee cancelled his fundraising dinners because friends bought entire tables but were too scared to attend. Instead, he sells raffle tickets outside department stores, raising about $2,000 (Canadian) an hour. Still, some donors stay prudently in the shadows, pushing their children forward with the money.

The anxiety is seeping into Canada. At a fundraiser last Saturday night in Markham, Ontario, 650 people raised $100,000 for the Hong Kong Democratic Party, but some donations were anonymous. Even on this fifteen-city tour of Canada and the United States, Lee's last before the Chinese takeover, Western leaders avoid him. So far, the no-response list includes President Bill Clinton and Prime Minister Jean Chrétien. "Every government is looking starry-eyed at the China market," says Lee, winner of the American Bar Association's 1995 International Human Rights Award and the National Endowment for Democracy's 1997 Democracy Award.

With his credentials and wealth, Lee could easily obtain Canadian, U.S., British, or Australian citizenship. But he has decided to cast his lot with Hong Kong. He has no foreign passport. He is not asking the same of his family. His wife, Amelia, a former schoolteacher, has a British passport. Their only child, Joey, fifteen, is safely ensconced at Winchester College, an elite English private school founded in 1382.

Lee believes his prominence will protect him from arrest. The party rank and file are in greater danger, he thinks. "That's why I want to stay. When they are put into prison, I will yell." But China has never shied from jailing its top dissidents, including Tiananmen student leader Wang Dan (now serving eleven years) and Democracy Wall activist Wei Jingsheng (now serving another fourteen, after already having served fourteen and a half).

Is Lee ready for jail? He nods. For twenty years? "Nelson Mandela went to prison for twenty-seven years. If I went to jail at my age, and spent twenty-seven years there," he jokes, "when I come out I'd be old enough to be the ruler of China." He laughs. But with the Chinese takeover just twelve weeks away, the jailhouse jokes don't seem so funny.

Martin Lee stayed on after July 1, 1997. He was free to travel overseas but was denied visas to mainland China. As expected, Beijing disbanded the elected legislature in Hong Kong and appointed a docile provisional body dominated by pro-China businessmen. In May 1998, Hong Kong voters gave Martin Lee and his

Democratic Party two-thirds of the popular vote. The prevailing electoral structure, however, meant that his party won only one-third of
the available seats.

In local council elections in late 1999, the largest pro-Beijing
party in Hong Kong doubled its strength, breaking the string of
electoral routs Martin's party had enjoyed since 1991. Still, the
Democrats won eighty-six seats, compared to eighty-three for the
pro-Beijing party.

In 2000, China continues to exercise its power, but in more subtle ways than many had imagined. Chinese troops keep a virtually
invisible presence in the territory. Mandarin has become the official
language in schools, as opposed to Cantonese, the local dialect. And
on one occasion, dissatisfied with a ruling by Hong Kong's highest
court, Beijing ordered the court to reverse itself. The court complied
with alacrity.

rayson huang

SPITEFUL AS THE SUN SETS

July 3, 1997

During the 1997 handover of Hong Kong to China, journalists
poured into the British colony. As hotels hiked their rates to $500
a night and more, a Canadian journalist friend, Janet Brooks,
found me a room at Hong Kong University. The faculty dining
room turned out to be a treasure trove of illustrious people. Some
were apprehensive about the Chinese takeover. Others exulted in it.
One of the latter was Rayson Huang, the former head of Hong
Kong University.

Rayson Huang, the former head of Hong Kong University and your typical helpless male, arrived in the visiting-faculty dining room at noon and announced: "My wife isn't feeling well. What should I do?" Hmm. What about getting her something to eat and taking it back to her room?

A scholarly man in his mid-seventies, with half-rim glasses and a slight British accent, he's also typical of the Hong Kong elite. As the sun sets on this colonial outpost, he has turned abruptly—and ferociously—anti-British and pro-Beijing.

Huang joined a group of us at a communal table. Like me, he was bunking at the university to observe the handover of Hong Kong to China. As waitresses brought out platters of sweet-and-sour spare ribs, steamed fish, and rice, everyone introduced themselves: a woman from France, another from Brazil, a professor from Hawaii, myself and Janet Brooks, another journalist from Canada.

It was just four days before the July 1 handover. Huang noted proudly that he had been invited to all the ceremonies. Without prompting, he added that he wouldn't attend Governor Chris Patten's 6:30 p.m. farewell and neither would many of his friends. It was a final, apparently orchestrated, snub by the pro-Beijing group.

"I'm an old man. It's too much," sneered Huang, who wore a jacket to lunch despite the humidity of the monsoon season. "It starts at six and doesn't end until two. But I'll go for cocktails and the banquet afterward. And the handover ceremony at eleven-thirty is very important. Then I'll watch Prince Charles's boat leave, dragging Governor Patten with him." He laughed sardonically.

Huang, who studied chemistry at Hong Kong University in the late 1930s, fled inland to China during the Japanese invasion. He obtained his doctorate at Oxford University and in the 1960s became provost at Singapore's Nanyang

University, where he earned a reputation for suppressing radical students. In 1972, he became the first ethnic Chinese to head Hong Kong University, the most prestigious seat of higher education here. Later, he helped draft the Basic Law, the Beijing-approved mini-constitution for Hong Kong. Now retired, he had just flown in from his home in England to witness the historic moment.

Under the British, the ruling class was a cozy elite. Under the Chinese, it will remain a cozy elite. The British governor appointed Huang—as a corollary of his university post—to the colonial government's law-making Legislative Council. Perhaps it rankled that although he occupied the mansion at the highest point of the mountainside campus, his title was merely vice-chancellor. By tradition, the British governor was always chancellor. Now, like the compradors of old China, Huang has switched allegiance.

Despite the long evening of scheduled events, Huang didn't consider ducking out of the last one, the 1:30 a.m. swearing-in of Beijing's appointed legislature. "I want to go," he said, helping himself to some fish with ginger and scallions. "I worked on setting it up. Besides, a lot of my friends are coming down from Beijing." By "friends," he meant the Chinese Communist officials in charge of ensuring that Hong Kong remains docilely under Beijing's thumb. Like an increasing number of Hong Kong's pro-Beijing elite, Huang's hatred of Patten was almost palpable. The way he sees it, the last Hong Kong governor's introduction of democracy was a deliberate provocation.

"He's ruined relations between China and Britain. He's ruined relations between Hong Kong and China," said Huang, an enthusiastic chamber-music violinist for whom Hong Kong University's performing-arts theatre is named. He criticized Patten for loosening restrictions on demonstrations a few years earlier. The Chinese have vowed to reimpose them immediately. "That is only right," said Huang, wagging his finger at everyone at our table.

Didn't he find it jarring that China was adopting the antiquated laws of a once-repressive colonial ruler? Huang shook his head. The law was the law. Patten should never have changed Britain's colonial laws one iota. They suited Beijing just fine. That isn't exactly how he put it. He said the people of Hong Kong were too naive, too unsophisticated, too illiterate to vote.

"Are you qualified to vote?" the other Canadian journalist couldn't help asking.

"Well, people ..." he began.

"No. You," she said. "Are *you* qualified to vote?"

He nodded. "I am. But others aren't."

He compared Hong Kong to Africa and predicted mayhem would ensue if people here were given the vote. "Democracy would bring chaos to Hong Kong," he declared. The others began drifting away from the table. Huang, who retired as vice-chancellor in 1986, pointed to the elections in Hong Kong a few years earlier. "I was there. I saw old amahs [grandmothers] being led in by their children. They voted. They couldn't even read the ballots."

Actually, 25 per cent of Hong Kong kids now go to college, compared with just 3 per cent a decade ago. As for the Third World comparison, Hong Kong's annual per capita gross domestic product exceeded Britain's years ago. Hong Kong also has one of the world's highest densities of cellphones, faxes, and beepers, not to mention Rolls-Royces.

Huang looked annoyed when this was pointed out to him. "Hong Kong can't be changed overnight. It needs to go slowly, step by step. Why should Hong Kong become like Britain or Canada?"

"Why not?" I asked. As for the pace, it was nearly the end of the twentieth century. Why shouldn't Hong Kongers have the same rights as other people?

"You're typical of the Western press," he said, now that Janet and I were the only ones still at the table. "I've spoken to many young people like you in Britain. You don't know Hong Kong." He sipped his glass of jasmine tea and sighed, as if explaining simple truths to children. "Democracy would bring chaos to Hong Kong. Hong Kong isn't ready for it yet. It would be a disaster."

Hong Kong already has had direct elections, in 1991 and 1995. But Huang couldn't point to a single example of ensuing chaos. He had to admit the stock market was booming, real estate was at record highs, and everyone had a job. "It's not chaos yet, but it will come in the future," he said irritably.

By now, the dining room was empty. He was wagging his finger with every sentence. We weren't exactly pleasant, either. Our voices were rising. The waitress politely asked us to move so she could clear away the dishes. Huang gathered up the ham sandwich he had ordered, as directed, for his ailing wife. As we went our separate ways, he said, "Talking to you is like talking to a brick wall." Then he walked off.

Rayson Huang started a letter campaign denouncing me to The Globe and Mail, *but it went nowhere because virtually no one wrote in.*

MOVIE MAKERS

sarah polley

TURNS LEFT AT FORK IN ROAD OUT OF AVONLEA

December 12, 1996

Sweet Sarah Polley of *Avonlea* fame does her best to act against type. During the Gulf War, while lunching with the president of the Disney Channel, Polley, then twelve, refused a direct order to remove her peace-symbol necklace. After that, auditions at Disney dried up. "We hear you're a communist," a Disney executive later phoned to tell the child actress. ("He didn't phone my father," she says. "He phoned me.")

At fourteen, she left home, or rather, she stayed behind in Toronto, when her father relocated north to Aurora. Polley, whose mother died of cancer when she was eleven, didn't want to switch high schools. She lived first with a female classmate, then a boyfriend, then alone. At fifteen, while playing the innocent heroine of *Road to Avonlea*, she hawked copies of *Socialist Worker* at Toronto's Kensington Market. "Get a job," someone shouted. She shot back, "I've been paying taxes since I was five." At sixteen, and suffering from scoliosis—she has since had an operation to straighten her spine—Polley hopped the barricades at a protest in front of the Ontario Legislature and squeezed her way to the front. In the ensuing violence, a cop clubbed her in the stomach and another elbowed her in the jaw. She lost two teeth.

Which ones? She stops chewing to show me. There is no gap. "They were baby teeth," she says, looking embarrassed. "I still have baby teeth." Baby teeth? How many people have had baby teeth knocked out by the riot police? Guess there's no point asking when she stopped believing in the Tooth Fairy.

We are lunching at Matisse, a noisy Toronto restaurant, where Polley, now seventeen, attracts zero notice in her black sweater, blue jeans, and Doc Martens combat boots. For a day of interviews to promote her latest film, *Joe's So Mean to Josephine*, which opened briefly last month in Toronto, she has bent her principles to apply what she calls make-up. "Chapstick, mascara, and something to cover my zits," she says.

Why would a cop club someone as fragile-looking as Polley? At five foot two, she has fine bones, grey-green eyes, and straight blonde chin-length hair. She also has great diction. "I was harassing him a bit. I told him: 'Don't you feel weird? There are only thirty of you and seven thousand of us.'"

Polley has dropped out of Earl Haig High School and plans to attend university eventually as a "mature student." She recently stopped joining every socialist splinter group she could find. "I've been to them all, every little sect in Toronto," she says. "Middle-class guilt," she adds, originally spurred her social conscience. "Having this life of acting, I just wanted to feel like I was doing something." Nowadays, Polley brings sandwiches to homeless kids on Yonge Street. "It's really a tiny Band-Aid," she says, with embarrassment.

I first encountered Polley at a literacy fundraising event last spring sponsored by CBC *Morningside*'s Peter Gzowski. Polley read aloud a poem about her mother's death. As a preamble, she announced, "I've been told I can't be political this evening, so I'm not going to say that Mike Harris is an asshole." Gzowski winced. A few people booed. "I just couldn't stand the fact that I was in front of all those CEOs who could afford a $100-a-plate dinner and not say anything," she explains.

Despite her peace-symbol, jumping-the-barricades image, Polley isn't a vegetarian. "Actually, I eat a lot of red meat," she says. She even smokes cigars. "Big, thick stogies," she says with relish.

She began acting when she was four. She says she was insistent, and her parents, both actors, worried she would resent them if they held her back. On the set, everyone cooed over her. She had private tutors. She also was exploited. It wasn't just the eighteen-hour days. "My mother's death was used to bring tears to my eyes" in *Avonlea* when she was eleven. "I ran through explosions that I wasn't told were going off because they wanted a real reaction" in *Adventures of Baron Munchausen*, when she was ten. If she has children of her own, Polley says, she would never let them act. "You really have to stand up for yourself on a set. It's a really exploitative environment."

In *Joe's So Mean to Josephine*, a Canadian production directed by Peter Wellington and costarring Eric Thal, Polley plays her first adult role, a college student from the Toronto suburbs who falls for a punk. She was initially nervous about her first on-screen kiss. A body double stood in for what she calls the "rutting scene." *The Globe*'s Rick Groen said the film, which won the 1996 Claude Jutra Award, "grows on you."

Although *Avonlea* made her a rich girl, Polley doesn't own a car. She currently shares an apartment with an older brother. And she spends nothing on clothes (she's worn the same Doc Martens for four years, even with dresses). Last summer, she went on a bare-bones safari organized by an African travel agency. "It was great. I had a shower every four days," she says. "We slept in tents and cooked our own food."

But the absence of easy solutions and obvious good guys confused her. Polley returned to Toronto less certain about what to do about the wretched of the earth. She's also grown slightly

more tolerant. She says she loves her current boyfriend, a writer
in Georgian Bay, even though he actually voted for, horrors, the
Ontario Conservatives. Polley herself would one day like to go
into politics. At the moment, she's still too young to vote.

When the bill comes, she pulls out some money. I tell her
The Globe and Mail always pays for lunch. She remains uncon-
vinced. But I assure her it's morally okay to accept.

Sarah Polley's subsequent films, The Sweet Hereafter *and* Last
Night, *were critical successes. At some point after our Lunch, she
grew increasingly prickly with the media.* Vanity Fair *wanted her to
pose with other up-and-coming actors for its cover. Only Polley
refused to put on make-up and wear the designer outfit they chose for
her. I liked her for that.*

atom egoyan

STILL PREFERS THE STREETCAR TO A LIMO

February 19, 1998

Atom Egoyan orders garlic soup at his regular hangout. "I'm so
nervous," says the waiter at the Epicure Café. His hands shake.
His voice trembles. In fact, he's so overwhelmed by Egoyan's
two Oscar nominations for *The Sweet Hereafter*, he leaves without taking my order.

Every day, champagne and flowers arrive at Egoyan's twelve-
foot-wide Riverdale semi. Hollywood directors also phone,
including George Cosmatos (*Rambo*) and fellow nominees Curtis

Hanson (*L.A. Confidential*) and Peter Cattaneo (*The Full Monty*). But Egoyan's favourite was the guy in a ski jacket on the 504 streetcar. "He flapped his hand and mumbled, 'Congratulations.'"

At thirty-seven, Egoyan has short, spiky black hair and designer glasses. He is slight and slim, dressed entirely in black: Donna Karan stretch jeans, leather jacket, and a short-sleeved sweater pinched from his wife. Limos aren't his style. The last time he took one to a premiere, the stretch got stuck turning onto his street. Success means a move to a bigger house in a nicer neighbourhood, but Egoyan still rides the streetcar to work. And he and his actress wife, Arsinée Khanjian, have no nanny. Instead, they take turns caring for Arshile, their four-year-old son.

Last week, Khanjian was filming in Europe, so Arshile accompanied Egoyan to New York to accept yet another honour for *The Sweet Hereafter*. Egoyan partied into the night, then crawled into the hotel bed with Arshile, who let him sleep for a few hours. "I just get so crabby, so he knows about not kicking me in the mouth."

Arshile woke up early. A hungover Egoyan desperately surfed the television for cartoons. Suddenly, he heard the words "Academy Award." "I pleaded with him—if I could just watch a little." Too late. Arshile had spied "Curious George."

Egoyan stumbled into the bathroom, which had a tiny TV set. Frantically twirling the dials, he heard the dual nominations: best adapted screenplay and, incredibly, best director. "It is a genuine miracle," he says, sipping tomato juice. The Oscar nominations rescued *The Sweet Hereafter* in the nick of time. Last week, it was showing in seven theatres in Canada. This week and next, it opens in fifty more.

The one glaring exception to the flood of congratulatory calls is *Titanic* director and fellow Canadian nominee, James Cameron. "Why didn't the Canadian call? Canadians are supposed to be really nice. So is he really Canadian? Where are you, James Cameron?" Egoyan parodies his own screenplays: "Egoyan's face registered anguish and grief. Holding back tears, he looked off into the window, and sniffed: 'I'm still waiting for him.'"

Isn't he old enough to call and congratulate Cameron? "He can probably afford it more than I can," says Egoyan.

Cameron spent a record $200 million (U.S.) on *Titanic*, which grossed $371 million (U.S.) so far. *The Sweet Hereafter* cost $4 million (Canadian)—and has already grossed $10 million. To cut costs in his 1994 film, *Exotica*, Egoyan used his own grey Volvo station wagon in the scenes where the obsessed man drives home the babysitter hired after his daughter's death. That has made taking home real-life babysitters a tad awkward. "Especially if they had seen the movie, we'd have these tortured conversations."

Egoyan's Armenian parents moved from Egypt to Victoria, B.C., when he was three. His odd name reflected his artist parents' admiration for science. His classmates called him Atom Bomb, but "the worst thing was having a sister named Eve," as in Atom and Eve. Egoyan takes a bite of fusilli and goat cheese, and admits it could have been even worse. "My parents were going to call my sister Molecule. You know, Molly."

Even now, people mangle his name. One bouquet of roses arrived addressed to "Adam." At a gala in New York, director Francis Ford Coppola introduced him and "screwed up my last name," says Egoyan, noting his parents had already dumbed it down from Yeghoyan. Desperate to blend in as a child, he clapped his hands over his ears and refused to speak Armenian. He soon lost the language. Still, he ended up marrying a fellow Armenian immigrant. He met Khanjian in 1984. He was twenty-three and working as a $5-an-hour porter at the University of Toronto's Massey College. She was an actress, two years older, married to a dentist. When she acted in his first feature film, they began an affair. Since then she has been in all his films, playing a grieving mother in *The Sweet Hereafter*.

Egoyan says he won't move to Hollywood. He already spent a painful year there recently trying to make a thriller for Warner Bros. He wanted Susan Sarandon for his lead. Warner thought she was too obscure. Out came *Dead Man Walking*. Now Sarandon was too famous. Egoyan left in disgust to make *The Sweet Hereafter*, the first home-grown Canadian movie to garner a best-director nomination.

At next month's Oscars, what facial expression is he planning for the close-up shot? "Early Pierre Trudeau," he says. "I'll store food in my cheeks from earlier meals."

Egoyan will wear a Hugo Boss tux, his usual purveyor of celebrity-event free clothing. Canadian designers and at least one U.S. jeweller are vying to drape Khanjian in their wares. (She may be busy filming in Europe. In that case, Egoyan says his backup date is "Sheila Copps, I guess.")

Does he think he'll win best director? "Not a chance," he says, sipping a double espresso. "That will go to that terrible man who doesn't call."

Atom Egoyan was right. James Cameron, who never did call, picked up the Oscar for best director. Egoyan later told me his friends were horrified he had put so much stock in getting a congratulatory call from Cameron. I guess we need a typeface called ironic.

In 2000, Egoyan's Felicia's Journey, *about a predatory middle-aged Englishman and a naive Irish girl, picked up the greatest numbers of Genies at the awards honouring the best in Canadian film.*

Egoyan is still driving the old grey Volvo station wagon used in Exotica. *I sometimes bump into him because his Arshile and my Sam are in the same grade. From a safe distance, we exchange polite nods.*

It always reminds me how grateful I am that, in all these years, I've never once run into Jukka-Pekka Saraste at school.

robert duvall

CHOWING DOWN WITH A TOUGH GUY WHO LIKES TO TANGO

April 9, 1998

Robert Duvall sure can eat. At a dim sum lunch, we order lobster dumplings, stuffed shrimp steamed with bird's nest, and crispy beancurd-skin rolls. The Oscar-winning actor also wants a half duckling à l'orange, a stir-fry of jumbo shrimp with broccoli, steamed rice, and a whole lobster braised with e-fu noodles.

"Do you want soup?" Duvall asks.

"Do you?" I say.

"Do you?" he repeats. Clearly, he'd like some, but even the waiter at Lai Wah Heen, in the swanky Metropolitan Hotel, is shaking his head. Duvall looks disappointed. "Okay," he says. "No soup."

Good thing he does the tango every day. At sixty-seven, his navy blazer fits snugly over his belly. As he picks up a beancurd-skin roll with his fingers—a no-no in Chinese etiquette—he smacks his lips remembering all the great Chinese restaurants he's sampled in Buffalo, Houston, Pasadena, and L.A. To his regret, Duvall has never been to Asia, even when he was a spokesman for United Airlines and could fly free anywhere in the world. But he eats Chinese food religiously every Sunday. The shrimp dumplings arrive, shaped like goldfish and crowned with wisps of gelatinous bird saliva. "I'm going to ask a very prosaic question," he says to the waiter. "Can I have a fork?"

Duvall is in Toronto frantically promoting *The Apostle*, his acclaimed film about a Southern evangelist gone astray. He cut a ribbon at a new cinema, donated memorabilia to the Planet Hollywood restaurant, and threw the first pitch at the Blue Jays' season opener. Asked if he's ever done so much publicity for a film, he shakes his head. "Ever in my life," he says, adding he hasn't even had time to see *Titanic*.

He wrote, produced, and starred in *The Apostle*. He also invested fourteen years and $4 million (U.S.) of his own money in the film. That's because, despite four Oscar nominations and one Academy Award, he couldn't attract Hollywood bucks in a "Jesus film," as he calls it. Duvall, a believer in Jesus Christ, has made back his money. In three months, *The Apostle* grossed $18.7 million and ranks nineteenth at the box office. Duvall showed it at the White House on the January weekend that the Monica Lewinsky scandal erupted. "Clinton reminds me of a high-level Pentecostal preacher. He grew up going to those churches."

Duvall's roles include the vengeful husband in 1995's *The Scarlet Letter*, the Corleone family consigliari in *The Godfather* Parts I and II in 1972 and 1974, the prudish Major Frank Burns in 1970's *M*A*S*H,* and the country singer in *Tender Mercies*, for which he won his Oscar in 1983.

Off screen, his hairline has receded way, way back. His blue eyes are bleached with age. Liver spots dot his pate. This hasn't prevented him from wooing Luciana Pedraza, a twentysomething Argentinian. They met while Duvall was filming there two years ago. "In front of a bakery on a Saturday afternoon," he says. "Yeah. Yeah. She came up and we started talking. She came over the next day and we started practising the tango." He left Pedraza, a former Miss Elegant in a Miss Argentina contest, down on his 360-acre farm in Virginia because she is in the midst of applying for permanent residency in the U.S. Asked what she does all day, Duvall looks slightly embarrassed. "She rides my horses."

He could, of course, get her a green card through marriage. Duvall demurs. "I'm not too good at it." He recently dumped his third wife, a dancer named Sharon Brophy, after the tabloids reported she was fooling around with the pool installer.

The middle son of a rear-admiral, Duvall says his grades in college were so pathetic that his parents pushed him into acting. They were afraid if he flunked out, he'd end up as cannon fodder in the Korean War. Later, he moved to New York, roomed with Dustin Hoffman and Gene Hackman, and got his first big part in 1962 as Boo Radley, the spooky recluse in *To Kill a Mockingbird*. Since then, Duvall has made seventy films, including four that have opened in the past eighteen months: *A Civil Action, The Gingerbread Man, Deep Impact,* and *The Apostle.* The last won him an Oscar nomination for best actor. At the Academy Awards, Sean Connery and Charlton Heston said they had voted for him. "I got a beautiful letter from Marlon Brando," says Duvall, who's planning to frame it.

On the big night, another nominee came over to chat. "Jack Nicholson said, 'It's between you and me, but it doesn't matter.' I told him, 'Yeah, it does.'" Duvall chuckles. "He was sweating. He wanted to win as much as anyone." Nicholson did win. Duvall consoled himself by studying another nominee across the aisle. "Burt Reynolds took it pretty bad."

Duvall has devoured everything. He wants more jumbo shrimp, this time salt-pepper style. "Are they the really big ones?" he asks the waiter. "They're so big," the waiter assures him, "you order them by the piece." Duvall, who packs 180 pounds on his five-foot-nine frame, smiles. "How many should we get? Half a dozen?"

His true love is the tango, although he's partial to mambo and cha-cha, too. He installed a dance floor in his barn. In hotels, he sometimes orders in a portable dance floor. Four times a week, he practises with Pedraza, but often, he dances alone. "It's like doing scales on a piano."

By now, the dining room is deserted. With just one Diet Coke (his), the bill comes to $168.12. Duvall has had a great time. On his way out, he does a graceful solo rumba in his pointy-toed black boots. Who says tough guys don't dance?

I really enjoyed pigging out with Robert Duvall, whom I matched mouthful for mouthful. But in a letter to the editor, Valerie Wheeler called my style of prose "spiteful." She wrote: "Perhaps someone could tell Ms. Wong that commenting on a fellow diner's eating habits is a no-no in Western etiquette. The rest of the article did nothing to change my mind about her writing—not amusing, not satirical, and not even all that informative, unless you're of the school that takes pleasure in seeing someone smile with spinach stuck between his teeth."

Memo to Ms. Wheeler: Please read the introduction to learn my spinach-stuck-in-teeth policy.

samuel l. jackson

FACING THE DAY AT THE END OF THE TRIP

November 17, 1998

For Samuel L. Jackson, lunch at Pangaea is light and healthy: tuna tartare on mesclun, washed down with tap water. It's a world away from his former life as a drug addict, when he consumed acid, marijuana, angel dust, speed, uppers, downers, cocaine, and heroin, chased with tequila and beer. I confess my total sixties drug experience is hash, once, and I'm not even sure it took. The star of *Pulp Fiction* assures me I just didn't recognize a high.

"You should have been with me. I knew how to make it fun," says Jackson with a wicked smile. Alas, it's too late now. He's been clean for nearly nine years. But before then, he was a high-functioning addict who went to auditions stoned on reefers and crack. On stage, he says, he always acted under the influence. For twenty-three years, the trips were fun. Then one day in 1990, his wife and daughter found him slumped over the kitchen table, a rock of cocaine still unsmoked in his hand. He agreed to go into rehab for twenty-eight days. He's stayed off drugs and booze ever since.

"The majority of men in my family died from alcoholism," says Jackson, who turns fifty next month. He's resplendent in a black-leather Gucci blazer, tan Kangol cap, worn backwards, and Calvin Klein prescription sunglasses. Strapped around his chest is a canvas kit bag containing his money and passport. Conditioned by all his years in New York City, he won't sling it over his chair, even in Toronto the Good. But he does whip off his cap to let me feel his shaved head. Except for a little roughness behind the ears, his scalp is as soft and moist as baby skin. "I'm follically challenged," says Jackson, who first embraced the bowling-ball look in *Sphere* (released earlier this year).

He's in Toronto for the opening of the Canadian film *The Red Violin*, in which he plays a musical-instrument appraiser. These days, Jackson earns up to $7 million a movie. Were he white, he figures, he'd be paid double. "It may not be conscious racism, but it's just not wanting to give the Brother his due." He says he's no longer obsessed about racism, as he once was. In 1969, as a marine-biology major at Atlanta's Morehouse College, Jackson joined the campus Black Power movement. He and other radicals locked white trustees in a building for two days, demanding equal voting rights for black trustees. Morehouse expelled him. Two years later, when it was forced to accept him back, Jackson enrolled in drama at Spelman, its sister college.

He grew up in segregated Tennessee, attending separate schools and separate theatres and playing on separate sports teams. "I was used to being called 'coon' and 'nigger,' " he says. At four, he whistled at a white girl from his front porch. He remembers his grandmother snatching him up and slapping him "because I could have been killed for that." Back then, Jackson stuttered. In fourth grade, his classmates teased him into a year's silence. Diphthongs and plosives still trip him up, so he carefully plots his conversation—and lines. If a script calls for him to say, "What's happening?" he's liable to go, "Wha-wha-wha-wha-wha ..." So he'll automatically change it to "So what's happening?" Still, he deliberately leaves some stuttering in his films.

"It's a very human thing," he says.

Jackson met his wife, actress LaTanya Richardson, during the Morehouse lockup. In the 1970s, they moved to New York, where he supported his off-Broadway acting career—and his drug habit—with janitorial work. "Drugs in Harlem were relatively cheap back then," he says.

He also womanized, but managed to stay married, now twenty-nine years and counting. "It's easy to walk away from something. Whether we admit it or not, we are each other's best friend," Jackson says of his wife, with whom he has a sixteen-year-old daughter, Zoe.

As he broke into film, his roles were all stereotypes. In *Sea of Love*, for instance, his character was called "black guy." With his six-foot-three physique and raisin-dark skin, Jackson was a casting director's cliché of someone you wouldn't want to meet on a New York subway. Actually, you might meet Jackson on the subway. Success came so late—a 1991 Cannes award for Spike Lee's *Jungle Fever*, a 1994 Oscar nomination for Quentin Tarantino's *Pulp Fiction*—that he was already set in his humble ways. (Now living in L.A., he makes his own bed and takes out the garbage.)

In recent years, Jackson has managed to cross over to roles that aren't race-specific, including in *Die Hard with a Vengeance*, the highest-grossing movie in the world in 1995. Over coffee, he confesses that his personality tends to excess. He owns, for instance, nearly four-hundred Kangol berets. And he loves comic books, which he buys by the bagful. "Fertile ground for films," he says.

His latest obsession is golf. He starts at dawn and plays for twelve hours straight. To churn through fifty-four holes (as opposed to the normal eighteen), he never wastes time on lunch at the clubhouse. Instead, he chomps sandwiches, fruit, and cigars on the run. His handicap of ten puts him in the top 1 per cent of golfers in the world.

As for his old excesses, he still keeps alcohol at home, for friends. While he cringes when his wife squanders Dom Perignon on mimosas, he won't touch a drop of anything. "I could say: 'It's been nine years. I could have a beer.' But I have never had one beer."

He flashes a movie-star set of teeth. "Instead, I get up every morning, say a little prayer, and face the day."

Samuel Jackson was one of the most prolific movie stars of the 1990s. In April 2000, he was filming yet again in Toronto and complaining that the snow on the ground prevented him from ducking out to play golf.

anthony quinn

LUST FOR LIFE WITHOUT VIAGRA

December 1, 1998

Hollywood actor Anthony Quinn was in Toronto for the 1998
opening of his humongous one-man art show: nearly three thousand
paintings and sculpture priced between $2,100 and $132,000.
Were Quinn to sell out the entire inventory, he'd gross $30 million.
"Money has nothing, nothing to do with art," Quinn told The
Globe and Mail'*s art critic, Blake Gopnik. Then the actor joked,*
"I need all the money I can get."

Over Lunch, I learned why. In his eighties, Quinn was still
fathering children. He had a lot of alimony to pay, and a lot of
children to support.

When Anthony Quinn's smoked-chicken soup with tortillas
arrives, he gives a hearty Zorba-the-Greek laugh. "This," he
says, pointing at the delicate slivers in his soup, "is a tortilla?"
Quinn was born in Chihuahua, Mexico, to revolutionaries who
marched with Pancho Villa. At eighty-three, he remains a symbol of macho virility, partly because he's had fourteen children
with four women. His oldest is fifty-seven. His youngest are
two and five. Recently, he married their mother, his former secretary, a woman young enough to be his granddaughter.

Over a two-hour lunch at the Four Seasons' Studio Café,
the Hollywood actor boasts of his stamina. "Three times a
week isn't bad." At the same time, he professes to be
vague about Viagra. "What? You go around with an erection
all the time? I swear I don't know. I've heard jokes about Viagra

on Letterman, so I suppose it's something to do with sex."

His sixty-year Hollywood acting career won him two Oscars (*Viva Zapata!* in 1952 and *Lust for Life* in 1956). But three hundred movies later and counting (he's just finished *Oriundi* in Brazil), his first love is art. On Saturday, he'll open the first exhibition in Canada of his expressionist paintings and Henry Moore–like sculptures at Toronto's Columbus Centre.

Quinn always travels with his latest family, Katherine Benvin, thirty-six, Antonia, five, and Ryan, two. "I'll tell you a secret," he says, leaning across the table. "We all sleep in the same bed." Doesn't he mind getting kicked in the face? "The face?" he chortles. "I get kicked in the balls. Then Antonia says, 'You should wear something.'" At home in Providence, Rhode Island, he bikes with his daughter. But he won't change Ryan's diapers. "I can, but he has got a most marvellous mother."

Without tasting his soup, Quinn shakes a frightful dose of salt into it. When it does not pass unmentioned, his craggy chieftain's face darkens. "You're like my wife, for God's sake! What have I got to worry about? That I'll die two weeks earlier?" He quit smoking twenty years ago. He had a bypass operation ten years ago and a quadruple bypass a few years later. He's shrunk two inches, to six foot one, since turning seventy. And despite swimming, occasional tennis games, and a daily regimen of sit-ups and push-ups, he's gained 20 pounds to a current 215. The "tragedy," he says, is that he can no longer squeeze into his custom-tailored Italian suits.

"Oh, I love elastic pants," sighs Quinn, who's wearing Italian wool trousers, a yellow polo shirt, and a buttery leather jacket in bittersweet chocolate. "Why do they make stretch pants for women and not for men?" He orders a plate of curried chicken and waves away the breadbasket.

His parents emigrated to Texas when he was a baby. In California, his Irish-Mexican father worked as a cameraman on silent films. There was no money for an operation to correct Quinn's abnormally thick frenum, a fold of skin under his tongue. "I slurred and mumbled." Quinn, who always liked drawing, won a scholarship with Frank Lloyd Wright after high school. Wright noticed Quinn's speech impediment. Contending that architects needed to speak well to persuade clients of their ideas, Wright paid for an operation. Quinn then exchanged janitorial work for speech therapy from a drama teacher. She recruited him to act in her plays. One day, Universal Studios offered him a contract at $300 a week.

"In those days, it was like $3,000," says Quinn, whose father died when he was eleven. "I needed money desperately. I was the sole support of my family." Wright, who remarked, "I could never pay you that much," gave his blessing.

At first, Quinn's exotic looks confined him to playing swarthy villains and ignoble savages. He soon married the boss's daughter, Katherine De Mille. Cecil B. De Mille was not amused. The legendary director saw to it that the "halfbreed," as he called Quinn, remained stuck in B-grade movies playing Chinese, Filipinos, Greeks, and Italians. For his part, Quinn, who wasn't a virgin, was incensed to discover his wife wasn't either. He felt it entitled him to be endlessly unfaithful to her.

"I was an idiot," he says, sipping cranberry juice. The marriage lasted twenty-eight years and produced five children, the first of whom drowned at three in W.C. Fields's swimming pool. Quinn's main mistress during the waning years of his first marriage was Iolanda Addolori, his Italian wardrobe assistant. They had two children and she was pregnant with the third when he finally divorced De Mille and married her.

That marriage lasted until Quinn began an affair with Benvin, his secretary. During the ensuing divorce, two of Iolanda's sons turned against Quinn. Iolanda also contended that Benvin's two children, then four and one, couldn't possibly be Quinn's. "I hadn't had anything to do with my wife for ten years. I told her I was impotent," he says. "She ordered the blood test on Antonia."

Iolanda got $7 million (U.S.) and a villa in Italy. Quinn kept the Picassos. Through the years, he's bought homes for virtually all his children. But he thinks eighty-three is the outer limit for fathering any more. "I ain't too long for this life. I would hate to leave my wife with an infant." Quinn wants to introduce me to his young family, waiting upstairs in his suite. As we leave the restaurant, I ask if he really does it three times a week. He glances sideways.

"Maybe two." He laughs and squeezes my arm.

Anthony Quinn drew more than two thousand people to the opening of his Toronto art show. In his review, Blake Gopnik said this about celebrity art: "Their big names can sometimes help along their very modest art. From Sylvester Stallone to Gene Hackman, Sally Struthers to Peter Falk, Pierce Brosnan to Tony Curtis, the entertainment industry has a little sideline in budding Leonardos. And most prolific of them all is Anthony Quinn." Gopnik concluded: "Maybe we should think of celebrity art as autographs with a pretty (or pretty awful) picture attached."

And people think I'm *nasty.*

john hurt

DON'T WORRY, THIS LITTLE LUNCH WON'T HURT A BIT

June 9, 1999

John Hurt, fifty-nine, is happy to talk about *Alien*. He even reveals the secret of his famous chest-bursting scene, in which a hideous monster explodes from his thorax. "My feet were under the table. We had a fake body on the table. And there was a prop man under the table, pushing it [the alien] through with a stick."

But Hurt is unhappy talking about his life. At lunch in Toronto at Sassafraz, the temperature drops one degree with every question. Ask him, an infamous chain smoker, why he's not lighting up. (He recently quit for the third time.) Ask how much he used to smoke. (Two packs.) What brand? (Gitanes.) Filtered or unfiltered? (Filtered.) "Is this going to be about smoking?" he asks, slightly irritated.

He's told the point is to figure out what makes him tick. "I don't think you'll manage to do that over lunch," he says dismissively. Then he recovers his charm, crinkles his small brown eyes, and smiles. "I'll do my best to help," he says, adding that he's quit twice before and it's easy, providing he can get through the first day. "I smoke a pencil for a bit," says Hurt, who's dressed in a cream Paul Smith suit, dusty-pink linen shirt, and tasselled Italian loafers. To demonstrate, one of Britain's finest actors pulls a green pen from his pocket and puffs on it. You almost believe it's oozing nicotine.

Hurt, who has done eighty-five films in his thirty-eight-year career, has played a first mate on a doomed starship (*Alien*), a Victorian carnival freak (*Elephant Man*), and a jailed junkie (*Midnight Express*). The son of an engineer (his mother) and a vicar (his father), he decided at age nine that he loved acting. Asked why his father, now ninety-five, burned his mother's treasured collection of newspaper clippings about him after her death, Hurt's smile fades. He won't answer.

He's in Toronto to publicize the twentieth-anniversary video rerelease of *Alien*. Subconsciously, he sticks with the sci-fi horror theme at lunch. He orders a calamari appetizer and calf's liver, evoking the tentacled, face-hugging monster and its embryonic form created from—this is true—pig intestines, hearts, livers, and membranes delivered fresh each morning from a local slaughterhouse.

For years, Hurt looked young for his age. But the chain-smoking and dedicated drinking—he's been quoted as saying he drank seven bottles of wine a day during *Midnight Express*—have caught up with him. He's wrinkled now, with ravaged eyes and faded freckles. Asked to confirm the chronology of his love life, he stares as if I'm a chest-bursting alien. "It's full of complications," he says. "Marie-Lise died, then Donna and I got married, then I fell in love with Jo, then we separated. Sarah is my present girlfriend."

To be precise, his first marriage was a shotgun wedding to an actress named Annette Robertson, who was pregnant and later miscarried. Then he lived for sixteen years with Marie-Lise Volpeliere-Pierrot, a French model who died in a riding accident in 1983. Donna Peacock was a California barmaid for whom he built a house in Kenya while filming *White Mischief*. Jo Dalton was an assistant on the set of *Scandal*. He had two sons with her, but the marriage broke up after she had an affair with a gardener. He currently lives with Sarah Owen in Dublin. In between, he went back to Donna briefly and Jo remarried. But Hurt is right. It's too complicated. He sips some mineral water, which reminds me. Wasn't Sarah the one who got him to stop drinking? "Nobody makes anybody go off drink," he says, enunciating each word.

He puts down his knife and fork. Uh-oh. This is a man who took a swipe at a photographer at last year's British Academy Awards gala. "Nobody told me I was doing an in-depth interview." Glowering, he cites his right to privacy and denounces "glib" articles published "for the sake of selling newspapers. Not that I'm being churlish."

The maitre d' interrupts. "How is everything?"

"It was delicious, thank you," says Hurt pleasantly, demonstrating his fine acting ability. Once the maitre d' disappears, he continues. "I'm slightly annoyed now," he says icily. "As far as I knew, I came here to help [Twentieth Century] Fox get their wretched film off the ground. Don't put that down, for chrissake."

A soft question seems in order, but a tactless one pops out. Has he ever been confused with William Hurt, of *Big Chill* and *Broadcast News* fame? "It was," he concedes, "a Trivial Pursuit question: 'Which actor played the Elephant Man? William Hurt, John Hurt, John Heard?'"

For a moment, it seems the interview has driven Hurt back to nicotine. "Give me my cigarette," he says. He grabs his green pen and starts sucking on it and exhaling loudly. It's clearly a no-dessert meal. He orders a double espresso. Just then, the publicist shows up to escort him to his hotel for the next interview.

"Don't let him yell at you," I advise her. "Tell him to yell at your boss." The publicist giggles nervously. "I thought I was here to push a wretched film," Hurt explains cordially. "Doing a personal interview is not something I would do. It's put us both in a rather embarrassing situation."

The publicist's mouth is clamped in a smile. "Shall we go?" she manages to say. But Hurt's espresso hasn't arrived. "I think you should stay," he tells her, motioning to the empty table beside us. I also urge her to stay—and referee.

"Oh, come. We're not fighting," says Hurt. "But I did get a bit grumpy at one stage."

"You know what?" says the publicist, jumping up. "I'm going to head over to the hotel."

When John Hurt told me he didn't do personal interviews, I replied that I didn't promote movies. Some readers chided me for quoting his comment about the "wretched film" when he asked me specifically not to print it. To clarify, going off the record during an interview is something that must be requested by the subject—and agreed to by the reporter—before the off-the-record comment is made. And, as I said in the introduction, I don't go off the record at Lunch.

Hurt would have stomped out, except he didn't know the way back to his hotel. After his publicist fled, I walked him back the two blocks to the Four Seasons. (We both pretended everything was fine.)

But that's celebrities for you. Elmore Leonard, author of Get Shorty, *noted that celebrities don't know their own phone numbers or zip codes, either. When David Geffen, cofounder of DreamWorks, for instance, bought Jack Warner's old mansion, he had to ask his secretary for the address when someone wanted to send him a parcel. You'd think after spending $47.5 million on his new home, the most ever paid for a single-family dwelling in America, he'd remember the address.*

In 2000, Hurt was wowing London theatre audiences in a production of Samuel Beckett's Krapp's Last Tape, *about an old man with a weakness for booze who spends each birthday taping the memories of the past twelve months. Hurt decided to return to the stage, he told a British reporter, because as he got older, interesting film roles got rarer. But he complained that the role of Krapp required him to eat ten bananas each week. Did he even like bananas? "No!" he said. "And they're constipatory."*

WINNERS AND LOSERS

fred eaton

THE EMPEROR WEARS HIS OWN CLOTHES

May 15, 1997

In the spring of 1997, Eaton's department store was teetering on the edge of bankruptcy. For so many people, Eaton's was a Canadian icon, part of the fabric of the country. But for decades, the business had been slipping. The fourth generation of the Eaton dynasty, four brothers, had grown up in luxury. They had no drive, no feel for the down-and-dirty business of sales and shopkeeping. When the crisis hit, the brothers ducked. Only Fred Eaton responded to my invitation to Lunch.

Fred Eaton, great-grandson of Timothy E. and paid-up member of Britain's Polite Society, has nice manners. In the hectic days in March after the legendary department store chain filed for bankruptcy protection, he always returned calls. "I can't have lunch right now. As you can imagine, I'm rather busy," said Eaton, fifty-eight, executive-committee chairman of the family holding company.

"Don't worry. I'll pay," I said.

Eaton laughed politely and promised to meet when things calmed down.

Ten weeks later, he keeps his word, even arriving seventeen minutes early because he couldn't remember the exact time of the appointment and was afraid of being late. He has sandy-brown hair, deep blue eyes, and tortoise-shell bifocals. He is dressed in a checked shirt and double-breasted blazer—all Eaton's clothing, right down to his underwear. At the Senator Steak House, near his office at Toronto's Eaton Centre, he orders a Diet Coke and warily fields questions.

Is he saddened by the state of the family business? "No. Why would I be sad? Life is full of trouble. Trouble is only a challenge to overcome." Nor are his three brothers, John Craig, the oldest, Thor, third, and George, the youngest, devastated. "Nobody cries," he says. "They work harder."

Fred ran the store starting in the mid-1970s. From 1991 to 1994, he took a patronage appointment as high commissioner to Britain. That's where he joined the Polite Society, which, among other things, urges drivers to be considerate on the road. "I believe in good manners," Eaton says.

There are limits. The photographer asks: "Who do you want to look like?"

"Tom Cruise."

"I can't perform miracles."

Eaton is not amused. "You have three minutes to take a picture," he growls.

When Fred left for London, George, a race-car driver, became CEO. Last week, George said he would step down as soon as a replacement is found. Fred says the family hasn't given up the idea of taking the company public, adding: "Of course, this isn't the best time."

For a family that's been so private, it's been hard seeing friends. "They say, 'Good luck.' Or, 'Sorry to hear about your problems, but wish you the best.' " As his grilled swordfish arrives, I confess that perhaps I helped put Eaton's under. I recently bought a kitchen table from one of his Montreal stores. It was substantially reduced. A yellow tag took off an additional 25 per cent. Then the salesman forgave the GST. And because my sister charged it on her Eaton's card, delivery was free—from Montreal to Toronto. Eaton begins to look worried.

"The moving men lost the screws for the base," I add, "so they had to make a second trip to deliver new screws."

"Well, did you like the table?"

I love the table.

"That's good. You're a happy customer." He pauses. "And I doubt it's the table."

Maybe the breaking point was the incredible deal I got on a green wing chair.

But I haven't the heart to tell him. Canadians have an abiding affection for Eaton's. Just two years younger than Canada itself, it was once the country's fourth-biggest employer, after the government and the two railways. "Almost every family had someone at some stage or another who had worked for Eaton's, even if only a summer job," Eaton says.

The dynasty began in 1869, when an Irish immigrant named Timothy Eaton took over a Toronto dry-goods store. He offered two innovations—fixed prices and a guarantee that stands today: "Goods satisfactory or money refunded." Eaton's thrived, churning out cash, which the family invested into 20 per cent of the Eaton Centre, real estate valued at $1 billion, and a controlling stake in Baton Broadcasting Inc. But in recent times, the stores have hemorrhaged money. Eaton's strategy of "every-day low prices"—but no sales—failed.

A former staunch Conservative, Eaton plans to vote Reform on June 2, 1997. "I'm completely convinced Preston Manning will form the Opposition." In the past two years, Eaton has twice hosted fundraising dinners for the Reform Party leader, each attracting about four hundred people at $250 a head.

Eaton grew up in a household with a butler, cook, and maid. Never an A student, he partied so enthusiastically that he didn't finish Grade 13. The University of New Brunswick accepted his Grade 12 marks, and he earned a B.A. there—and an award for extracurricular activities. He was appointed the university's chancellor in 1993.

He credits the family's Protestant work ethic for keeping him from becoming part of the idle rich. As a kid, he worked on his grandmother's farm, collecting eggs and shovelling manure. "For all the fact my father was a very rich man, he went to work every day. He always taught us the value of work, and that work is fun and good, and everybody should work." Asked how he feels about presiding over the ailing family business, Eaton chews on a piece of swordfish. "That's a chapter that's only begun to be written," he says. "This is an episode that's a long way from being finished."

Correction: After the column ran, Fred Eaton called to say he had told the photographer he wanted to look like Robert Redford, not Tom Cruise.

The family eventually did take the company public. Selling the company was probably one reason Fred Eaton agreed to Lunch. Then, in the summer of 1999, Eaton's went bankrupt, leaving thousands of employees, creditors, and shareholders in the lurch.

Fred Eaton stopped returning calls and stopped going to his office. But when you go bankrupt with other people's money, newspapers must write about it. So two enterprising Globe reporters tracked Fred Eaton down at his ninety-three-hectare estate in Caledon, north of Toronto. There was no doorbell or intercom by the roadside, so they parked their car, ducked under the gate, and asked a security guard for directions.

Ninety-three hectares is equivalent to 230 acres, more than twice the size of Tiananmen Square, itself big enough to simultaneously accommodate all twenty-eight teams of the National Football League plus four hundred other teams, each playing separate games. The two reporters walked a good ten minutes through the vast grounds, past workers' quarters, a tennis court, a statue of a ballerina, an ornate fountain, and a black Rolls-Royce parked on a circular drive.

Susan Bourette and Andrew Mitrovica found Fred Eaton on the back terrace of his mansion, enjoying a leisurely Friday lunch. When my colleagues asked him to comment on the liquidation plan that Eaton's had filed one week earlier, he exploded. "Get a life … This is a gross, gross indiscretion on your part. I mean, this is my home." The reporters tried another question. "I'm calling the police," he warned as he went inside his house.

In the aftermath, I wrote an opinion column about 140 disabled Eaton's employees whose long-term disability cheques had been cut off. Some were dying of AIDS and couldn't afford the medicine. Others were sharing their parents' old-age pension cheques. Still others were about to lose their homes.

It turned out that, to save money, Eaton's had self-insured that part of its benefits program. Now that it was bankrupt, it stopped all disability payments. In response to the column, some Globe *readers sent cheques and cash. One reader suggested a fundraiser for disabled employees. Already busy with other stories, I passed her on to lawyers from Koskie Minsky, the firm representing Eaton's employees. To my astonishment, the lawyers volunteered to organize a benefit concert. Reporters are supposed to be objective, but I soon found myself drawn in by everyone's enthusiasm. I called back several persistent* Globe *readers, who instantly agreed to help. Four hectic meetings later, with zero experience among the dozen volunteers, we staged our fundraiser. The Nylons, Nancy White, and several Toronto Symphony Orchestra musicians donated performances. Including a silent auction and corporate donations, we raised $92,000 that night.*

Through an intermediary, the Eaton brothers said they would donate—but only if they received a tax deduction. Our seat-of-the-pants fundraiser did not have charitable tax status. In the end, the Eatons did not give a cent.

mel lastman

NOBODY BEATS HIM, NOOOO-BODY

November 6, 1997

In November 1997, Mel Lastman was mayor of North York, the separate municipality on the north flank of what was then Toronto proper. But provincial legislation had amalgamated various Toronto-area municipalities into a megacity, and a lot of mayors were losing their jobs. Lastman, who had been North York mayor for eons, decided to run for mega-mayor. He was in a tight race with the mayor of Toronto proper, Barbara Hall, who didn't want to lose her job, either. (She had also accepted an invitation to Lunch.) By the time I Lunched Lastman, it was a week before election day, and he was nervous about making a vote-losing faux pas.

Lunch was supposed to be sentimental: farewell bagels in Mel Lastman Square. "It's a great honour, and I promise not to take it with me when I leave," Mel Lastman had quipped when, like Stalin, he graciously accepted the naming of a civic square in his honour. The jokester mayor of the disappearing city of North York (pop. 562,000) is always kidding. But at lunch in a downtown Toronto café, the smile is fading just a bit. New polls show his initial two-to-one lead against his chief rival,

Toronto mayor Barbara Hall, has evaporated just days before this Monday's megacity mayoral election.

Last spring, the provincial Tories rammed through amalgamation legislation, effectively sacking Lastman and five other Toronto-area mayors. That's hard to take for someone who loves being called His Worship. As for Mel Lastman Square, "I had nothing to do with it," he says. He notes, however, that the city council vote was unanimous—like Stalin's Politburo.

Alas, campaign logistics force a last-minute change from bagels in Lastman Square to the Kensington Café, on the same street in inner-city Kensington Market where Lastman grew up. He's very short—five foot five—and very brown. Don't call him "tanned," he pleads. That implies he's always sunning himself in Florida. (He even flashes baby pictures to prove he was always dark.) Last winter, though, he spent twenty-five days at his Palm Beach townhouse, one of the longest vacations of his life. "When they came up with the mega-city, I wanted to see if I could retire," says Lastman, who turns sixty-five in March. "But I found out I couldn't retire. Marilyn couldn't stand me around the house."

Marilyn is his wife of forty-four years, source of his snappy one-liners and, perhaps, an ex–kidnapping victim. They met when he was sixteen and she was thirteen. "Her father wouldn't let me take her out until she was fourteen," says Lastman, munching on a grilled-chicken sandwich. "So our first date was on her fourteenth birthday." Both dropped out of high school. She quit to earn money. He left because of a reading disability. "I could figure out the word, but I couldn't comprehend what all the words together meant." (He later taught himself, he says, but currently has no time to read, even newspapers.) Lastman quit school at eighteen to get a job so he could marry Marilyn. They wed two years later, a few days after she turned eighteen. "At the time, you didn't sleep with the girl you were going to marry. Or any girl. I mean, woman."

He's wearing two chunky gold rings, suspenders, a silk tie, and a brown jacket. His fuzzy brown hair is a see-through cloud. Lastman began balding at twenty. As mayor, he used to have his hairdresser tease the remaining wisps and goop it in place. Disaster struck at a hotel opening when a helicopter hovered overhead. "It sucked up my hair," he says, holding his hand a foot above his head. "Miss Canada and Miss Japan broke into hysterics." Lastman sweated under a toupee. Finally, a doctor transplanted hair from the base of his head to the top. "I had over a thousand plugs," he says proudly. Unfortunately acreage exceeded seedlings, so Lastman also had three operations to slash the size of his scalp.

His Polish-immigrant father held down three jobs. His grandfather had a fruit store right across the street. "I was three, four years old and hawking pickles for a nickel over there," he says, gesturing to the window. Back then, Kensington Market was a rough-and-tumble neighbourhood. "A lot of my friends later went to jail for booking, for pimping. None of them robbed banks."

He credits Marilyn for keeping him straight. "She pulled me right off the streets." She was fifteen when she got him his first job, in an appliance store. A few years later, Lastman borrowed $2,000 and bought a bankrupt store, eventually expanding it into Bad Boy, a forty-store appliance chain with the slogan "Nobody beats Bad Boy, noooo-body." By the time he was first elected suburban North York's mayor twenty-five years ago, he was driving a Rolls-Royce and had assets of $4.4 million, not including his Bad Boy chain.

Marilyn herself hit the headlines in 1973 when she disappeared for ten hours. She returned home in a taxi, claiming she had been chained to a bed and injected with poison. In the face of widespread skepticism—and some discrepancies in her story—she took, and passed, a lie-detector test. Lastman says

Marilyn later picked out one of the kidnappers from a police lineup. "But they couldn't nail him."

Lastman, a child of the Depression, replaced the Rolls-Royce with an Excalibur, then a Jaguar, and now his-and-hers Mercedes-Benzes. For the bar mitzvah of their older son, Dale, the Lastmans transformed the entire convention floor of the Royal York Hotel into King Arthur's Court. Dale sat on a gold throne, wearing a frilly gold shirt and a crown topped with a Star of David. The bar mitzvah of their younger son, Blayne, "was bigger and better," says Lastman. Blayne's birthday cake was seven feet high and rigged with a champagne fountain. "I worked for that money. Nobody's going to tell me how to spend my money," he says, adding he has less now than when he went into politics. He blames low interest rates and a reluctance to invest "because people point fingers."

Lastman has won ten successive elections as mayor. (He lost only once in his life, when he ran as a provincial Tory in 1975.) He has no hobby, no life outside politics. Asked to define himself, other than as mayor, he sips his coffee. "A salesman," he says. Waxing philosophical, he adds that doctors sell their bedside manner, journalists sell their stories. "Everybody's a salesman," says Lastman. "I mean, a salesperson."

Mel Lastman won his race to be mayor of Toronto's first megacity. In the Fall 2000 election, he was re-elected by 80 per cent of the vote, and made it into the Guinness Book of Records *as the longest continuously serving mayor in history.*

A year or so after our Lunch, I attended a black-tie fundraiser for the arts at which Mayor Mel and his wife were guests of honour. As my date, I invited my mother, who'd heard a lot about Mayor Mel and wanted to meet him. She also felt sorry for Marilyn, who had been arrested for shoplifting some pants at Eaton's. (Marilyn

apologized. Eaton's decided not to press charges, a spokesman said,
because of her age and because she had no criminal record.)

As I introduced Mom to Marilyn, the mayor's golden-gowned
wife batted her eyelashes at me and said, "Please. Don't take my
husband to lunch any more."

Now I know why. In late 2000, two brothers and their mother
launched a $6-million paternity suit against Mayor Mel. Todd
Louie, thirty-eight, and Kim Louie, forty-two, accused the mayor of
fathering them during a lengthy affair with their mother, Grace
Louie, now sixty-eight. The brothers accused Lastman of letting them
grow up in poverty while he himself lived lavishly.

In a statement, Mayor Mel acknowledged his affair with
Grace Louie, then an employee in his Bad Boy appliance chain.
"In 1957, I was twenty-four years old. I made a terrible mistake.
I began a relationship with a married woman," said Lastman, who
was already married to Marilyn at the time. Mayor Mel did not
admit he was the father of the two boys, but he said he had paid
their mother $27,500 in 1974.

john cleghorn

HIS MARRIAGE IS HIS MOST PRIZED MERGER

July 21, 1998

John Cleghorn, chairman of the Royal Bank, became the point man
during a proposed merger between his bank and the Bank of
Montreal. That's partly because his counterpart there was reeling
from bad publicity over his marriage to an ex-model with a past.
(Matthew Barrett later became CEO of Barclays PLC in London
and split up with Anne-Marie Sten.)

*Barrett turned down Lunch, but Cleghorn accepted. He told me
he did so because he had read the Lunch column on Don Cherry. It
had made him cry. "I was on a flight," he said, "and I had to turn
and face the window."*

John Cleghorn motions to the mahogany table set for two in his
office at Toronto's Royal Bank Plaza. The chairman of Canada's
biggest and most profitable bank is scowling. He has mega-
mergers on the brain—but not the proposed one between the
Royal and the Bank of Montreal. No, he's thinking about the
1997 merger between Matthew Barrett, his counterpart at the
Bank of Montreal, and ex-model Anne-Marie Sten. A *Globe and
Mail* article two days earlier described Barrett's second wife as a
former companion of Adnan Khashoggi, the Saudi arms dealer.
It also ran a photo of Sten in a fur bikini that first ran in *The
Toronto Sun*, and later, *Frank* magazine.

"Since when did *The Globe* merge with *Frank*?" says
Cleghorn. At fifty-seven, Cleghorn has just marked the thirty-
fifth year of his own matrimonial merger. His wife, Pattie, is also
fifty-seven. So why hasn't he traded her in for a younger, um,
model? "We're very close," he says, "and she's my best friend."

Their marriage has endured, for better or worse, for richer,
for poorer, in sickness and in health. The year they were married,
Cleghorn earned $9,000. Last year, he made $3.2 million. In the
early 1990s, Pattie developed diabetes. In 1995, she was hospitalized for two months, first with pneumonia, later for two
operations that removed part, then all of one lung. Cleghorn,
who had just been named chairman of the Royal, worked out of
a room at the Montreal General Hospital. "Don't lay it on too
thick," he says. "I just brought my in-basket there."

But he takes every holiday he's entitled to, usually at their
twenty-hectare property in Quebec's Eastern Townships. This
year, their June 29 anniversary fell on a Monday. Cleghorn took

the day off to be with her. "Just the two of us," he says.

At lunch, Cleghorn steadily eats his way through a plate of sandwiches—roast beef, turkey, and tuna-shrimp—sent down from the corporate dining room on the fortieth floor. With Pattie away, he skipped breakfast. She's supervising his thirty-fifth-anniversary present to her—an extension on their A-frame cottage, so their three adult children and families can visit at the same time.

He met her on Boxing Day, 1960, at a ski resort in Ste-Adèle, Quebec. He was in commerce at McGill. She was in arts at the University of Toronto. They were both nineteen, out for dinner with college chums. "Pattie was going steady with someone else and so was I. But hers was back in Toronto, and mine was doing something else. A friend said, 'Why don't you two sit together?'" He says he liked her spontaneity and her intelligence. "And she's a Scorpio. So were my mother and father." He also liked her height, all five feet. "She was the right size. My mother was five foot eleven and a half inches. God indicated that's what the gene pool needs," says Cleghorn, six foot two and a former college football player.

He promised to fetch her the next morning, but his car wouldn't start in the cold. She waited for him. They ended up skiing that afternoon, and all evening. He serenaded her on the chairlift with "The Green Leaves of Summer." "By the Brothers Four," he says. "That was the big hit that year." Pattie's family was "normal, and normal-sized. They had family dinners on a regular basis," he says enviously. His didn't. His mother was an actress and a dietitian at the Montreal General. Because she worked the noon-to-8-p.m. shift, supper for Cleghorn and his younger sister often consisted of peanut butter sandwiches. His father, an accountant and artist who painted the sets for his wife's performances, was associate director of the Montreal Museum of Fine Arts. The family lived in an apartment on Côte des Neiges and later in a house on the fringe of Westmount. They never owned a car.

While other bank chairmen ride in limousines, Cleghorn sometimes hops the subway to work. He also ditched the Royal's corporate jet and flies economy on short-haul flights. He married Pattie in 1963. They were twenty-one, and got to work on the gene pool right away, producing three children in five years. Although she has a teaching certificate, she worked sporadically because they were always moving. Still, she staked out her ground. When Cleghorn once suggested he'd like to golf with the guys, she responded tartly, "You're going where? That's all day." So he played tennis instead—with Pattie.

He also sang the kids to sleep, when he didn't fall asleep himself first. But he made them work their way through college. And when they borrowed money, he charged interest. "Cheaper than commercial," he says of the rate, "and only after they were earning income." Early on in their marriage, he and Pattie had a big fight. He went to a friend's for commiseration. Meanwhile, she packed her bags and drove off in her green second-hand Datsun. She changed her mind an hour later. When Cleghorn returned, he asked what the bedroll was doing at the foot of the stairs. "The joke in our family is that Pattie ran away and nobody noticed."

You know it's true love, though, because Cleghorn sticks to her diabetes diet when he's with her. He says they've stayed together all these years because there were "no hidden agendas in our house. If anybody disagreed, you heard about it," he says, finishing every scrap on his plate except the raw broccoli. "Friends tell me we're the worst example of a good marriage."

My Columbia journalism professor taught me the interview doesn't end just because you've shut your notebook. As Cleghorn walked me to the elevator after Lunch, he told me how Pattie had once walked out on him "and nobody noticed." It was a moment that a lot of readers could identify with. As soon as the elevator doors shut, I whipped out my notebook and wrote it down, finishing the last bit on a bench in the Royal Bank lobby.

As I was leaving The Globe *that day, the bank's chief publicist called, asking for my home phone number. I gave it to him, but cautioned that I wouldn't be there until quite late. I knew what was coming. I got home at midnight to find a message from Cleghorn telling me to call his home no matter what the time. With a sinking heart, I dialled the number. He answered immediately.*

After our Lunch, he explained, Pattie had debriefed him and was horrified to learn that he had spilled the beans. Even their closest friends didn't know about the bedroll incident. Now, the chairman of the Royal Bank of Canada confessed, he was in deep doo-doo. He begged me not to use the anecdote. I felt bad. But I also remembered that this was a man with an entire P.R. department at his disposal. I told Cleghorn that I wouldn't know until I wrote the column whether or not I would use the anecdote—but I said I was pretty sure I would. Cleghorn said he'd become confessional only because I'd told him about my own parents' long-lasting marriage. I told him that bonding with one's subject was a time-honoured journalism technique.

"You tricked me," he said, cordially.

"You're a big boy," I said, cordially.

I can't believe I said that to him, but it was late and he was so nice that I was afraid I'd crumble and agree not to use it. Pattie Cleghorn apparently didn't hold a grudge. A year later, she bought my second book, Jan Wong's China, *and had me autograph it for her.*

Incidentally, the federal government eventually quashed the merger between the Royal Bank and the Bank of Montreal. In 2001, Cleghorn shocked the bank world by retiring at the age of fifty-nine.

george cohon

McNuggets of Wisdom

June 23, 1999

Ahead of time, George Cohon is given a choice: Wendy's or Burger King. "You know what?" the senior chairman of McDonald's Canada says from his car phone two days later. "I want to take you to Variety Village." On the drive out to this centre for disabled children, Cohon, sixty-two, talks up his memoir, *To Russia with Fries*. His book on McDonald's expansion into the former Evil Empire was published just as the Diana grief industry swamped the 1997 bestseller lists. Undaunted, Cohon persuaded his franchises in Canada to buy 12,500 copies.

"That's a bestseller in and of itself," he says, slowing his blue Mercedes wagon down to eyeball the lunchtime crowd at a McDonald's on Kingston Road, in Scarborough, the east flank of Toronto. Cohon, whose royalties go to Ronald McDonald Children's Charities of Canada, unloaded another thirty-thousand copies during three months of fundraising breakfasts, lunches, and dinners. "I'd lay guilt trips on people. I was shameless."

The same relentless McOptimism led him to Moscow in 1976. After fourteen years of byzantine negotiations, he opened his first outlet in 1990. Today, there are forty-nine. But with Russia's current economic crisis, McDonald's has doubled prices, slashed wages, and cut this year's openings to five from a projected twenty. A Happy Meal now costs two days' pay. "It's a Russian success story," insists Cohon, who travels there with a bodyguard. "I think we're a great employer. I'm sure the people who work at McDonald's make more money than most people—and they get paid on time."

He's permanently upbeat and permanently tanned, with mottled brown-blue eyes and a greying comb-over. He even flogs fries with author namecards in the shape of a Big Mac (good for one free Big Mac in Canada). Another reproduces the cover of his book (good for free fries in Canada—or Russia).

In 1906, his grandparents fled czarist pogroms in Ukraine. In the United States, an Ellis Island inspector mangled Kaganov into Cohon (pronounced Co-HOHN). Cohon was a thirty-year-old lawyer in Chicago when his life changed. After a client declined to buy the McDonald's franchise for eastern Canada, founder Ray Kroc offered it to Cohon instead. In 1967, he scraped together $70,000 (U.S.) and moved to Toronto with his wife and two young sons. Five years later, Kroc offered Cohon $1 million to buy back the franchise. Too late. Eventually, though, Cohon accepted McDonald's stock. For a time, it transformed him into the corporation's second-biggest shareholder, after Kroc.

Today, Cohon is a Canadian citizen. He's also rich enough to own five cars and three homes with an undisclosed number of bathrooms. (David Macfarlane, his ghostwriter on the book, remembers thirteen bathrooms, but isn't sure if that includes the Florida house. "Much more than thirteen," Cohon later jokes.)

At Variety Village, where his wife was once chairwoman, he greets several athletes by name and folds his six-foot-one frame into a wheelchair to race around the indoor track. (He beats me after one circuit.) Then he tells Joe Millage, the managing director, that we need something to eat. "The last person George brought here for lunch was Mikhail Gorbachev," says Millage.

"She wanted to take me to Burger King or Wendy's and I didn't know what to do," Cohon whispers.

In the cafeteria, he loads a Styrofoam plate with two hot dogs and a bag of chips. He shuns the raw vegetable platter. Like a true McDonaldite, he hates vegetables but loves ketchup. With huge, hairy hands, he rips open five packets of ketchup and squeezes them onto a single hot dog. Our only company is a circle of tube-fed toddlers surrounded by their caregivers. Then several dozen kids—abled and disabled— invade the cafeteria. We escape into the sanctuary of the director's office and eat over his blotter.

Opening in the Soviet Union took tenacity, Cohon notes. He first arrived during the Brezhnev era and hung in as the country lurched toward glasnost and perestroika. He learned only five words of Russian, but bet, correctly, that 258 million people on a meat-and-potato diet would embrace Big Macs and fries.

He's been a shrewd risk-taker all his life. In the U.S. Army, when his redneck sergeant persisted in calling him "Jewboy," Cohon challenged him to an arm-wrestling match. With those huge hands, he snapped three of the man's fingers. In 1971, Cohon was returning from a business trip when he overheard his next-door neighbour remark, through an open window, "The dirty Jew is home." Using a WASP law firm and a shell company, Cohon bought the Forest Hill Road house and bull- dozed it. Now it's his reflecting pool. He also dumped his Paris law firm after the senior partner snubbed him. And he went toe-to-toe in Toronto with Prince Philip when he told Cohon that McDonald's destroys rain forests. (The Prince eventually backed down.)

He's also fiercely loyal in return. McDonald's sells Coke. The competition sells Pepsi. So a few years ago, Cohon refused to close on a dark blue Jaguar with a celebratory Pepsi from the dealer's vending machine. Instead, Cohon smilingly demanded the dealer replace it with a Coke machine. The stunned dealer acquiesced—and only then did Cohon buy the Jag.

"Some people think I used too much clout," he says, rushing off to fetch me a refill of grape drink from the cafeteria. (There's no Coke.) "I do what I have to do."

Cohon objected only to the description of his hands as "hairy." For days afterward, he showed his hands to friends and asked their opinion. I stand by my reporting. His hands are hairy.

Andrew K. Harvie Sr. wrote this letter to the editor, published June 25, 1999.

> *I am the "next-door neighbour," and I believe this particular anecdote is more fiction than fact! Here is my recollection:*
>
> *As a savvy businessman of the seventies, George made money quickly and one of the first fruits of his labours was the Forest Hill Road property. I was his neighbour to the south and, over the next twelve to fourteen months, I watched as George renovated and added to the structure until every square inch of his property was utilized.*
>
> *In the fall of 1971, I was contacted by Richard Levinsky, a realtor who, on George's behalf, presented "an offer I couldn't refuse." We packed up within thirty days and moved up the street.*
>
> *I don't think it's rocket science to figure out that George wanted a garden and had the financial resources to solve the problem immediately. There were no covert operations; in fact, after I signed the deal, we both met George in his driveway to shake hands and chat.*
>
> *Regarding the "open window" anti-Semitic comment: It makes great copy in a rags-to-riches epic but has no foundation in the story of a Canadian "burger king" who huffed and puffed and blew his neighbour's house down to make a garden!*

George Cohon wrote about the "dirty Jew" story in To Russia with
Fries *and I asked him about the incident at Lunch. When I subsequently told him that his old neighbour had gotten in touch with me
and would be writing a letter disputing his version of events, Cohon
was unperturbed. He stood by what he told me at Lunch.*

fred goldman

RON GOLDMAN'S FATHER BANS O.J. FROM
THE BREAKFAST TABLE

April 17, 1997

*The Goldmans showed up with a publicist and a stranger in tow.
"And you are?" I asked. He shook my hand and gave me his name.
He was a Toronto policeman, in plainclothes.*

"That's off the record," Fred Goldman interjected.

*Flabbergasted, I opened and closed my mouth like a goldfish. Off
the record only applies—in advance—to quotes, not something that*
happens. *But as I hesitated, Fred Goldman snapped, "Yes or no? If
you don't agree, we're outta here."*

*I'm reporting it now. As I say, you can't remove events from the
record. Who knows why he was so secretive about having a bodyguard, but Fred Goldman's ultimatum set the tone for our breakfast.*

Fred Goldman orders scrambled eggs, sausage, toast, and coffee. Some orange juice? the waiter asks. "Tomato juice," says
Goldman. He won't drink orange juice. Not any more.

"It's in my subconscious. The thought instantly goes
through my mind," he says. Kim, his daughter, adds: "If a

waiter says, 'Want some O.J.?' I correct him. It's orange juice."

To them, O.J. is "the killer," the man who murdered Ron—her brother, his only son. The Goldmans are in Toronto as part of a thirteen-city North American tour to promote their book, *His Name Is Ron.* Goldman's coauthor and third wife, Patti, is with them, but has made a stop at the ladies' room. Time is tight—they will do eight interviews today—so I try to start without Patti. Fred and Kim refuse point blank. So we sit in awkward silence. Patti arrives, everyone smiles again, and the Goldmans segue from hardball to grief.

They are your average dysfunctional American family, only more so. These are not people who set out to be famous. But not only have they been struck by tragedy, they have been star-struck by celebrity in the most ghoulish way. Each wears a large button with a colour photo of Ron. It says, "In Our Thoughts Every Day—Ron." Patti's youngest daughter wore one her first day of junior high. To the Goldmans' dismay, the criminal-trial judge banned Ron buttons in court. The book cover shows the family posed on a grassy knoll, each with a button above the heart.

Maybe it's the awkward opening or the Ron buttons, but the interview feels eerie. This is the American way of death. A celebrity murders a twenty-five-year-old waiter in L.A., making him famous. By extension, the victim's mom and dad and sister become celebrities, too, providing they do Oprah and book tours. The hype surrounding Paul Bernardo's trial was on a kinder, gentler Canadian scale compared with O.J.'s. It's hard to imagine Leslie Mahaffy's mother buying a vanity plate. The one on Kim's silver Nissan says: MSNG RON. Her step-brother, Michael, has one that says: RMBR RON.

It's also hard to conceive of Kristen French's father signing a book contract. Nearly everyone involved with O.J. (the initials are now a registered trademark) has written a quickie book: Simpson himself, jurors, lawyers, purported friends, and now even the grieving family. Fred Goldman, a former packaging salesman with large glasses and a grey handlebar moustache, got a $630,000 advance. "Try to paint me as a money-grubbing celebrity seeker," he writes in the book as he describes steeling himself for cross-examination by Simpson's lawyers. "I had my written answers memorized."

The Goldmans say they want to tell the world who Ron was. According to their book, he was an easy-going, good-looking college dropout who was jailed once for unpaid speeding tickets. He ran up debts of more than $16,000, then filed for bankruptcy. Even Kim was annoyed when he never repaid her for springing him from jail.

In February, Fred Goldman made a dramatic offer: He would forgo his share of the $47 million in compensatory and punitive civil damages if O.J. would confess. Of course, O.J. wouldn't, but the story was impeccably timed and made front-page news. The next day, *His Name Is Ron* ($32.95) hit the bookstores. When it is suggested that Fred Goldman is a public-relations genius, he frowns. "That sounds like it's a business," he says, with a touch of modesty. "We just do what we think is necessary. Money isn't the issue for us."

The book has since made the *New York Times* bestseller list. What will they do with the profits? "We don't have a clue," says Kim sullenly. Fred Goldman adds: "We haven't discussed any of these issues, which seem to be important to others." Important to others? This is the family that needed lawyers to divvy up the $12 million they were awarded for compensatory damages. Ron Goldman's mother, Sharon Rufo, who in the decade before his murder had spoken to him just twice—by phone—got 15 per cent. Fred Goldman, who raised Ron, got 85 per cent.

This is also the family that urged the civil-trial judge to let them collect punitive damages separately from the Browns, the family of victim Nicole Brown Simpson. It's now a first-come, first-served scramble for O.J.'s assets, pitting Fred Goldman against Nicole's two young children.

Of course, you feel sorry for the Goldmans. Their first glimpse of the accused was not in handcuffs and orange prison overalls but in an expensive tailored suit. Outside, placards proclaimed, "Free O.J.!" Vendors hawked T-shirts and mugs emblazoned with Ron's now-famous photo ID. Then there were the reporters camped out on their lawn. But the family soon embraced the media circus. They held press conferences. And they went on talk shows, even after the civil-trial judge imposed a gag order. "Just as we were discussing how to get in touch with her, Barbara Walters called us," Goldman writes. The *Oprah Winfrey Show* was next.

Sharon Rufo appeared on *Inside Edition*. Later, on *Larry King Live*, she described her closeness to Ron. Incensed, daughter Kim called the show, using a special number to zip past the switchboard.

Kim: "You were not close with me, and you don't have a right to sit here on national TV and claim your fame to Ron's death."

Rufo: "There are two sides to a story. I am sick and tired of hearing all this brainwashing that your father has done."

Kim: "I'm sick and tired of you, honey."

Since the trials, the Goldmans' lives have changed. Fred is now a $140,000-a-year spokesman for Washington-based Safe Streets Coalition. Patti, the stepmother, took an electrolysis course during the civil trial and has opened a business. And Kim, through her media contacts, landed a job with the *Larry Sanders Show*, a comedy about a talk-show host.

As they rush off to their next interview, Fred Goldman shakes my hand with practised warmth. He actually winks. On the way back to the newsroom, it hits me: We never talked about Ron.

The Goldmans were deeply infected by celebrityitis. A CTV producer told me that when their limo showed up at the studio, the family demanded that someone walk out to meet them at the parking-lot gate or else they wouldn't go in. During their interview on Canada AM, the Goldmans wept for the camera, but joked during commercial breaks.

After the column ran, it occurred to me that the parents had never visited Ron's restaurant. Checking out your son's new workplace is a bit like attending his school play. Wouldn't you have dinner there at least once, if only to leave him a big tip? In their book, the Goldmans say they went to the restaurant for the first time only after Ron's death.

At last report, Fred Goldman was pursuing a career in broadcasting.

sheila bujold

LIVING WITH A EUPHEMISM

September 29, 1998

A reader called to ask why I never wrote about the mentally handicapped. She put me in touch with a social worker, who in turn suggested Sheila Bujold. I explained to both Bujold and her social worker that I intended to ask all kinds of questions, not just the politically correct ones. They both agreed, but only Bujold came to Lunch.

Like many who are illiterate, Sheila Bujold ignores the menu. "I'll have a hot dog," she says. "I know they have hot dogs." But Bujold, thirty-one, isn't illiterate. Pressed to read the menu aloud, she does, stumbling only over "halibut." That done, she decides to order fish and chips instead.

Bujold is mentally handicapped, and sometimes needs a little push to accomplish what she already can do. This fall, she's getting a big push: making speeches to raise funds for the Toronto Association for Community Living, which marks its fiftieth anniversary today. The euphemism forces fundraisers to keep explaining it isn't about retirement housing. A decade ago, political correctness forced its name to be changed from the Toronto Association for the Mentally Retarded. The terminology remains touchy. Asked if she objects to being described as "mentally retarded," Bujold studies her pink nail polish. "I know what it means, and it doesn't bother me. It means I'm handicapped. That I have ways of not understanding things. Of not learning things."

In fact, Bujold understands a lot. She works four days a week as a receptionist. Until recently, she had a steady boyfriend. And she takes public transportation by herself across Toronto. She's also fluently bilingual, having grown up in New-Richmond in the Gaspé region of Quebec. But socially, she has the maturity of a twelve-year-old. In terms of life skills, she functions on the level of a fifteen-year-old. And she has epileptic seizures.

When she was three, doctors diagnosed her with brain cancer and removed a plum-sized tumour. "I lost half my memory," she says, sipping a Diet Coke. "As they say in Quebec, *c'est la vie*." Medication controlled the seizures, but also made it easy for her to gain weight, she says. At school, the other kids shunned her. "They'd tease me as retarded," she says in unaccented English. "They'd tease me because I'm big. They would make me feel terrible." Bujold held her tears until she went home. She failed Grade 5, but soldiered on. After Grade 10, she dropped out. She can add, subtract, and multiply (but not divide).

Her fish and chips arrive, and she eats carefully. The restaurant, a greasy spoon, was her choice out of all the restaurants in Toronto. She chose it because she's been there a couple of times before.

Until recently, her best friend was her boyfriend, who is also mentally handicapped. They dated on and off for ten years and had planned to get engaged. But recently he dumped her for someone else. "I'm pretty heartbroken," says Bujold, who has a girlish voice and curly brown hair that keeps falling into her blue eyes. Like a child, she sometimes has little control of her life. After her case worker dreamed that Bujold was pregnant, Bujold was sent to the doctor. She wasn't. "If we do it, we use condoms to be safe. We're not cuckoo," she says, chewing on some fries.

Her previous boyfriend was also mentally handicapped. "He was always telling me, 'Why don't we have sex?' That's all he would think of doing. Excuse me, men don't have the right to push women into that." She watches as I scribble notes. "Am I going too fast? Sorry."

Bujold is shocked when told of the mass sterilization of mentally handicapped people in Alberta between 1928 and 1972. "Oh, gosh, that's so sickening. I wouldn't agree with it." She avoids pregnancy, she says, only because she's overweight. She would like to adopt a child. Could she care for one? "Actually, I've worked in day care. I love kids," she says, adding that she used to make lunch for her younger brother and sister back in the Gaspé.

Grease clouds the dining room, so we go to a Tim Hortons next door for coffee and Timbits. Bujold says she moved to Toronto in 1982 for social services that weren't available back home. Each summer, her parents, an electrician and a secretary, send her a round-trip train ticket home. Asked how she changes trains in Montreal, Bujold says patiently, "I look what gate, and get in line."

For ten years, she's been a receptionist at two jobs, both at centres run by the Association of Community Living. She's paid token amounts, less than $1 an hour. (But she must be good. While writing this column, I drew a complete blank on the fish-and-chip restaurant's name. I called Bujold. "You're very lucky. I have a card of it," she said, putting down the phone. A moment later, she was back: "The Four Seas." Thank goodness someone's on the ball.)

Bujold finishes a frosted Timbit and sighs. She yearns for some independence—a bank-machine card, for instance—and resents her social worker always accompanying her to the bank. "It's an awful pain in the neck. I'm thirty-one years old. I feel like I'm getting treated like a pet. That's why I sometimes get upset. They never give me a chance." Bujold's dreams aren't outrageous. She'd also like her own apartment. Currently, she pays $500 of her $708 monthly family-benefits cheque to live with a foster family. With what's left, she buys her transit pass, sees Jackie Chan movies, and buys the occasional newspaper to check her horoscope.

She'd like a better job, too, perhaps teaching French. But she's reminded of her limitations every day. After work, when she boards the city bus with her coworkers, some of whom are visibly retarded, she hears the comments. "I wish people would not call us stupid," she says, her blue eyes brimming with tears. "God made me this way. Am I making any sense? I have a heart and feelings, too."

Sheila Bujold faxed me to say how happy she was with the column. "My sister Chantal said she had went to see her doctor and he had

*seen the article and he said is Sheila Bujold your sister? And
Chantal had said yes, why? Well, I think she's a smart sister!"*

*Jeff Rush, an executive with Famous Players Theatres in
Toronto, noticed that Bujold was wearing an Indiana Jones T-shirt
in the photograph. He sent her a stack of complimentary movie passes.*

nancy lynn hallam

SHE BEGS TO DIFFER

December 19, 1996

*For Christmas in the first year of the column, I invited a beggar for
a wonderful meal.*

Nancy Lynn Hallam hadn't been begging at her regular spot,
so I left voice-mail inviting her to Christmas lunch.
"Thursday," she said, returning my call, "cuz I don't have nothing booked for that." She especially liked Italian food. Let's go
Italianissimo, I figured, and made reservations at Centro, where
lunch for two, without wine, easily costs $100 and up.

I first met Hallam, thirty-eight, last summer when I pro-
filed her as the quintessential Canadian panhandler—polite,
friendly, and living on social assistance. She was fat—277
pounds on a five-foot-two inch frame. And she always begged
from a government-supplied $4,000 Ultramatic wheelchair-
scooter, less a necessity than an accessory. Hallam could walk.
I wondered what had happened to a person that the media—
well, I—had made famous. On the appointed day, I went to
her government-subsidized apartment in St. Jamestown, a
high-rise, low-income Toronto neighbourhood. Hallam, her

copper-dyed hair mussed as usual, was wearing blue eye-shadow, pink stretch pants, a teal-blue sweatshirt, and a soiled white hockey sweater. She grabbed a cane.

"Hi, Albert," said Hallam, waving to an old man in the lobby.

"Where's your wheelchair?"

"Left it at home. I'm going out with my friend today." As we got into a taxi, she pointed across the street. "Somebody was murdered in the building over there last week."

Centro was filled with the gentle murmur of expense-account diners. Yet the staff was courteously class-blind, from the stunning blonde who checked Hallam's hockey sweater to the suave maitre d' who pulled out her chair. "Thank you," said Hallam, twisting around to give him a smile. He smiled back.

She lit the first of many cigarettes. "I like this place," she said, blowing smoke at the thirty-foot-high cobalt blue ceilings. She ordered organic Cookstown greens on a poppadom crisp with aged balsamic vinegar, and hesitated over salmon. "The only fish I can eat is fish and chips," explaining that other kinds give her indigestion. Instead she chose caramelized breast of free-range capon with roasted winter vegetables and truffle juice. But, first, she wanted an explanation. "Chicken," I said. "You know how you fix dogs and cats? Capon's a rooster that's been fixed."

Hallam, who says she never worked a day in her life, pan-handles $500 to $900 a month, in addition to her $990 government cheque. She subscribes to deluxe cable television and every three months receives a $99.50 GST rebate. She would like a cell phone, but settles for voice-mail—she doesn't want to miss calls from her doctor or family-benefits counsellor while out begging.

"Fresh pepper?" the waitress asked, setting down a salad.

"Yes, please," she said.

Hallam, who has only three teeth left, munched on a tangle of frisée, mache, and arugula and tried to avoid the F-word. "Ever since that article got into the newspaper, this one guy harasses me. He said that I should be cut off family benefits, booted out of Metro housing, and Revenue Canada should sue me for $500,000. Nice guy, huh?"

After *The Globe* story ran, the government docked Hallam $158.25 a month in "overpayments" and ordered her to keep daily panhandling records. Each month she must bring them to a government office for clerks to photocopy. To her delight, after examining her records, the government restored the monthly $158.25 overpayment. Hallam bore me no grudge for her troubles. She blamed the provincial Tories.

Starbucks had recently opened in the building behind Hallam's regular spot at the corner of College and Yonge. When she vanished, I assumed the coffee bar had shooed her away. In fact, foot traffic was up. And Starbucks customers sometimes brought her coffee and muffins while she panhandled. The reason I hadn't seen her, she explained, was because she had been sick. Doctors had diagnosed her with cancer. Last October, they removed her uterus. "I'd like to have another child, but I can't now," she said. She gave up her first baby, the result of a rape by her stepfather. Children's Aid took away her second baby. "I'll get her back in two more years," she said confidently, when her daughter turns eighteen and is told Hallam's identity.

We both drank tap water. Hallam's husband and sister are alcoholics. So was her mother and stepfather. "When I was a child, my stepfather always cashed my mom's cheques on booze." To prevent her husband, George, from doing that, Hallam has her government cheque deposited directly into her bank account. "What's more important? Having a roof over our heads? Or booze and living in the streets?"

I was struck again by her normalcy, given how damaged her life has been by poverty, violence, and alcohol. For Christmas, she has invited four friends for ham with Stovetop stuffing, boiled potatoes, and canned mixed vegetables. Her capon arrived, a golden hunk atop a mound of creamy mashed potatoes. Hallam sampled it, kissed her fingertips, and sighed, "Yep, this is chicken."

She and George have been married nine years. He works nights, collecting empty beer bottles in parks. They met at a his-and-hers shelter, when she hurt her hand in a fight with another woman. "I whipped a chair at her," she said. George gallantly walked Hallam to and from the hospital. "Then he upped and asked me for a date," she said. "You heard of Fran's?" I nodded. It was a home-style restaurant not far from Centro. "He paid," she said softly.

Our desserts arrived, hers a Decadent Dark Chocolate Pyramid with hazelnut ice cream, which came on a huge hand-blown glass plate. She also ordered a cappuccino, her first.

"I'd like to steal that wine glass," she sighed, nodding at some sparkling glassware on a table near us. "And I'd like to steal each a one of them bottles." I looked at the gleaming wine cabinet beside me. Was she pulling my leg? I told her I coveted the heavy, damask tablecloth. She laughed. I relaxed.

As I paid the bill, $101.67 before tip, Hallam told me she plans to be back on the street this week. She expects to pull in $200 on Christmas Eve. On New Year's Eve, she'll beg until 4 a.m. "This time of year," she said, "everybody's in a cheerful mood."

Ooh, the hate mail. Half the people thought I was making fun of Hallam. The other half thought it was obscene to spend so much when others were homeless and hungry. Dr. David Kinahan, in a letter to the editor, wrote: "Jan Wong's piece on Nancy Hallam was nothing short of offensive. Her condescending and patronizing tone was made only worse by her smug little face smiling out over the piece in proud ownership."

Hallam had a great time, and so did I. She was pleased with the Lunch column. I know, because my Aunt Ming lived near her corner and always stopped for a chat. Hallam carried photocopies of the column in her waist purse and showed them to anyone who was interested. Lunching people like her is, for me, one of the great rewards of writing this column.

FAMILY MATTERS

alisha ling-wong

My Niece is Smart, Accomplished and Nice—and She Has No Friends

May 6, 2000

Alisha Ling-Wong, eleven, folds the cloth napkin. Presto! A floppy white tulip emerges. What can't this sixth-grader do? As a pianist, she plays a mean Mendelssohn. She scored in the ninety-ninth percentile in Canadian math and verbal aptitude tests. And she was runner-up this week in Quebec's Royal Commonwealth Society essay competition. She just tied for second place in a National Mathematics League test, taken by one million students annually in Canada and the United States.

But Alisha has no friends. As smart kids everywhere know, brains are a mixed blessing. Her classmates call her, sarcastically, The Improved Einstein. "I'm not a genius. I'm human," she protests.

Let me say right off that Alisha is my niece, and that I was the first person, after the obstetrician and before her mother, to hold her. So when I say that's she's cheerful and pretty, with glossy hair, doe eyes and straight white teeth, I may be prejudiced.

At an Easter weekend lunch at Trapper's Restaurant in Toronto to celebrate her math victory, she orders a huge platter of char-broiled lambshanks. At Lower Canada College, a private school in Montreal, she's house head, sings in the school choir and acts in the school play. She's also a member of the soccer team. She's no sixty-seven-pound weakling, either. As a volunteer "peacekeeper," she helps mediate schoolyard conflict.

But none of this has made her any friends. That is the mystery of kids. Excluding someone else can make you feel better about yourself. If we ostracize others, maybe by default we'll be "in." And so kids, (and private clubs, too,) create rigidly enforced hierarchies of unimportance. Montreal is a long way from Littleton, Colorado, and Taber, Alberta, where rejected kids murdered other kids. But not all pain involves guns. Sometimes it's just a slow withering of childhood. You can become an outcast for your hair, your acne or the way you walk. You can suffer because you're too stupid, or too smart.

While boys openly bully—body slamming, underpants wedgies, punching and taunting—girls are more sneaky. They condemn you to permanent solitary confinement, something that adults may not notice. They may conduct a whisper campaign about your slutty sex life. Or they may slip in a cutting remark about your chest size or your choice of footwear. The hottest interactive game on the Internet right now is Sissyfight 2000. Players assume the persona of schoolgirls about Alisha's age, then scratch, tease and humiliate each other until they break down in tears (interactively) and quit.

At lunch, you know Alisha isn't cool when she eats all the broccoli and turnips on her plate first. The last time she was invited to a sleepover was half a lifetime ago, in Grade Two. The class had just four girls. The other three formed a clique. "I cried a bit at home, not at school," she recalls. "In Grade Three, it hurt a little less."

In Grade Four, the other girls once gloated that they had a "secret clubhouse." It was just a spot behind a schoolyard tree. "Can I join?" Alisha asked, walking into the trap. Of course, they told her "no." That same year, she invited five girls to her birthday party. Only one showed up. In Grade Six now, she says, "I'm indifferent." To be sure, other kids call. But they just want help with their homework. One night, five of them phoned. "They know I don't forget my homework at school," she says, without resentment.

It's not strictly true that Alisha has no friends. One girl, the one who came to her birthday party two years ago, gave Alisha gifts she's wearing at lunch: tiny pierced earrings and a green t-shirt that says: "Be different. Be yourself." But the girl is in another class and the two haven't gotten together since March break. And while this kid has other friends besides Alisha, she's Alisha's only friend.

At recess while other kids play games of "Truth or Dare," Alisha curls up with a book. She finds solace in reading, but there's no denying her competitive streak. The school's reading program requires a minimum of thirty points, based on the number and complexity of books read. Last year, the runner-up, a boy, earned one-hundred-forty points. Alisha earned two-hundred-eighty points.

Naturally, that doesn't win her friends. Still, she tries to be tactful about her achievements. When the teacher called on Alisha to tell the class about her math victory, she began by announcing LCC's overall high ranking. Amid the cheers, she slipped in the fact that she came second nation-wide. Her score, she tells me at lunch, was thirty-nine out of forty. Here's the question she muffed: Every even number over 0 is divisible by a) 0; b) 1; c) 0 and 2; or d) 0, 1, 2. I confess I'm stumped. On the test she guessed "d," which sounds good to me. But the correct answer is "b," she explains, because she now understands "you can't divide by 0."

Alisha's mother explained that to her. My sister is a chartered accountant and a computer expert. A single parent, she quit her job at a big accounting firm and took a job teaching at Dawson College so her schedule would match her children's.

"My mom did give me a lot of moral support. She was always there," says Alisha. (Her father moved to Toronto when she was two years old. She and her brother Willie, thirteen, see him one weekend a month and three weeks each summer.)

It's suggested she might have friends if her marks weren't so fabulous. "Having friends is good," says Alisha, who would like to be a surgeon. "But I wouldn't drop my marks purposely, because it won't guarantee you'll have friends.

This is her last year in junior school. But middle school might be worse. According to a 1994 study in the U.S., the majority of middle-school students are bullied. After Littleton and Taber, many schools have a zero-tolerance policy on physical bullying. But there's scant consciousness about psychological cruelty. Other studies show that if a deep-freeze starts and adults do nothing it spreads like a contagion, engulfing the entire school.

In a few weeks, Alisha's teachers will likely choose a class valedictorian for the junior school. "I guess I have a chance," she says. She doesn't smile.

I thought a long time about the danger of writing about my niece in Canada's national newspaper. That Easter weekend, I told Alisha and my sister that if I were to write about Alisha's accomplishments, I would also have to write about her loneliness. We discussed the potential fall-out. I told them that there were three possibilities. Nothing could happen. Her classmates could retaliate. Or things could change for the better. At the very least, by going public, she might be able to help other kids.

Alisha and my sister were both willing to take a chance. I told them to sleep on it. But that night I hardly slept. The next morning, before I took Alisha to lunch, I warned her that this would be an official interview. I would ask blunt questions. And nothing would be off the record. She agreed. Still, I had misgivings. After I wrote a

draft, I showed it to several colleagues who thought it should run, as
did my editor.

Well. That first week after publication, the school was in an
uproar. Many parents, and some teachers, were outraged that I had
mentioned LCC in the same breath as Littleton, Colorado. The
parents of Alisha's only friend phoned me to complain that I had
named their daughter. (I didn't this time around.) They felt I
had portrayed their daughter in a bad light. They also insisted
she had never attended Alisha's birthday party. Perhaps they feared
their daughter would be contaminated by the friendship, and end up
ostracized, too.

The story ran on a Saturday. That Monday, many female classmates became openly hostile. Some parents suggested that Alisha was
fantasizing and required therapy. The next day, she begged my sister
to let her stay home. She said her stomach hurt. My sister, who was
deeply upset, told Alisha that skipping school wouldn't make things
better. I felt helpless. One colleague suggested I visit the school, apologize and explain my motivation but I thought that would only
worsen the situation.

At work, other reporters told me about their unhappy childhoods.
Wherever I went, parents stopped to tell me how their children were
shunned, too. At a dinner party, a former deputy minister in the federal government related how he'd been beaten up at school on a daily
basis, and no one had done a thing. He thought the experience had
made him a meaner human being.

At the same time, readers from all over the country asked me to
forward their letters of encouragement to Alisha. Adults urged her
not to lose hope and assured her that brains would eventually pay
off. Kids wrote to say that they were struggling with the same loneliness. A schoolboard in P.E.I. asked if it could reprint the column in
an educational package it was preparing on bullying.

That Friday, Alisha's teacher asked all the girls to stay in for
noon recess. They sat in a circle, and everyone talked and cried. The

other girls said they hadn't known that Alisha had no friends.
Alisha cried, too, and promised to stop hiding behind a book at recess.

I'm delighted to report that in Grade Seven my niece began to
make friends. They're not close ones yet, but they're friends. She's even
back on speaking terms with the friend-that-cannot-be-named. And
maybe, just maybe, I helped another lonely kid somewhere else.

aunt ming

FAMILY POLITICS RULE THE DAY

March 27, 1997

"Lunch With" always puts the focus on my guest. In this column,
and the next, I'm the one in the hot seat. By the way, no one in my
family believes me when I say I didn't plan ahead of time to write up
Aunt Ming's party. I didn't. But once the thought occurred, it was
irresistible.

Aunt Ming is my favourite aunt. I'm so proud she was the
third Chinese woman in Canada to earn her medical degree.
When she turned eighty-three recently, I decided to throw her
a birthday lunch. Now, some people might see me as a scary
person with whom to have lunch. But, believe me, my relatives
are much, much scarier. Families, in big or small doses, are like
that. They reduce you to an insecure, incompetent, immature
version of your everyday self.

I asked Aunt Ming whom she wanted to invite. I've
learned not to take on that risk myself. We have a very big family. My grandparents—Aunt Ming's parents—had twelve children. Twenty years ago, one cousin daringly invited only aunts

and uncles to his wedding, thereby permanently offending all his first cousins. Recently, another cousin annoyed all the aunts and uncles by restricting her Christmas party to cousins. (We cousins number, I think, more than one hundred if you include spouses and offspring.) When Aunt Ming's guest list hit twenty-five, I began to make stricken noises. Even with three tables scattered around my house, I couldn't seat more than that. She insisted I tell everyone not to bring presents. Naturally, I obeyed. Naturally, almost everyone disobeyed.

My main worry was food. I didn't want two weeks' worth of leftovers, nor did I want anyone to go hungry. My generation, the cousin level, always makes clear any planned contributions. Cousin Janet announced she would make a stuffed salmon. Cousin Andy brought a pot of hot-and-sour soup. Cousin Colleen made the birthday cake. The problem was the older generation. My aunts and uncles are all in their seventies and eighties. Uncle Ying turns ninety next year. Maybe familial piety makes it impossible for me to broach the subject. To ask if they were bringing anything would be misconstrued as a rude request. I would never live it down. "Oh, Uncle Ying will bring lots of food," said Aunt Ming reassuringly. "He always does."

That Sunday, Uncle Ying arrived bearing the proscribed birthday gift, but no food. In a panic, I told my Cousin Lily to throw on a second pot of rice. No matter that my main offering, other than shrimp and snow peas, was spicy sesame noodles. Starch fills. Cousin Mary brought no food either, but she did bring the only hostess gift, a huge box of deluxe chocolate-dipped cookies. I showed it to Ben, my six-year-old. I wanted to cheer him up because he was running a fever and had to stay in bed.

Soon, everyone was happily eating Aunt Ming's poached ginger chicken and Aunt Helen's poached ginger chicken. (That's what happens when you don't coordinate the food.)

Cousin Lily urged steamed rice on everyone, but we didn't even finish the first pot. My aunts and uncles sat in the best seats in my formal dining room. We cousins clustered at tables in my kitchen and sunroom. It was a rare get-together that gave us a chance to chat about each other's lives. I told Cousin David about my "Lunch With" column. "I haven't read *The Globe and Mail* since 1989," he said.

As an employee, I'm entitled to seven half-price subscriptions. Would he like one? "Nah," said Cousin David. "I can read it at work."

Somewhat deflated, I checked Cousin Colleen's birthday cake. She had brought the batter because she hadn't had time to bake it before she came. When it was finally ready to come out of the oven, everyone was so impatient that she stuck the candles in the hot cake, melting them.

My son Ben came down from his sickbed when we sang "Happy Birthday." He looked longingly at the cake, which was fast disappearing, and asked me to save him a piece. I cut a slice. To reassure him, I wrote a note and put it on the plate: "Save for Ben."

It was time to open the gifts. Only Cousin Mary had taken me at my word. "You said no presents," she whispered, mortified. I grabbed the box of cookies she had given me. "Here," I said. "Give this."

Everyone lingered over coffee. I put out heaping platters of home-made baking: brownies, chocolate chip cookies, muffins, and cinnamon buns. My mother, who came from Montreal for the party, regaled her elderly siblings with the story of how she recently cracked a tooth when she fell flat on her face in a Florida parking lot. "I didn't break my glasses!" she exclaimed.

An uncle asked me for some paper plates. I didn't know why he wanted them—I had set out plenty of china—but I've learned not to question my relatives. After everyone left, I broke the news to Ben about how our box of fancy cookies morphed from hostess gift to birthday present. He nodded understandingly. Then he went to check on his piece of cake. Someone had eaten it. He burst into tears. I suggested he have a brownie. That's when I realized that two of my relatives had swept all the desserts, except for one muffin and three chocolate chip cookies, onto the paper plates and taken them home. When I called my mother, who was spending the night at Aunt Ming's, she laughed. "They were going to take your plate, too," she said. "But I stopped them."

After everyone had long gone, the doorbell rang. One of my cousins, who had left a few hours earlier, was back. "Can I borrow some rice?" he said. I assumed he had run out. I began to fill a container with raw rice. "Uh, I mean, the cooked rice," he said. He knew about my surplus because I had borrowed his electric cooker to make the second pot. I was just about to use up the cooked rice for dinner. But I smiled gamely and gave him half.

Never mind. It's Easter this weekend. I'm going to his house for dinner. I announced weeks ago that I was coming with my sister and her kids from Montreal. That's when he extended me an invitation.

This Lunch reminded many readers of their own chaotic family gatherings. At first, Aunt Ming was chagrined at the thought of being in the newspaper. She was somewhat mollified after hearing from several long-lost friends from the University of Toronto's medical school, class of 1942. Aunt Ming had gone there on a church scholarship, one of only seven women and the only non-white out of 122. She became Canada's first female anesthetist of Chinese heritage.

After graduation, she married a Chinese research scientist in New York. As Dr. Ming Yao, she travelled to north China with the

United Nations Relief and Rehabilitation Agency. There, she treated victims of the civil war between the Communists and the Nationalist KMT. In China, she also gave birth to one son, Ted. While fleeing the Communist advance, she delivered her second son, Tom, cutting the umbilical cord herself on a freighter in a storm-tossed Yellow Sea.

Aunt Ming was my role model. She was smart, kind, and funny. She was the linchpin of our family. My two young sons saw her so often they believed she was their grandmother. Aunt Ming passed away on January 5, 2000, after a massive stroke, surrounded by her loving family. She was eighty-five.

the family

PLAYING HOST TO SIXTY-FIVE OF YOUR CLOSEST RELATIVES

January 8, 1998

Holidays are when you take leave of your senses and invite over too many people. This past Christmas Day, my mother turned eighty. So last Saturday I invited four generations of my closest relatives to lunch. On my mother's side, I have a dozen aunts and uncles, forty or so first cousins, and at least a hundred second cousins. My late Uncle Harry, for instance, had nine children. One of them had seven. And one of *them* had four. You get the picture.

My husband, an only child, blanched. But I had learned my lesson after bruising feelings last year by inviting a mere twenty-five to my aunt Ming's birthday party. This time, she helped with the phoning. But I had to call Aunt Sue myself, penance for omitting her the last time. She knew because I had written about that party. Aunt Ming, a retired doctor, wasn't thrilled either by that column. "Now the whole country knows I'm eighty-three," she moaned. "Yes," I commiserated, "and before, everyone thought you were seventy-nine."

At eighty-eight, Aunt Sue is hard of hearing. Or maybe she was exacting revenge. I made the mistake of calling her from *The Globe* newsroom, where eavesdropping is considered a point of honour. "Auntie Sue? This is Jan Wong, Eva's daughter."

"Who?"

[Louder] "Jan Wong. Eva's daughter."

"Who?"

My colleagues began standing up to watch. Aunt Sue finally admitted knowing me. I volunteered Cousin John to drive her in from Dundas, Ontario. But she was noncommittal. A few days before the party, Aunt Sue announced she couldn't possibly get dressed before 2 p.m. Could we push back the time of the party? Too many aunts and uncles drive badly enough in broad daylight, never mind at night. So I played the feudal-Chinese card. Uncle Ying, a year older at eighty-nine, ordered Aunt Sue to be ready on time.

To stave off panic, I refused to speculate on how many would show up. My parents and sister came in from Montreal. We packed off my unsuspecting mother to Aunt Ming's for a sleepover the day before. We wanted to surprise her, but not too much—Mom has had a quadruple bypass operation. My sister baked thirty-six lemon and chocolate tarts. We bought a ten-kilogram ham and a thirty-cup coffee urn. We also found "Happy 80th Birthday" napkins and balloons. (Thanks to the boomer-with-aging-parent market, you can buy 90th, 95th, and 100th versions, too.)

Last Saturday, Aunt Sue arrived on time, beautifully coiffed. One brother and his family came in from Montreal. My other brother heard about the party and flew to Mexico. I counted sixty-five guests scattered throughout the house. My nephew Willie, eleven, and my son Ben, seven, stood outside telling people not to park in the driveway so Mom wouldn't be forewarned. The bus drivers on our route even began dropping relatives right at the door. The only blight was a stranger on one bus who commented aloud on my cousin's mixed marriage. "You're a racist," the white woman told my cousin's white husband. "You should have married someone who looks like me." My cousin's little girl arrived in tears, but cheered up when she saw the chocolate tarts.

Unlike last time, I wasn't shy about asking people to bring food. Uncle Ying made his famous minced pork with preserved Chinese mustard greens. Cousins Andy and Phyllis brought smoked salmon. Someone brought a giant pan of macaroni and cheese. Almost no one drinks, so I chilled one bottle of Chardonnay.

Many of us in the third and fourth generations were meeting for the first time. We solved the identity crisis with name tags, complete with multigeneration genealogies, improvised from computer-disk labels. No-name kids disappeared into the basement to watch *Star Wars*. Bobby, my second cousin, arrived with a shell-shocked young woman. "She's, um ..." With guests pouring through the door, there was no time for subtlety. I scrawled "Significant Other" on a label and stuck it on her sweater. They blushed. It turned out they had just started dating.

Then Mom arrived. Everyone clapped. She was genuinely shocked. "I'm not wearing any make-up," she gasped, crying a little. Then she grinned. Unlike some of my Lunch victims, who either fly in from Hollywood or are illiterate, or both, my relatives were wary after the last writeup. Cousin-in-law Colleen, who runs a multibillion-dollar pension fund, had suffered national humiliation when I reported that she had served Aunt Ming's birthday cake hot from the oven, melting the candles. This time, her cake was already baked. It was also gigantic. "I used a lasagna tray," said Colleen, a pointed reference to the last party. Not only had someone chowed down the last slice—labelled "Save for Ben," who had been sick—but my aunts had stripped me clean of cookies.

Naturally, I savaged them in Canada's National Newspaper. This time, as the party wound down, I noticed everyone leaving empty-handed. We had gone through two urns of coffee and one glass of Chardonnay, but mounds of macaroni remained. I urged my cousins to take the leftovers. "No way," said one, recoiling. "I don't want to read about it in *The Globe and Mail*."

So now we're eating macaroni for breakfast and lunch, although I draw the line at supper. That's when we eat Uncle Ying's minced pork with preserved Chinese mustard greens. He's turning ninety this month. Out of my husband's hearing, I offered to throw another bash. But his son, John, and daughter, Mary, will give the party.

"Just bring the coffee urn," said John.

On July 1, 2000, I issued, or rather, my Uncle Fay told me to issue, an open invitation to all my one zillion relatives for a Canada Day barbeque. Everyone came over for a late lunch following a visit to Toronto's Mount Pleasant Cemetery. (Chinese always combine ancestor worship with food.)

The occasion for this family reunion was our first visit to Aunt Ming's gravesite. We also wanted to pay our collective respects to Chang Hooie, the family patriarch who had changed the course of all our destinies 119 years earlier when he left his village in south China and came to Canada as a coolie.

At lunch, Aunt Ming's son Ted handed out red bound copies of our extended family tree, a project that had taken him months. Our aging relatives were passing away. Aunt Edna, eighty-seven, died within a few months of Aunt Ming. And then Aunt Nova died a few months after Aunt Edna. Others had fallen ill. Uncle Ying, ninety-two, had had a stroke. So the next generation began to cherish our family ties even more.

Mom, eighty-two, had planned to come in from Montreal. But in June she too suffered a stroke. By July 1, she was able to speak haltingly and was even tossing a basketball with her physiotherapist. But she couldn't make this Lunch.

Her absence, and that of my favourite aunt, reminded me once again of the importance of lunch. The midday meal should be a special occasion, a time to talk and think, a time to size-up everyone and everything in broad daylight. When I visited Mom in hospital the week before Canada Day, I showed her the galleys for this book. I just wish I could have showed them to Aunt Ming, too.

acknowledgements

"Lunch With," the column, was the brainchild of Cathrin Bradbury, features editor of *The Globe and Mail*. John Pearce, editor-in-chief of Doubleday Canada, suggested *Lunch With*, the book. Both John and especially his assistant, Kendall Anderson, provided talented and tactful editing.

I'm deeply grateful to *The Globe and Mail* for granting permission to reprint my "Lunch With" columns, and to Richard Addis, the editor, for his support.

Globe copy editors, including Kim Honey, Derek Raymaker, Christopher Harris, Andrew Gorham, and Sue Grimbly, dreamed up great headlines and saved me from errors big and small. For tips, advice, and suggestions on what to ask and where to eat, I thank many colleagues, including Gay Abbate, James Christie, André de Treville, Dan Driver, Dave Roberts, Liz Renzetti, Doug Saunders, Alan Freeman, Miro Cernetig, Victor Dwyer, Brian Gable, Phil Jackman, Mike Kesterton, Tony Jenkins, and William Houston.

My colleague John Saunders first drew my attention to Jeffrey Archer's ill-fated Aquablast investment and dug up a yellowed typewritten draft of a story he had written about it years earlier. Martin Powell, an ardent Archer fan who works in *The Globe*'s mailroom, lent me a stack of His Lordship's novels. After reading them, I was able to confidently label them "airport literature." Sorry, Martin.

For their wisdom, I also thank these colleagues: Sue

Andrew, for reining in some of my worst excesses; Johanna Boffa, for sharing her common sense and trawling through the databases; Edward Greenspon, for suggesting I study the wonderful columns of Lynn Barber in the *Sunday Independent*; Greg O'Neill, for policing first-person references; and Stephen Strauss, for reassuring me it wasn't shameful to do Lunch.

My sister has been my unflagging cheerleader, bucking me up whenever criticism rained down. Without Mercedita Iboro on the home front, this book would not have been possible. But the biggest thanks go to my husband, Norman, and my sons, Ben and Sam, for not groaning too loudly when I announced I was going to do yet another book and for happily eating Kraft Dinner as I neared my deadline.

ABOUT THE AUTHOR

Over the past five years through her tremendously successful "Lunch With" columns, Jan Wong has been able to combine two of her favourite things: good food and a good story. She is the recipient of a National Newspaper Award, among many other honours, for her reporting. Wong is also the author of two best-selling books—*Red China Blues*, and *Jan Wong's China*. She lives with her family in Toronto, where she is a reporter and columnist for *The Globe and Mail*.